TV News Off-Camera

TV News
Off-Camera

An Insider's Guide to
Newswriting and Newspeople

Steven Zousmer

Ann Arbor   The University of Michigan Press

Published in the United States of America by
The University of Michigan Press and simultaneously
in Markham, Canada, by Fitzhenry & Whiteside, Ltd.
Manufactured in the United States of America

1990   1989   1988   1987   4   3   2   1

Library of Congress Cataloging-in-Publication Data

Zousmer, Steven, 1942–
   TV news off-camera.

   1. Television broadcasting of news. 2. Broadcast
journalism—Authorship. I. Title.
PN4784.T4Z6   1987   070.1'9   86-27263
ISBN 0-472-09372-X (alk. paper)
ISBN 0-472-06372-3 (pbk. : alk. paper)

For Alice and, of course, for Ruth and Jess

Preface

This is a guide to the off-camera side of television news. It mixes specific instruction in TV newswriting with informal discussion of the texture and substance of the career.

I have tried to make it the book I looked for but couldn't find when *I* was still in school and later when I was starting out—a book that answered my questions about the "real world" of the career I was heading into, a book that perhaps lifted my awareness and skills a notch or two above what I had barely mastered in the classroom.

It is an insider's view, written for insiders and would-be insiders. It focuses on the level where most careers begin and unfold, the newsroom level—the domain of writers, editors, producers, and executives up to local station news directors and network executive producers. It is about the newsroom's inherent values, personalities, politics, psychology—the unseen currents and motivations that explain so much about what it is like to work in TV news.

I think this world is best seen through the eyes of the newswriter, and that is the orientation of this book. For most TV newswriters, writing is only part of a job that usually includes production functions such as working with editors composing stories on tape or producing in the field.

Very few TV newswriters do nothing but write, and newswriters are unlikely to think of themselves as writing specialists. Indeed, many beginning newswriters are reluctant when it comes to writing, because they'd rather get on to something more glamorous and because they doubt their skills. These doubts are often well founded, which is a shame for journalism and for the individuals.

I say this not to moan about the breakdown of syntax and grammar or to lament the demise of the coherent sentence. Prose quality is important and writing well is satisfying, but there is a larger dimension. As I once heard an executive producer say to a disheartened newswriter, "We don't need you just because you know where to put the comma or know the difference between 'imply' and 'infer.' We need you because you can *think editorially.*"

Thinking editorially is the essence of TV news off-camera. It is the fundamental skill of journalism; everything else flows from it. The traditional way to learn it is by learning to write. Writing is not just arranging words; it is a thought process, a structuring process, a decision-making process. Seeing TV news through the newswriter's eyes is the best way to approach technique and broaden understanding at the same time.

Many TV newspeople who are not themselves polished writers succeed because they understand how a writer thinks. Knowing the values of writing gives them a built-in editing sense. They are able to compose a story in the field or editing room, to have useful ideas, to make the many editorial judgments that come up, to do the writing themselves if necessary.

Knowing the writer's structuring process, they know what facts and quotes they must get. They know they must talk, let's say, to a victim, a doctor, and a public official—and maybe to a disgruntled former employee. They know what to ask them. They recognize what is and isn't news. They know what the camera should show. They know how to fit it together. They know how to tell a story.

On the editorial side of TV news (as opposed to the technical or logistical sides) *everyone* is a writer. Anchors write, reporters write, producers write—and many of them have moved up to their current roles after experience as newswriters. In some news shops there are no newswriters; the writer job is done by all of the above or by associate producers who also function as field producers. Most executives have graduated from one or another of these jobs, so they can write too.

When it comes to getting a job, lack of writing skill is quickly exposed. You are not expected to be a master stylist on your first day (or ever, for that matter), but there is an unmistakable difference between "promising" and "not promising." Outsiders would be amazed at how difficult it is to find job applicants with acceptable writing ability. At the networks (and allowing for network stodginess) there is dismay over the uneven and generally unimpressive writing skills of many younger generation correspondents. It doesn't take a genius to realize that learning to write well is an investment that will pay off quickly and lastingly.

All the familiar principles and pointers about newswriting are covered in these pages, but I have learned that miscellaneous instructions tend to float off into the blue yonder unless they are incorporated into larger themes. This I have tried to do, as indicated by chapter headings, avoiding random rule-giving as much as possible and stressing the *why* of different writing solutions with hopes of creating awareness, taste, and discriminating appreciation of good newswriting.

For several reasons, there are not a lot of the usual examples showing how-to and how-not-to. There are many ways to write every story; many are fine, many are not, and there aren't enough pages to show them all. Picking just one or two—saying *Do it this way!* or *Don't try that!*—seems arrogant and arbitrary.

Another reservation about examples is that broadcast scripts are not meant to be read in a book. Like songs, they are written to be heard, not read; taking them out of their natural medium can be as distorting as a quotation out of context. The best newswriting is so seamless and stripped-down for the voice and ear that examples of it often seem thin and unremarkable on the printed page. Examples of bad newswriting are so flagrant that a student is unlikely to believe he could ever make such mistakes (though sooner or later he probably will).

Regarding the chapters that are not strictly instructional, I should say that despite my occasionally dogmatic tone they are meant not as the last word on these subjects but as consciousness-raisers, to be further developed by teachers in classroom discussion. I hope it will be understood that the topics of these chapters required considerable generalizing, subjectivity, and personal opinion. Journalists distrust such departures from the code of objectivity unless they are openly acknowledged, and I do so without reservation.

For every sweeping statement I make in this book I've imagined veteran newsmen shaking their heads and saying, "No, that's not how it was where I've worked." Well, it's not even exactly how it was at the individual places where *I* have been. It is, of course, a composite.

My TV news experience is confined to only one city (New York) and only one company (ABC), but within that framework my resume is diverse. I have worked for local news (WABC-TV) and network evening news (under Harry Reasoner and Howard K. Smith in the mid-1970s and Peter Jennings in 1983). I have worked for morning television (as chief writer of *Good Morning America*), late night (as senior producer of *Nightline*) and very late night (the short-lived *The Last Word*), for a TV network news magazine *(20/20)*, and for ABC's monumental three-hour documentary *FDR*.

Except for some free-lance producing and *Nightline*, my experience is mainly as a writer and editor, both of which (like most TV job titles) have different meanings in every shop. I took the *Nightline* producership with misgivings, which were justified: my ears longed for the staccato music of the typewriter keyboard, my typing fingers twitched, I wasn't happy, and I quit.

The TV jobs I've had account for only a part of my background in journalism. I grew up in a journalism family. My father, Jesse Zousmer, had a distinguished career in broadcast journalism at CBS and ABC, including a long association with Edward R. Murrow, which I describe in chapter 1. My mother was a prize-winning feature writer for newspapers in Ohio. Most of the visitors in our home were journalists. I went to graduate school in journalism and reported for two newspapers, the *Providence Journal-Bulletin* and the *San Francisco Chronicle,* before going into TV. I saw reporting from the other side as a Navy information officer at the United Nations and in Vietnam. I met my wife in a TV newsroom. Most of *our* friends are journalists. For as long as I can remember, I've been hearing, reading, arguing, and gossiping about journalism.

I have resisted advice to be "positive" in writing about journalism, just as I would resist a suggestion to write a news story in a positive light. Young people coming into TV news have more enthusiasm than I could possibly dampen. They need no propaganda, but good advice might save them from sour experiences, and I have tried to give it without fretting over whether it is upbeat. I would be disappointed if my attention to imperfect aspects of TV news were construed as personal negativism. On the contrary, I believe in TV news as someone might believe in his family, not uncritically or unpeevishly but with the firmest faith in its goodness and value.

On one point I would ask forgiveness, or at least understanding. Throughout these pages I refer to news*men* and anchor*men,* and I use *he* and *his* in most cases when I am talking about typical journalists or journalists in general. De-sexing all such references would have been consistently awkward and tedious—both especially undesirable in a book that immodestly attempts to tell other people how to write. A passage from Strunk and White's *The Elements of Style* (3d ed. [New York, 1979]) supports me: "The use of *he* as a pronoun embracing both genders is a simple, practical convention rooted in the beginnings of the English language. *He* has lost all suggestions of maleness in these circumstances. . . . It has no pejorative connotation; it is never incorrect." *Whew!*

But I'm uncomfortable anyway, and I apologize. It may be that my sensitivity to this matter is related to my experience at *Good*

Morning America where I headed a department that for a long period consisted of twelve women and me. If I had sexist tendencies, they were beaten out of me. In terms of the people you work with in journalism, I think the notable difference between men and women is that when you go to lunch with them women tend to have salads.

Acknowledgments

Special thanks to Bruce Armbruster, Betsy Aaron and Richard Threlkeld, Nick Archer, Patricia Berens, Edward Bliss, Jr., Bob Blum, Richard Clurman and Shirley Clurman, Dan Cooper, Bob Davis, Elmer Lower, and Perry Zousmer.

The author further wishes to thank the following experts for their advice in the writing of the chapter "Dealing with Numbers": Dr. J. Michael Cayton, economist; Dr. Kathleen Frankovic, Director of Surveys, CBS News; Philip McGuire, Director of Crime Analysis, New York City Police Department; Edward R. Tufte, Professor of Statistics and Political Science, Yale University; and Dr. Margaret Wright, computer science, Stanford University.

Contents

PART 1

Newspeople

1

Murrow

Murrow. A book about broadcast journalism should begin with his name.

When Edward R. Murrow died in 1965, I was a twenty-two-year-old student at the Columbia University Graduate School of Journalism. I went to his funeral with my parents. My father, Jesse Zousmer, had been co-producer with John Aaron of Murrow's popular television interview show, *Person to Person,* and a producer under Fred Friendly of Murrow's historic documentary program, *See It Now.* Between 1947 and 1954, he wrote the hard news half of Murrow's nightly radio broadcast. Murrow himself wrote the second half, the commentary. *Edward R. Murrow and the News* was the principal news program on radio and the forerunner of the network evening newscasts on television.

After the funeral, my father excused himself and went to walk alone in Central Park, to come to grips with the loss of a deeply admired hero who was also a treasured friend of nearly twenty years. They had spent thousands of hours together, faced many journalistic storms, emptied many bottles of scotch and many cartons of Camels. (Less than a year later I took the same walk in Central Park after the funeral of my mother and father, who died in the crash of a plane returning from Vietnam. At that time my father was vice president of TV news at ABC.)

My personal memories of Murrow are few but vivid. I met him in visits to the CBS offices in Manhattan and in annual family weekends at his farm in Pawling, New York.

Murrow loved the farm, which must have reminded him of his youth in the farming country of North Carolina and the logging country of Washington State. It surprised many people that this formal and urbane gentleman who wore impeccable British suits and seemed the personification of Indoors Man was a proud product of rural America. He was eager to introduce his son Casey to the activities of country boyhood, but in the summers I remember Casey was only six or seven, too young for Murrow's robust curriculum. My age, however, was just right; I was four years older than Casey and ripe, and Murrow was ready.

As my parents looked on with what must have been considerable nervousness, Murrow put me in the saddle of a huge horse and jogged alongside as I thrilled to my first horseback trot. After that it was pistol marksmanship, Murrow crouching next to my gun arm as I blasted away at a woodpile.

We toured the farm, inspecting its machinery and its various animals. We played softball on a vast green lawn and I slugged home runs off easy pitches from the living god of broadcast journalism. I ran the bases gleefully, his applause in my ears. Another time he extolled my agility in making a quick catch of a falling lamp when his farmhouse was jolted by lightning.

Like most children, I was awkward and uncomfortable with adults, especially the famous and imposing CBS newsmen I met often. But the most famous and imposing newsman of them all put me at ease with his open affection and unpatronizing conversation. In my memory I see him tall and elegant even in an old short-sleeved shirt and rolled-up farm trousers, cigarette and drink in hand, laughter dissolving the handsome gravity of his face.

I knew he was a great guy before I realized that he was a great man. What I regret is that the profession chose to remember him not as a man but as an immortal paragon. Broadcast news has produced many stars and worthy contributors but Murrow is its only towering hero, so perhaps there was a need to chisel his image into marble. I suppose it's also understandable that, after his death, it didn't seem heroic enough to remember his faith in fundamental values. There had to be, instead, a Murrow Legacy, a creed so high-minded that it seemed to insist on impossible purity.

The Legacy was seldom permitted to inspire. More often it was used to shame and punish. Whenever there was a charge of departing from the High Road, Murrow's memory was invoked to expose the alleged sinner to damning contrast. The Legacy became a moral and ethical whip in media combat. Many an on- or off-camera bigwig felt its lash. Many a newcomer was taken behind the woodshed for a stinging dose of Legacy. To young journalists the implicit message was that Murrow was beyond emulation; no matter what heights they might reach, they would always fall short of the Murrow Ideal.

The generation of TV newsmen who were so personally stirred by Murrow pressed his memory to the point of overkill, clearly because they feared that future generations would not be equally stirred by his memory. Generations will always behave this way, trying to preserve their heroes in a condition of eternal homage by pumping them up so much larger than life. It doesn't work.

My impression is that today's young TV journalists regard Murrow as some sort of ancient dragon slayer who appeared in the mists of TV folklore and now seems more mythic than real. His memory has become an abstraction, too lofty to have meaning in the course of an unlofty day in the newsroom. When you face an urgent situation and need to refer to a useful model, you do not turn to a figure Beyond Emulation.

Time gets some of the blame for this but even guiltier is the Glorification Committee. Murrow should not have been turned into an abstraction or a myth. He worked in the real world and it wasn't *that* long ago that he did so. The world he faced as a journalist was different from today's in style and perhaps in complexity, but in any larger sense it is the same world that newsmen will always face. Murrow was exceptionally gifted but what made him great was that he was a decent man who had the courage and intelligence to follow his own highest instincts. Many less-heralded journalists have done the same thing. So can you. If you want to emulate Murrow, you can. It is a wonderful thing to try to do. But don't expect it to be easy. It wasn't easy for Murrow to be Murrow.

Television newswriting owes a great deal to Murrow and his colleagues in radio news in the 1940s and early 1950s. In those days broadcast journalism was still in the process of inventing itself. Fortunately the inventors were brimming with the talent and creative energy that always seem to appear in the ferment of big new things. They came to the new medium, adapted their skills, and helped establish— among other things—a style of newswriting that has never needed changing.

It is no accident that they did such a good job. They had grown up in a period when a well-developed skill at writing opened possibilities for exciting careers and public acclaim. If they lacked the literary gifts of the Hemingways, Fitzgeralds, Faulkners, and Steinbecks, there was still the mystique of the trenchcoated newspaper correspondent. They had learned their trade with newspapers and wire services (Murrow was an exception—he never worked in print journalism) and they put great value on the written word. Later the creative vigor of television news would shift from the writer-report-ers to the producers (today the producers must struggle to keep the upper hand against the surging innovations of TV technology), but the Murrow era was the prime time for writers. Murrow was a strong writer himself and he was served by strong writers. One of them was Edward Bliss, Jr., co-author with John M. Patterson of the re-spected textbook *Writing News for Broadcast.* Another was my fa-ther, of whom Bliss writes (forgive my pride in including this quote) "Zousmer was recognized as the best news writer in the business."

Of course Murrow's contribution went much deeper than writ-ing technique. Possibly because he started out as an educator and was never trained as a journalist, he was attuned to meanings and morals as well as events. Photographs of Murrow in his twenties reveal the face of a man who had already shouldered the solemn burdens of his times and would never be comfortable with anything of less consequence. He believed in high-minded, substantial, re-sponsible reporting. This principle was not new to journalism but it had not been established in television. A figure of Murrow's stat-ure was required to establish it and become its symbol.

His stature was built on his legendary radio reporting during World War II, his unmistakable intelligence and integrity, and, no small factor, his extraordinary "performer qualities": a voice and delivery that gave him dramatic, illuminating impact on radio and a physical presence that gave magnitude to everything he did on television.

Young people are surprised that he was never an anchorman. In fact, he did not take part at all in daily news coverage on tele-vision, preferring radio, which he thought superior for reporting breaking news. (Given the state of TV technology in the 1950s, he was probably right.) Murrow was at his best as a commentator or long-form (documentary) correspondent. He was not well suited for anchoring: he was too grave, too intellectual, too challenging. In contrast to today's stereotype of the plastic anchorperson, he was *too real.* He would have exhausted viewers with his intensity and his palpable discomfort: he was miserably nervous during broad-casts and perspired profusely, and he was ill at ease with the per-forming requirements of appearing on camera, feeling (as many TV journalists have felt) fraudulent and embarrassed by the Show Busi-ness of *acting* like a newsman.

Another reason for his stature lay in the enhanced stature of journalism, for which he was partly responsible. Americans have always demanded a free press but not necessarily a *distinguished* press. The notion of journalism as a *profession*—practiced by a corps of educated, ethical, skilled, dedicated men and women—is fairly new in the public's mind and was not widely held until the era when Murrow became such a standout.

In the period between the prime of radio and the full emergence of television, when Americans became familiar with the voices of journalists and then got to know them on television, the foremost figure of broadcast news happened to be the most impressive man broadcast news ever produced: Edward R. (for Roscoe) Murrow! Not only was he a superior journalist, he was also *American* in a sense that would raise patriotic goosebumps on the flesh of the coldest cynic. He was at his finest in 1954, when Senator Joseph McCarthy was conducting a rampage of terror that now seems unbelievable, wildly charging that Communists had infiltrated all corners of government and that many eminent Americans were acting as Soviet agents. These accusations were based on hearsay or no evidence at all, but they devastated the lives and careers of the accused and fostered a dangerous climate of national paranoia. The White House seemed intimidated, and only a few public officials and print journalists spoke out. Murrow's stunning *See It Now* attack on McCarthy was a turning point. In his conclusion Murrow said in part: "We will not walk in fear one of another. We will not be driven into an age of unreason if we dig deep into our history and our doctrine and remember that *we are not descended from fearful men . . .*" (emphasis added).*

Talk about a legacy! He found his guiding values in "our history and our doctrine." His journalism was a function of his citizenship. That may be why he struck such a deep chord. His name became associated with a morality in which being a journalist meant bearing a heavy public responsibility. He embodied this elevating purpose, adding mightily to the dignity of journalism and the self-esteem of journalists. His voice and later his image traveled thousands of miles into peoples' homes where, figuratively, he was an honored visitor, a minister of news. There was never a greater advertisement for a profession than his presence in it. To this day, TV journalists reap (and sometimes abuse) the benefits.

---

*Two days after the *See It Now* broadcast, McCarthy attempted to smear Murrow with the "Soviet agent" brush, but by this point the tide was turning against McCarthy and Murrow was not seriously damaged.

The people at CBS News in the Murrow era were caught up in a dynamic moral and professional climate. If they were occasionally righteous and prideful, so be it. They were also ferociously dedicated and exacting. The news, for them, was holy. There would be no trivializing, no pandering, no breaches of integrity or quality, no vacillating when it came to doing what was right. Intimidation would be resisted; intimidators would be challenged. The most scrupulous standards would be applied to everything. At times there would be terrible discord among colleagues, but it was worth it: this was serious work. It was *moral* work. To play fast and loose with its morals would be to invite the unforgiving and clamorous contempt of your peers, your superiors, and even the lowliest desk assistant.

Right away there were compromises. There always are. Reality, like gravity, has an inevitable way of bringing down the level. The colossal success of television created two such realities: a desire for more and more success and a dread of something going wrong. The bosses, and especially CBS's Number One Boss, William S. Paley, were excited by the high ratings and vast profits brought in by some of the most boneheaded entertainment shows in TV history. But Murrow kept rocking the boat with his trouble-making journalism. So it had to be curtailed. In the face-to-face showdown following the emasculation of *See It Now,* Paley reportedly told Murrow, "I don't want this constant stomachache every time you do a controversial subject."

Call it the Stomachache Rule. It is pervasive in every big organization and corporation. In television it has always existed and always will, at just about every level, from the network headquarters in midtown Manhattan to the local stations, right down to the producers, reporters, and writers. It becomes ingrained and reflexive to try to spare your boss that stomachache. Don't put him under pressure he might mishandle. Skip the risky thing, do the safe thing. Cover other peoples' controversies but don't get pulled into them and don't start any of your own.

The Stomachache Rule says: soften that tough verb. Let's not use that sound bite—it might bring on a libel suit. And forget that ghetto story—the reporter and crew are leery about setting foot in the ghetto anyway, but even if they go the story is so complicated and depressing that viewers won't understand it or even try. Why produce a downer like that when it's so much safer and cheaper to cover a boat show or a fire or a street crime or the mayor deploring whatever he's deploring today?

It goes on: Why get the boss all shook up? You'll have to go in and explain it to him, and he'll be sitting there upset and fidgeting and waiting for an upset and fidgeting call from *his* boss. Why send a reporter and crew back to re-do an interview because the reporter didn't think fast enough or because he didn't quite have the nerve to ask the key question? It costs time and money to send the crew back and they could be doing something else with less chance of a washout. And hey, face it: Reporter Jones can't handle it anyway. Jones was hired for his or her sex, sexiness, appearance, age, voice, eye contact, race, ethnic origin, nice smile, audience warmth rating. Expect something from Jones? Are you kidding? And besides, Jones has made it clear that he/she won't be available to do any reporting this afternoon because he/she absolutely must get to the hair stylist to get ready for—get this—tonight's awards dinner!

Corruptions of this ilk take place every day. They are exasperating and sometimes appalling. But make no mistake: they are piddling compared to what might have been. If you doubt that, consider what actually *is* in most other countries. Political pressure, censorship, government or sponsors meddling with content—these dragons may not be entirely dead in this country, but they have been whipped into submission and whenever they stir, a warning cry goes up. The warning cry that followed Spiro Agnew's fire-breathing attack on the news media was more of a flustered squeal than a clarion call to arms, but by the time good luck and good prosecutors had driven Agnew into disgrace, TV news was probably re-immunized in its resistance to external villains.

Murrow is a symbol of the victory against these villains, who were defeated before they could dig in. In a time when television journalism was a baby giant groping for identity and values, he led the way. He set a very high level. We have not always stayed on that level, but at least we know what a high level is. No other country, to my knowledge, has had a Murrow.

There is an assumption throughout TV news that the moral code Murrow symbolized is a permanent and secure part of the fabric—that it is universally understood and embraced, that it passes along by osmosis to each generation of newcomers, and that the elders of the profession remain steadfast in their commitment to it. Well, maybe. It has worked pretty well so far. There have been many stalwart keepers of the flame. Some, like Walter Cronkite,* have

---

*Cronkite was an outstanding wire service reporter in Europe during World War II, and Murrow tried to hire him at CBS. Cronkite passed up the offer and didn't make the move to CBS and broadcasting until five years later.

kindled flames of their own. But now the guard is changing, and one must wonder how readily volunteers would mobilize to defend the code if doing so involved real personal risk.

As for the leaders of TV news, certainly they didn't get to the top by being weaklings (although that need not mean they are strong on defense of principle). High position brings out the best in some people, but remember the seductions. All of them have been cradled in the lush bosom of the corporation. They have presidential or vice presidential titles. They have power and prestige. They can pick up their living room phones and impress their guests by ordering on-the-air changes in news coverage. They can have tape cassettes, or lesser executives, delivered by helicopter to their summer homes. They can phone the White House and probably get through to the Chief himself. They can set people in motion all over the world. They can read their names in newspapers, be quoted in magazines, receive awards and tributes on a regular basis, travel overseas on the company tab, and be treated like lords wherever they go. For all this they receive large salaries, bonuses, stock deals, etc. It's a lot to risk, particularly when the alternative is probably oblivion—early retirement or a teaching job or an insecure and ornamental position in public relations.

The leaders are not the only ones who might have to face a test of values. It goes all the way down. Executive producers and senior producers. Station managers and news directors. Globe-trot-ting network correspondents who need their nightly "fix" of air time the way an addict needs heroin. Six O'Clock producers and report-ers in remote stations who feel their career momentum rushing them toward the Big Time. And writers too. The test comes suddenly and the response might shape the pattern of your future. Does that young journalist's vow to emulate Murrow fall by the wayside? Does that network vice president's resolute posture melt into a scramble for compromise?

It is not enough to hope that challenges from powerful au-thority (external or internal) will always be courageously rebuffed. It is a romantic illusion (inspired to some degree by Murrow himself) that journalists, because of their presumed idealism, will always re-spond idealistically. Every confrontation raises the possibility of ac-quiescence. When it comes down to an individual situation, self-preservation tends to push other motives into the background. If a stand on principle endangers your job or standing, what does it get you, other than self-respect and a round of applause from some of your colleagues as you head out into the cold? Will they name a legacy after you? Where will the next paycheck come from? *Gulp.*

I have taken part in my share of minor stands on principle but I recall only one clear-cut incident when, all alone, I took an inflexible I-shall-not-be-moved moral position and got a sense of the hot anxiety it generates. It happened in my first year as a newswriter. I was supervising the editing of a film story (this was 1972, before videotape replaced newsfilm) that I judged to be grossly incomplete and one-sided. I stalked out to the producer and firmly advised that the story be killed. To my surprise there was strong resistance to killing it—it was an important subject and the reporter was a star with a fiery temper who tended to explode in rage when his pieces were tampered with, let alone killed. Everyone wanted the story; no one wanted the explosion.

The assistant news director followed me back to the editing room to see the film for himself and apply his cooler judgment. After screening it he said, "I see your point, but let's use it anyway. It's not that bad."

I should stress that this pragmatic decision is fairly common (though rarely articulated so candidly). But I resented it and vehemently pressed my case against the piece. An animated argument ensued. The noncommital film editor sat between us turning left and right as if watching a tennis match. Finally the decision to proceed with the piece took the form of a direct order—and I rejected it. Soaring with indignation I announced that I would take no part in this contemptible breach of principle, I would not complete the piece, and I would not be quiet about what had happened.

The assistant news director now had mutiny on his hands. That reflected poorly on his leadership. And he knew the piece was bad. So he tried to back off, suggesting a compromise. I have forgotten now what the compromise was, but I distinctly remember where I told him to shove it. In this excess I crossed the line between defense of principle and brazen insubordination. He was infuriated. Suddenly he was screaming at me. He was normally amiable and I had never seen him upset, so seeing him red-faced and spluttering with rage was a shock.

I stood there shaking my head in silent defiance, knowing that silent defiance was all I could muster because my righteous courage was beginning to deflate. I started asking myself uncomfortable questions. Who was I, with six or eight months of television experience, to be firing a torpedo into a major story by a major reporter in direct defiance of a major executive? Was the story really so badly done that it couldn't be salvaged or repaired? Couldn't I be fired for insubordination? Wouldn't a certified insubordinate have difficulty getting another job? Would potential employers be impressed by my lofty principles or would they identify with the assistant news director?

Then the whole crisis ended in a single sentence, an abrupt reversal. The assistant news director said, "Aw hell, you're right, let's kill it" and walked out of the room.

So I had won. But it felt more like a reprieve than a victory. I stood there thoroughly rattled, watching dumbly as the editor rewound the film. He stared at me, shaking his head in wonder at the reckless things people do. Then he unlocked a cabinet and produced his secret bottle of vodka, which he kept on hand for calming-down purposes after frantic "crash-and-burn" editing sessions. I took an eye-watering slug and lingered for another moment and headed back to the newsroom, hoping it would be a while before my next great moral confrontation.

Looking back now I see that in my anxiety I exaggerated the probable consequences of the situation. I doubt very much that I would have been fired, though I might have been disciplined. It helped my case that I was indisputably right, though if my obstructionism had come close to airtime or caused a gap in the newscast, being right would not have been enough. As it happened, there was an unspoken agreement to forget the incident. My insubordination would be regarded as only a tempermental flare-up (of which there are many in a newsroom), but I would get the message that continuing in the same vein would lead me to grief.

Yet I think there was more to it than that. The incident was small, small even in the context of that single day in the newsroom, but I think it was more than a growing-up experience for a junior newswriter or a transitory office problem for a junior executive. I think it reminded both of us, as well as a veteran film editor, that we worked in a business that was more than just a business. Indeed it was a public institution with real moral obligations and its own code of ethics—a code usually known by its all-encompassing shorthand label, Murrow Legacy. Such high-falutin matters are almost never mentioned in newsrooms, partly because they make for tiresome conversation, partly because they make people too solemn to function. A climate of morality is presumed to be present but a newsroom prefers not to test it, just as a motorist would rather not put his brakes to the test when he is driving in a pouring rain. The test asks the question: are the brakes there or are we now hurtling out of control and into something dark and dangerous?

In my little showdown, the brakes worked. The question was asked, and for whatever reasons, the right answer was given. Undoubtedly the word spread beyond the tiny editing room, traveling via office grapevine. I like to think that it modestly reassured the news staff that the code was still intact. That assurance is vulnerable; in the newsroom I'm remembering, it later did break down, not entirely but enough to disturb anyone who wants to believe that the standards associated with the Murrow era are safe and secure.

My feeling is that rather than relying on individuals to be reckless or heroic in spectacular confrontations, the key to deterring intimidation, venality, or slipshod standards is a general awareness of the effectiveness of moral disapproval. Nobody, including a boss, is comfortable with the moral disapproval of the people around him, especially if it threatens to undermine his position.

For instance, the general manager of a local station knows that he can probably take his subordinate, the news director, into a private session and bully him without repercussion. He is probably not concerned about a few individual hotheads on the news staff, but it would moderate his behavior if he perceived a danger of igniting the idealism of the newsroom community. This is trouble and he doesn't want it. He doesn't want to have to explain or defend himself to protesting staff members. He does not want to be embarrassed by newspaper stories (leaked by staff members) which lead to editorials that beat him over the head with the Murrow Legacy. He does not want phone calls from nervous sponsors. He doesn't want union grievance sessions or anchormen fretting about damage to their "image." He doesn't want worried questions from his wife or children or behind-his-back whispers at his country club. Most of all, he doesn't want corporate bosses discussing the way he blundered and lost control of the situation. Wary of these repercussions, he avoids igniting them in the first place. But if he has no reason to be wary, there is no restraint on where temptation or expediency might lead him.

I do not mean to suggest that station executives or anyone else come to the office scheming to perpetrate treacherous abuses of the Murrow Legacy. In fact, dramatic abuses are uncommon. If you are hankering to take a stand in a clear-cut moral showdown, you may have to wait a while for the occasion. And even then ambiguity creeps into the picture. Most abuses stem *not* from calculated evil but from intentions or ideas that seem genuinely sensible to someone else (Paley surely thought it was sensible to increase profits and avoid stomachaches). The matter is not simple, and you're not fully confident in your cause. You don't know if it's worth the fight and the risk. And there is always that handy rationalization about holding off today to fight the bigger battle tomorrow.

And what happens tomorrow? When that bigger battle starts taking shape you might figure out that the risk is also bigger. So maybe you hold off once again, waiting for another day when you will fight a *smaller* battle. Or maybe you trade in your white horse and forget about riding off on intrepid crusades.

In the narrow context of the newsroom, the question is: when do you squawk and when do you walk away? Certainly it is excessive to reject all compromise or to prowl around pouncing on others in their less than noble moments, setting off little dramas in which you become the incarnation of virtue. This is self-serving but also self-defeating. You will be considered a crank and isolated from everything important. People will tell you to "grow up" or be "realistic." Your crusading becomes a bore or a joke, and you become a Don Quixote tilting at assistant news directors until they stop putting up with you.

But consider the other extreme, which is basically a decision to acquiesce in anything that will keep you out of hot water. This approach, which is what is meant by being "grown-up" or "realistic," is taken instinctively by most people who are apprehensive about jeopardizing their positions. This is understandable, but it's also sad. What is sadder is that it doesn't protect them from trouble. Fearfulness is an invitation to bullies, as Murrow noted when he challenged McCarthy. Spinelessness makes you vulnerable. You get demoted, mistreated, insulted, toyed with, maybe even discarded. At the end of your career you have to say, "I stood for nothing, I went along, I did everything they wanted, and finally they screwed me anyway."

A simple definition of the Murrow Legacy is: *conscience*. When your conscience tells you to act, that is a strong signal that you must do it or rue it. Journalists, who savor their role in forming judgments on others, must be accountable themselves. Particularly the newswriters. They are the bedrock of the internal community of the newsroom. Morality must be secure on their level. They must have it themselves and be ready to offer it in support of those above them who face greater pressures—reporters, anchormen, producers, executives. They can help preserve the best in the system or they can let termites devour the foundation.

2

Common Mistakes of Neophyte Writers

In the previous chapter I noted that I grew up listening to Edward R. Murrow. Murrow's style, enhanced by his electrifying delivery, created a strong echo in the writing "ear" of many future writers; I didn't realize that I had absorbed his sound and rhythms, but I had; and it gave me an unexpected advantage when I started writing words to be read aloud by others.

Except for classroom exercises, my first experience writing for someone else took place when I was a junior officer in the Navy, drafting a speech for a three-star admiral. Even among admirals he was a deadly speaker, an intelligent man but stuporous and reluctant on the public rostrum. He knew he needed help, but he could not have been optimistic about what he would get from me. We were worlds apart: he was in his sixties, I was in my early twenties; he was a true Navy man, I was one year out of graduate school and ill at ease in my uniform. He requested short sentences; that was all the sophistication he would ask of me. Little did he suspect that I would furnish him with a text designed for one of the foremost communicators of the twentieth century: what I wrote was pure Edward R. Murrow. Correction: pure *imitation* Edward R. Murrow.

I did not mimic Murrow intentionally, or even consciously. But as I wrote, his sound played in my mind, like a background melody. All I had to do was fill in the words. It came so naturally that I never paused to consider what I was doing or what the consequences might be.

When the admiral began his speech—eyes glued to the text in the manner of all unconfident speakers, his voice flat as an aircraft carrier's flight deck—I felt a flash of horror and realization. Something was terribly wrong. Something was missing. *Murrow* was missing! Where in this flow of Murrow sentences were the Murrow resonances, the Murrow tautness and intensity? I did not hear the admiral—what I heard was the *difference* between the admiral and Murrow. And what a difference! To my ear it was resounding, painful; the admiral was unbelievably inadequate, and he was being humiliated! What had I done to this nice old man? And since this nice old man had the power to dispatch me to the Vietnamese jungles or the Antarctic with a single phone call, what had I done to myself?

But it turned out fine. The possibility that the admiral was up there doing an imitation of Edward R. Murrow was suspected by no one, including the admiral himself. His speech, while not enthralling, was listenable and solid. No one dozed off; the admiral was thrilled to finish a speech in front of awake people. He was overjoyed with my work. I looked to the heavens and whispered a word of thanks to Murrow for planting in my ear a rhythm and syntax so clean and true that it would work for even the most untalented readers.

The Murrow tones are no longer ringing in my writer's ear. And that's fine: no more imitation for me. Still, imitation is an excellent learning method. I'm sure that every writer has gone through imitation phases. Creative writing teachers have seen whole generations of students imitating Hemingway, Faulkner, J. D. Salinger, Norman Mailer, Tom Wolfe (and many a newsroom editor has spotted the laconic cadences of David Brinkley). I've heard of creative writing exercises in which students are *assigned* to imitate top writers or simply retype exemplary literary passages. Both are ways of getting deeper into the rhythm and character of an accomplished writer's work.

Imitation can be enormously helpful to neophyte newswriters because it helps them find a voice, a consistent and confident way of saying things. If they do not have a style to imitate, or it they imitate poorly, their writing is erratic and tentative. They try everything, all at once, like a shopper feverishly trying on hats in search of "the real me."

I have seen some phenomenally out-of-control scripts by new writers in this predicament. In just a few sentences they manage to be both too literary and too colloquial, too formal and too flippant, too wise and too naive. They bog down in qualification or they forget to qualify; they are stiffly objective one moment, injecting personal opinion the next; trying to showcase a special gift for powerful descriptive writing, they fall back upon the weakest weapon of oral communication, the adjective. And they choose the wrong adjective.

This is not imitating, because no professional writes like this. It is a mishmash of unexamined *impressions* of what the news sounds like. Self-conscious desperation jumps up from the page; the writer is acutely conscious that he does not have a self (voice) of his own.

That's the time to borrow one and use it as a crutch until a mature style of your own emerges. And make sure you borrow a real one, not some foggy notion of how newsmen sound. Get some scripts and read them thoroughly. If you can't get scripts use a tape recorder and transcribe. When you see it on paper you'll start developing a trustworthy "ear." One other thing: if you're going to imitate, imitate someone who is conspicuously good. Don't teach yourself to be a hack.

Having blessed imitation, I must also warn against it. It has at least two major drawbacks.

The first is the probability that you will imitate that most imitated element of newswriting, the cliché. Telling a new writer to banish the cliché is like telling someone, "Don't catch a cold this winter"; like the common cold or the weed or the cockroach, the cliché can be attacked but never stamped out entirely. For even the best newswriters, resisting the cliché is an eternal struggle, a struggle that merits a chapter of its own later in this book.

The second major drawback to imitation is that you can steal someone else's outward style, but you cannot steal that person's substance. Judgment, knowledge, perspective, and wit are theft-proof. In my speech for the admiral I may have achieved Murrow-esque style, but God knows what I used for substance in view of my shallow background in naval affairs. Imitation is hollow, and the best reason to grow beyond it as fast as you can is that it exposes your hollowness and calls attention to the disparity between you and the genuine article.

Here are five more pitfalls awaiting the beginning newswriter.

1. The assumption that mankind's experience began the day you became a professional chronicler of it.

As a beginning journalist you have almost no context to fit things into and thus have difficulty telling the special from the ordinary. Your youthful discoverer's zeal tempts you to react as if the things you encounter are being encountered for the first time, not just by you but by the world at large. It is like arriving at a baseball game in a late inning and marveling over the first play you see, which everyone else in the stadium recognizes as routine.

In your eagerness you think that every story that comes your way is fresh and new, but of course what is fresh and new is *you*—your professional consciousness. The stories, well, they have happened many times before, in many variations, and they have been covered in all the predictable ways. The stories that most appeal to beginners' imaginations tend to be the most unreliable—clichés, melodrama, hokum, crackpot antics, blazing rhetoric, tenth-of-a-point statistical fluctuations that entice the writer to announce historic trends or changes. The newcomer dives into such material seeking splashy displays of his talent, but what he displays is his innocence.

That story about the buffalo chip olympics is hilariously novel the first time you do it—but a year later you're doing it again, and you figure out that it's an annual dumb event that gets attention only because it's so hilariously novel to first-timers.

That heart-wrenching family story moves you so earnestly the first time—but the same story happens every day, and sometimes it turns out that the poor sweet victimized grandmother who aroused so much of your compassion actually runs a numbers racket and tortures the starving dog she keeps locked in a closet.

That exciting "first" is not a first, or even a second. Best, worst, biggest, smallest—beginning journalists are suckers for bogus superlatives. (Some never outgrow the temptation.) How well I remember my eleventh grade English teacher, William B.T. Mock, chalking in giant letters on the blackboard ESCHEW THE SUPERLATIVE, an admonition that was all the more memorable because of the odd-sounding new vocabulary word *eschew*—the message was not to *chew* the superlative but to *abstain* from it.

So, restrain your discoverer's zeal. But don't choke the life out of it. A good news organization depends heavily on young people who are open to discovery. Your seniors would rather cope with an excess of zeal than with the premature world-weariness of a twenty-four-year-old who thinks he's seen everything. If Thomas Edison had agreed that there was nothing new under the sun, we'd be writing news by candlelight.

2. The assumption that because you know what you're trying to say, you've succeeded in saying it.

The basic challenge in all kinds of writing might be: Can you say exactly what you want said? Can you *control* what you're saying? Most writers think they can, but often there is an element of wishful thinking or benefit-of-the-doubt about your own copy.

You know what you want to say (or think you do), and you write something down. But do these words really capture the thought? Have you articulated successfully or only put down some kind of approximation or shorthand language that makes private sense to you but will be vague, incomplete, or baffling to viewers?

All writers struggle with this problem. Those who communicate most effectively learn to hear a story as the audience will hear it, without any supplemental coaching or explaining. They know the story must stand on its own and that the audience cannot and will not read the writer's mind. All the right words and facts must be there, concretely, like physical evidence in a courtroom, or the point will not get across.

So, when you read over your copy you must suspend the impulse to adore it uncritically. You must learn to muster as much detachment as possible, searching for flaws, gaps, ambiguities, and possibilities for misunderstanding. E. B. White, a master of control and clarity, wrote, "When you say something, make sure you have said it. The chances of your having said it are only fair" (*Time Magazine,* 14 Oct. 1985, p. 105).

3. Becoming a victim of your eagerness by seeing only what you want to see.

As a newspaper reporter in San Francisco, excitedly covering my first murder, I wrote a hair-raising front page story about a mother who had been stabbed to death defending herself and her little boy (also dead) from a brutal intruder. I went whole-hog with the dramatics, impressing my fellow reporters and terrifying the community where the brutal intruder was presumably on the prowl.

The next day the police disclosed that there had been no brutal intruder. The mother, for whatever dark reasons, had crushed her son's skull with a brick and then attempted suicide by swallowing drain cleaner; the drain cleaner created such an agonizing fire in her throat that she attacked it with a knife, stabbing herself sixteen times in the neck, until she was dead.

So my story was horrendously incorrect. The police at the crime scene had pointed out that there was no sign of forced entry into the house, no sign of robbery, no sign of sexual assault. These facts were left for me and one other young reporter to add up. We let them go by as unexplained curiosities. We were not inclined to deal with an ambiguous story when a sensational story dangled in front of us. Eagerness triumphed over restraint: we saw only what we were looking for.

In my own defense I should note that one is slow to suspect a mother in the slaughter of her child, and one who barely notices a can of drain cleaner in a cluttered and bloody room is not likely to connect it with sixteen knife wounds in the throat. But the police made all the connections. When I questioned them they must have been already dubious about the brutal intruder theory. I suppose they were within bounds to withhold their speculation, but it would have spared a community a day of fear if they had said to me and the other reporter, "Look, you two don't seem to be catching on but there's a chance this isn't what you think it is. Just bear that in mind."

But the fault was ours; we should have kept asking questions as long as there were question marks. Instead we dashed off to our typewriters. Since then I have never finished an interview without asking, "Is there anything I should know that I haven't asked about?" If the source is withholding information, this question pressures him to choose between revealing it or lying—a choice he can otherwise avoid on grounds that "You never asked." Even if he doesn't reveal it, he might give you a signal, intentional or not, that there is more to the story.

It should be noted that esteemed veteran journalists are not immune to overeagerness when sensational stories beckon—for instance, the brief but embarrassing episode involving the faked "Hitler Diaries" in the spring of 1983.

4. Myopic omission of major points.

I mentioned that newcomers lack the frame of reference that facilitates judgments about what is important in a news story and what is only secondary. In the absence of an established structure for fact selection, there is a kind of mental free-for-all in which various story elements go up and down in value. In this stock market atmosphere main points tend to lose glamor, supplanted by bewitching lesser details. The newswriter becomes fascinated with, say, an earthquake's Richter scale rating and forgets to report where it took place or what damage it did.

Of course this happens to experienced writers too, not so much because the story is a muddle to begin with but because they get involved in trying to refine their telling of it. Somewhere around the third or fourth draft the main points start being nudged aside to make room for the writer's tangents or flourishes.

When you find yourself bogging down like this, it is wise to take a breather, clear your mind, and ask yourself just what you're trying to say. It might help to try the tell-it-to-your-aunt technique: Imagine picking up the phone, calling your aunt, and telling her the story. Instinctively you gear it for her comprehension, trimming away the tangles and complications. You will hear yourself telling the story naturally. It's an especially good way to sort out your thoughts about where a story starts or how you should phrase the lead.

Of course this technique will get you into trouble if your aunt is particularly atypical. In that case pick someone else. Turner Catledge, the late executive editor of the *New York Times,* suggested imagining "a curious but somewhat dumb younger brother."

5. Not knowing enough.

When I began this book I sent postcards to the faculties of sixty-five college journalism and TV departments asking what they considered the major deficiencies of students planning to go into journalism. Many of the replies complained that students were shockingly ignorant about basic institutions, namely government, police, and the courts.

When you consider how much daily news flows from these institutions, it is unforgivable if beginners are lax in finding out about them. I suggest getting someone in your newsroom to explain them to you; after that you should *go* to city hall, the police station, and the courthouse and aggressively seek out people who will show you around. You may feel shy about doing this but you'll find that people like to discuss their jobs. You'll return to the newsroom more confident and less ignorant.

What's worse than not knowing enough is not realizing how little you know. Trying too hard to be impressive, a young writer or reporter may puff up his copy with offhand statements that seem accurate at the moment (but are not) or tidbits of conventional wisdom that seem to ring true (but collapse under scrutiny). He leaps confidently into subjects that turn out to be whirlpools of complexity. He tries to go too far with too little knowledge. And he gets caught. It can be very embarrassing.

He will learn to stick to what is concretely in front of him and not to flavor it with loose thoughts. He will learn to hesitate before embracing assumptions or forcing the neat conclusions writers naturally yearn for. He will come to recognize the wisdom of the old saw, "When in doubt, leave it out." He can learn the easy way or he can wait for the mortifying kind of lesson I learned when I covered my first big crime story that afternoon in San Francisco.

3

The Newswriter and the Fundamental Duality

F. Scott Fitzgerald was hardly groping for the essence of TV news, but I think he hit the mark anyway in his much-quoted suggestion that "The test of a first-rate intelligence is the ability to hold two opposed ideas in the mind at the same time, and still retain the ability to function."

TV news has a split personality. It is not one idea but two. Draw a line between TV and News and there it is: it is television *and* news. It is Show Business *and* journalism. It is production *and* reporting. It is highly paid performers wearing makeup as they read scripts before a camera *and* it is a words-and-pictures, facts-and-figures account of the day's events.

It is image *and* substance, experience *and* information, theater *and* data. It is, for example, the classic *60 Minutes* piece in which Mike Wallace nails a Bad Guy: investigative journalism *and* gripping drama as the villain attempts to squirm free.

The key is that it is always both. An anchorman reading a script is performing, but he is also telling the news. A TV station wants its newscast to get the best ratings and profits, but it also wants to do well journalistically. The values of TV and of journalism are often in opposition and the balance between them is forever fluctuating, but the point is that they are always there together, uniquely intertwined.

Virtually everything about TV news reflects this double identity, which I will call the Fundamental Duality (I would have preferred a Quintessential Dichotomy but they were all taken). I believe it uncomplicates many of the conflicts and contradictions that muddle our thinking about TV news.

It is a simple concept, yet in practice people flunk the Fitzgerald test of holding two opposed ideas in their minds at the same time. They insist on trying to understand TV news as reflecting almost exclusively the values of television *or* of journalism. Critics will tell you TV news is strictly Show Business, entertainment in the guise of news. Defensive TV journalists will tell you the Show Business aspect is only peripheral and doesn't influence the journalism. But the truth is that it is what it is: both.

The Fundamental Duality applies to almost every decision and almost every job in a news department. It will be mentioned frequently in this book. In this chapter the subject is how it affects the working environment of the newsroom and, particularly, how it affects the writing and those who write.

In the newsroom the dual processes are reporting the news and producing the TV show—journalism versus production. They work in close parallel, sometimes indistinguishably, and it often seems that one has eclipsed the other. If you come into the newsroom late in the day it should be clear which process has the greater dynamism: production.

It is not that journalism is consciously disdained but that production is the more frantic imperative. The momentum of putting the show on the air overrides all other considerations. The greatest nightmare is not a deficiency of journalism but a breakdown in production: if important journalistic details have been omitted they can be plugged in later (the odds are that their absence will hardly be noticed anyway), but if the cameraman has missed the big shot, if the tape is not delivered or edited on time, or if a lead-in to Tape A is followed by the roll of Tape B (or worse—I once wrote a lead-in to a gasoline prices story and what rolled was a Texaco commercial), this is a catastrophe, painful and humiliating.

Whenever there is a conflict between TV production values and journalism values, TV values have the more natural claim and will usually and unsurprisingly prevail. Production is urgent, exciting, concrete; journalism tends to be intangible. Production requires a high-powered team effort; journalism usually comes down to the effort of a single Lone Ranger. The momentum of production yanks this Lone Ranger along; he learns to tailor his journalism to the needs of the production machine.

The production machine is operated by the journalists of the newsroom but also by many people who are *not* journalists—the director and assistant director, tape editors, tape librarian, production assistants and associates, graphic artists, control room technicians, engineers, and studio crew.

Some are savvy about the news (especially the director), some are not—it's not a requirement of their jobs. Non-journalists dom- inate the studio and control room, and they are an integral presence in the newsroom—a major difference from newspapers, where the workers who actually make the newspaper seldom have contact with the people who report for it.

The non-journalists tend to be alert, extroverted, forceful peo- ple who exert a strong influence on the atmosphere and values of the newsroom. Their paramount value is production, so it's no sur- prise that production skill becomes the measure of a person's contribution.

Journalism-minded staff members do not seal themselves into editorial enclaves as they might on a publication. On the contrary, they become avid connoisseurs of production. Watching their news- cast together they grimace in unison at a bad edit or a late tape roll or a "super" (superimposed printing) that comes up at the wrong time, and they award professional praise when they spot a nifty piece of work. They don't say much about the news itself. They take pride in mastering and implementing production technique and learning production jargon. If they go overboard with dazzle or gim- mickry, that is only a small offense, an excess of creative enthusiasm.

And that brings up another factor in production's sway over journalism: it is generally more fun. It's a large part of the attraction of working in television and it is probably the reason most TV news- people chose television instead of print. A friend of mine who started as a local station newswriter and rose to success as a network pro- ducer fondly recalls his writing days but remembers his hurry to break away from the typewriter and start doing "real TV stuff"— standing over editors, taking crews out on stories, doing back- timings and rundowns, racing the clock, rushing to the control room in a tingle of nerves and excitement and grappling with the explosive contingencies of a show on the air.

A show. The news is the subject but the show is the action, the experience, the proving ground. Banging on a typewriter or trying to dig out the facts on auto accidents or fires is dreary stuff by contrast with the roller-coaster exhilaration of production.

At this point it is time for an emphatic reminder that everything I have said above applies to the *internal* values of a newsroom. The gems of production that inspire such whoops of internal appreciation may seriously mislead the newsroom's journalists. They come to think that their audience is the newsroom and its connoisseurs of production. What they tend to forget is that there is also an outside world. The values of the people *out there* are diametrically different from "inside" values.

Audiences do not watch TV news to admire the production. No doubt production (including the composition of the on-air "news team") affects the quality and success of a program. But it is not why people watch. Unlike the viewers in the newsroom, the people at home watch the news to get the news. Indeed it is a famous statistic that 67 percent of all Americans say they get their news mainly from television. Thus the Fundamental Duality, internally tilted toward production, now tilts the other way, toward telling the news.

This brings us to the newswriter.

Amid the noisy sweep and swirl of the newsroom, the writer sits in frozen concentration. His desk top is cluttered with wire copy, coffee containers, overflowing ash trays. He stares at his typewriter or word processor, mumbles to himself, pecks at his keyboard, or pounds away at it. While he struggles to write he is all alone; the action flows around him like water flowing around islands in a stream.

If he is at all perceptive he has come to question whether he is at the core of the news operation (as he hopes) or on the periphery (as he suspects). It occurs to him that he is theoretically expendable—anchormen and reporters should do all the writing, reporters and associate producers should oversee the editing of tape stories (in newsrooms that do not employ staff writers this is exactly how it works).

At his lowest moments he wonders if he is an anachronism, if the TV newswriter is an endangered species bound for extinction as TV journalism sheds the obsolescent fixtures of the past. And what figure is more obsolescent than the old-fashioned newswriter—the practitioner of a Print Era job in a No Print medium?

What I am calling the Writer's Secret is the one invigorating positive that offsets a slew of negatives about the writer's perception of his place in the newsroom. (It also applies to reporters and anchormen when they are functioning in their roles on the journalism side of the Fundamental Duality, as opposed to their roles as on-camera performers.)

This is the Writer's Secret: that while he is writing for an anchorman who receives many times his salary, that while his judgment is rarely sought and not always welcome when he expresses it, that while his work is hardly noticed unless it is conspicuously bad or absolutely haywire, *he* controls the words. And despite all the sophisticated technology and organizational complexity of TV, the age-old truth of journalism prevails: *the words are the freight.*

Try relating facts without words and you find yourself at the pre-caveman level of human communication. So you would assume that words and the people who are employed as specialists in the orchestration of words (and thoughts—don't forget thoughts) would enjoy a position of creative prominence in the TV news process.

But it doesn't feel that way to the newswriter. On the contrary, he feels that he is regarded, within his own news organization, as an unskilled laborer.

There are several reasons for this. In a way, newswriters *are* unskilled, because they lack the technical training or production management skills of others in the newsroom. A college graduate with decent writing ability might be able to get by as a writer after a few weeks on the job, but it would take many months, probably years, before he could survive a single day of producing or directing an hour-long newscast. Of course writing is a skill, but a newswriter churning out blurb-length stories rarely gets the opportunity to display his range as a craftsman (if he is one). There is also the irony of the newswriting style: it exalts simplicity, but if the writer consistently achieves simplicity, others will think it was simple.

Because he lacks premium skills (and can easily be replaced) the writer receives less pay. TV is a financial gold mine, and the writer's pay is generally nothing to moan about, but the writer who places high values on his journalistic contribution may be surprised at his low position on the salary scale.

He is outearned by a majority of his colleagues: on-camera "talent" because they are stars, producers and assignment editors because they are his newsroom seniors and have much greater professional knowledge and responsibility, executives because they are executives, technicians and engineers and especially the director—the kingpin of the production side of the Fundamental Duality. The newswriter's pay may be on a par with film or tape editors. The only group he clearly outearns are the assistant-level people, the researchers, production assistants, and desk assistants.

Newswriters also tend to fall into the unskilled category because they are new. The newswriter job is a coveted entry position for beginners who manage to skip over the desk assistant level. And it is a high turnover job because newcomers who do well quickly graduate to producer or on-camera jobs and are replaced by still newer newcomers. Writers who do not go on the higher jobs are of two kinds: a small number who enjoy what they do and don't want to switch to something else and a larger number who have no other choice—either no one wants to promote them or they are veterans whose careers are going down, not up. The older writers are vaguely discredited and the younger ones have not yet earned credit; if they are taken seriously, it's only tentatively. Individual writers may stand out, but the writers as a group do not have potent status in the newsroom hierarchy.

And it gets worse.

In an organization whose designated function is the gathering of news, the writer does not take a primary role in newsgathering. He doesn't go out on stories (mainly he *processes* news gathered by reporters for his organization or from wire services), which means that he is always operating from the weak and beholden position of indirect or secondhand knowledge.

His decisions are small ones. He doesn't make assignments or give orders. He doesn't initiate. Because he writes copy another person will read aloud, he must submerge his own ego and efface his personality (which is not to say that he cannot be the life of the party in the newsroom). And there is a further blow to his ego: in many newsrooms the writers are not the best writers. They can be beaten at their own game by at least a few other members of the editorial team.

Most producers started out as writers and would not have risen unless they had done well, but the best writers are found among reporters and anchors. Not that all of them are good. Some are only good talkers and fall apart when there is a need for disciplined writing structure.

Others simply lack talent and need an embarrasing amount of help from writers and producers. Too little help and constructive criticism is available to local station reporters; for network reporters there may be too much of it, in the form of meddling, nit-picking, and sometimes bullying by senior producers and editors on the network news desks. This accounts for occasional "defensive writing" by network correspondents who become overly inhibited by the prospect of news desk criticism. They write and deliver such self-conscious copy that they seem to be strangling as they say the words—or, if not strangling, wearing extremely tight underwear.

If there is an element of self-importance in network style, it's also true that the networks *are* important and feel a palpable responsibility to protect their reputations as prestigious and unimpeachably credible news organizations. This sobering consideration and the compression of network reports (local stations have far more airtime for news) explain the tense formality of network writing. The local station has more freedom and more airtime and should be a better place for talented writers.

Writing for on-air anchormen or reporters who are superior writers themselves might seem to be a daunting challenge. *(Me? Writing for him?)* But in my experience, good on-air writers are most likely to recognize and appreciate good off-air writers. They will not feel threatened by you or competitive with you. In fact, they will be delighted if you give them something especially well written because good copy reflects well on them no matter who wrote it. Further, they tend to be deft editors and copy-fixers, and that's good for both of you.

Many of the best on-air writers also turn out to be topnotch on-air readers. It is a rewarding feeling for the newswriter to have his copy well delivered, just as it is annoying or even infuriating when an anchorman flubs all your best lines. Harry Reasoner used to astonish me with his virtually foolproof reading style: if you wrote it well he would read it well, but if it was hasty or mediocre, he would *still* read it well. A run-on sentence that would leave anyone else gasping for breath was effortless for him. A carelessly written story with potential trip-ups, such as confusing pronouns (which "he" does this "he" refer to?), would come out with perfect clarity. It may be intimidating to write for a master, but in the end *you* look like a master too.

So here I am talking about writers as masters. Only a moment ago it was writers as second-class citizens. Which are they?

The Fundamental Duality answer is: both. Production may be a roaring locomotive that the writer can barely cling to, but the words are the freight, and that is where the writer comes to the fore in terms of journalistic content. Because he is largely bypassed in the hurtling momentum of production, he comes closer than anyone in the newsroom to being free to function purely as a journalist. (Reporters, producers, anchors, and anyone else who writes also belong on the journalism side of the Fundamental Duality, but unlike the writer all of them also have consuming obligations in production.)

In this role he is not an unskilled laborer. Nor is he an anachronism in a No Print medium: almost every word of TV news is in print, though of course viewers don't see the written scripts. As a journalist he does what he has been educated and trained to do: dealing with the *content* of the news.

In the tumult of production, the writer sometimes experiences a delicious feeling that he is *sneaking in* with the substance. While everyone else is screaming and having conniptions over production, his script slips through and—boom!—it is on the air, going out to a vast audience. In the bedlam of the control room, maybe no one is listening. But the public is listening.

4

Faction and Friction

Tempers run high in a daily news operation, especially in the compacted environment of television. Big egos collide, purposes conflict, the countdown towards airtime creates explosive tension. Annoyances and animosities that would ordinarily fester slowly are accelerated by the general pressure and burst out in sudden fury. But then they subside. There is too much urgency to dwell on them, too many intervening distractions to even remember them.

The greatest blowup I've witnessed in television took place in a crowded elevator. I was squeezed into the elevator with another writer and our boss, the executive producer. The other writer made a casual wisecrack about a piece that had gone badly on the previous day's show. The executive producer was a wisecracking type himself, but the writer's flippancy hit a tender nerve, and he erupted in an astonishing tantrum. His face turned red, his features contorted, his voice cracked. Heedless of the many strangers packed around us, he left no obscenity unyelled as he cursed the "negativism" of writers. The other passengers pressed back to make space for him, as if they had found themselves standing too close to an unhinged psychotic.

The elevator's short trip seemed endless and miserably claustrophobic. At last we reached our floor, but when the doors drew back the executive producer was still cursing and screaming, and a dozen or so people waiting for the elevator were visibly shocked by the violent language blasting out at them. The executive producer, trapped by his own momentum, had no choice but to redouble his rage and charge out of the elevator like a wild bull. The wild bull was followed by two sheepish and mortified writers, furtively exchanging glances that ignited a mutual desire to break loose in gales of laughter. We had to wait until the boss cooled down, but ten minutes later the tension gave way and the three of us laughed until we ached.

The story illustrates the Roman candle temperment that exists in television (and probably in most other highly pressured occupations). More specifically, it illustrates the vein of resentment that many TV people feel about writers. It was remarkable in the elevator incident that this resentment was expressed by an executive producer who was sympathetic to writers—a former writer himself who fondly understood the writer's irreverent personality and had often defended writers accused of negativism.

This attitude toward writers has much in common with the public's attitude toward journalists in general—expressed with memorable alliteration in Vice President Spiro Agnew's 1969 attack on the news media's "nattering nabobs of negativism" (translation: carping know-it-alls who won't let well enough alone).

Why do people feel this way about journalists?

Answer: because it is true, at least superficially.

Why is it true?

Answer: because the writer-journalist is a relentless and aggressive skeptic. Carping and not letting well enough alone are his ways of probing for the flaw, and when he finds the flaw he pounces on it triumphantly, even if it is trivial. His instinctive assumption that there is a flaw may seem negative, but it is frequently correct—most valuable reporting stems from this assumption. As for being a know-it-all, the writer-journalist resents *not* knowing it all; he is personally and professionally affronted by his suspicion that secrets are being kept from him, that meanings and ulterior motives are being concealed, that he is being swindled by fast-talking salesmen peddling spurious goods.

Skepticism is an indispensable trait of a good journalist. Tell him the sun rises every morning and he'll give you a scrutinizing look and say, "Yeah, sure, I'll have to check that out." Skepticism is part of his professional equipment. In a chicken-and-egg relationship, it also reflects his personality. He has a neurotic inclination to doubt and to challenge. One impolite but emphatic judgment is always on his tongue: *"Bullshit!"*

As I've said, TV news is a team effort in which many team members are not journalists. Like good team members, their attitude stresses the positive. They have little affinity or affection for the journalist who goes around suspecting everything of being bullshit. The writer's unceasing skepticism is unattractive to them; they don't mind when he applies it to proper journalistic targets like politicians and police chiefs, but when it comes out in the office, newsroom people find it just as obnoxious as do harrassed news figures.

When an idea comes up in the newsroom the writer is not likely to respond in a can-do spirit (unless it is his own idea). His approach is to look for minuses while everyone else is admiring the plusses. He knows that at some future point he will have to execute the idea in words, and he must convince himself that it is not an illusory, wonderful-seeming bubble that will burst in *his* hands when the time comes to frame it in the unyielding concreteness required by language. His flaw-seeking approach is felt by others as negativism, even when it is ultimately constructive and positive. Not that it always is.

Writers do not help themselves with their erratic behavior, which reflects the swinging pendulum of their self-esteem: they feel at times that they are the only pure journalists in TV and at other times that they are downtrodden word-mechanics. On the upswing they are argumentative objectors, on the downswing they are sullen followers. They are abrasively cynical and vulnerably innocent. They feel unappreciated and stifled—most writers would nod in brotherly agreement with Mozart who, forced to write compositions unworthy of his musical genius to preserve financial support from his patron Emperor Joseph II, ironically complained, "Too much for what I do, too little for what I could do." Classic grousing from a classical master.

There is one other odd bit of behavior that afflicts writers and reporters too: occasional lapses from reality in which their scripts seem to read like surrealist monologues or personal diatribes. I'm not sure why it happens, but most producers will confirm that it does. Usually the writer or reporter insists that what he's done is especially good and usable, and he won't be convinced that he's wrong. It's a strange phenomenon; the producer can only shrug and reassign the story.

The personality I've ascribed to writers is pervasive among journalists in general. They question everything, they are always contentious and ready to disbelieve, and most of them never get over their sense of being aggrieved outsiders, chip-on-the-shoulder truth seekers. Of all journalists, I think the most likely to drift away from this mentality is the prominent on-camera TV news figure who, in his affluence and acclaim, might come to identify more with society's insiders and winners than with its underdogs. More later about the on-camera personality. This chapter is about the main *off-*camera characters of TV news, except executives, who are covered in the next chapter.

Almost every statement I make here is a generality, and I'm sure that every TV news operation would provide variations and exceptions. But I think these generalities reflect *tendencies* that are consistent with the different jobs. Each job attracts the same types of people, and even when the people are different, the job instills the same type of thinking. I suspect that if there is a TV news operation in a distant galaxy where creatures look like bugs or clouds or fire hydrants, the writer-creatures act like writers, producer-creatures behave like producers, director-creatures like directors, and so on.

Producers

Basically, there are two types of producers in TV news, producers who go out on stories and producers who stay inside and run the show. The former are informally called "field producers": they make advance arrangements, get to the story with a crew and with or without a reporter, guide the coverage, return to headquarters or work at a "remote" location to "cut" the piece with film or tape editors, and write or help write the script. Networks assign field producers to every story. Local stations assign them when available; when local stations cannot afford field producers, the reporters do the producing themselves.

The field producer's relationship with the reporter varies from network to network and station to station, and it may change with different pairings of producers and reporters. Sometimes the producer is considered senior, and the reporter follows his instructions. Sometimes the reporter is dominant, and the producer assists. Sometimes they take pains to avoid confrontations over who has the upper hand. Some producer-reporter teams work in constructive harmony; some clash bitterly and come back bad-mouthing each other. I've seldom heard of a field producer who is not a former writer, and most program producers have field producing in their backgrounds.

The other type of producer is the boss of the show. In his book *Air Time: The Inside Story of CBS News* (New York, 1978), Gary Paul Gates describes the evolution of the producer function and title in the late 1940s and early 1950s, when Don Hewitt (later the executive producer of *60 Minutes*) was the director of *Douglas Edwards with the News,* the predecessor of *CBS Evening News with Walter Cronkite:*

Hewitt believed that if the Edwards show was ever going to amount to anything, there had to be more cohesion . . . the news or editorial side had to relate to what was being done on the production or technical side, and vice versa. In taking steps to bridge the gulf, he eventually assumed control over both the editorial and technical operations . . . this made him something more than a director. . . . Indeed it was mainly to define Hewitt's enlarged role on the Edwards show that the term "producer" came into common usage. (Pp. 59–60)

Thus the solution to the recognized problem of bridging the gulf between the two sides of the Fundamental Duality. The producer, with his immediate and direct supervision over news content *and* the production apparatus, had no counterpart in print journalism.

The job called for a unique double orientation. But, to paraphrase George Orwell, one orientation was more equal than the other. It quickly evolved that news producers would be chosen *from the editorial side*. The technical and production side would work *under* a journalist. We now take this for granted, but it was an important step: we could have had non-journalists—directors and technicians and entertainment-minded showmen—producing the news. (Don Hewitt's original title was director, but he had journalistic as well as control room credentials. He had been a newspaper correspondent and editor, and his father was an advertising man for the Hearst newspapers. According to Gates, Hewitt's childhood dream was to become an ace reporter in the get-the-scoop, stop-the-presses tradition of Hearst journalism.)

Except for appearing on camera, producing is *the* job in TV news, the job to which most off-camera TV journalists aspire. The producer is a news program's chief journalist: he supervises assignments, "reads in" to wire copy, checks scripts, consults with reporters, tries to find time to critique the editing of films and tapes, plots the order and flow of stories, and uses his overview—he alone has this overview—to construct a balanced and complete newscast.

Because the producer is probably a former writer himself, there tends to be a strong bond between producers and newswriters. The producer is more likely to understand, tolerate, and stand up for writers than any other power figure in a news operation. He is most likely to be receptive to a writer's suggestions or reservations about a story; in return, he may be the only authority to whom the writer feels personal loyalty. I have gotten into antagonistic situations with just about everyone else in the news operation, but I don't recall a single serious dispute with a producer.

Not that producers are benevolent or too cool to express vehement disapproval. It may be that they simply don't have time to revel in anger. Each day's mounting pressure propels them forward at a dazzling tempo. I recall a thirty-year-old producer whose hair had turned white, who smoked three packs of cigarettes per show, drank black coffee two cups at a time, barely finished gulping down his brought-in sandwich, and made such a post-show rush to the bar across the street that he was usually into his second strong drink before other post-show drinkers arrived to join him. He was a man of many stimulants, but his foremost stimulant was the show itself. He was a glutton for the action and pressure it provided. And while his case is extreme (and unhealthy), most producers seem to thrive on frantic pressure and glide over aggravations that would reduce more deliberate types, including many writers, to hysteria or catatonic collapse.

Sometimes the news is routine and dull, but producing is *always* an intense experience. Therefore it's not uncommon for a producer to become obsessed with "the show" and bored with the news. He does not go out on stories, so it's no surprise if the stories become less real to him. What *is* real are the challenges and pressures of producing. He becomes fascinated by intricacies of production or razzle-dazzle technical gimmickry—the package instead of the contents. Writers and reporters then complain to each other, "This guy doesn't care what we're saying. All he cares about is how long it is and how it fits into his lineup and how he can tease it," etc. (To "tease" a story is to make viewers stay tuned by teasing their curiosity with catchy lines about what lies ahead.)

Ask these questions about the producer of the Six O'Clock local news: does he have more than a headline-deep knowledge of news events? Does he retain personal contact with news figures or news sources? Has he ever seen the mayor or fire chief or local congressman at anything other than chitchatting social events? In moments of relaxation, does he discuss the news with genuine interest? Is his sophistication as a newsman equal to his sophistication as a producer?

In most cases the answer to these questions is no. Producers are always quick to grasp the gist of a story, but frequently that is the extent of their interest. However, this is not necessarily an indictment of the producer. His job does not permit exclusive concentration on *either* side of the Fundamental Duality. He has editorial and production staffs to do that concentrating and provide whatever help or information he needs. As long as he keeps both sides in balance, he is doing a good job. If he tends to tilt that balance in his fascination with production (just as when a writer takes off on flights of unreality or a reporter becomes emotionally involved in a story), it is up to the rest of the team to pull him back on an even keel.

Assignment Editors

The producer stands over the Fundamental Duality, but the assignment editor embodies it. He has dual priorities in almost every decision; every news judgment entails a television judgment, and vice versa. The stories he selects must be newsworthy, but they must also offer visual or action elements for the screen. He must figure out what those elements are, and then he must solve the journalistic, logistical, and technical problems of getting them covered. And he must have a solution when things go wrong, as they often do. He has many headaches.

At some stations the assignment editor has free rein, but that's not the way it's supposed to be. A disciplined news organization tightly controls his decisions. Strong producers and executives take part in choosing stories, deciding how to cover them and which reporters are most suitable to which stories. Then the assignment editor makes it happen. He passes on instructions, sets up interviews and other shooting details, moves reporters and crews around, keeps in touch with them, and gets them back in time.

An assignment editor must be aggressive and creative; he must be instinctive because there's usually not much time to think things over. He should be closely familiar with his locality, knowing the right people to call and the right places to go. He must be good at giving journalistic directions, production directions, and street directions. I think he should be from the city he works in, or at least experienced in that city's journalism, yet stations persist in hiring assignment specialists from other cities. I have seen this done in New York, probably the most complicated city in the Western world, with results that call executive wisdom and sanity into serious question.

The assignment editor must be a salesman for his ideas and others people's ideas, but he rarely gets the enthusiastic response he would like. He is constantly second-guessed and criticized, so he must be thick-skinned and resilient and able to put up with unbelievable frustration and minimal appreciation.

He tries to please everyone but knows it's impossible. The executive wants all key stories covered plus some great new feature ideas. The producer wants a balanced show—in his nightmares the assignment editor provides him with nothing but crime stories, or political stories, or soft features. The reporter going out on an assignment wants a briefing and a preview of what to expect. The crew wants to be finished shooting in time for lunch at a favorite restaurant. And then the writer strolls by and points out that a certain story falls short of his journalistic standards. If it is a story the assignment editor has engineered with great duress, the writer is in for a nasty confrontation.

After a good day, the assignment editor can go home with the satisfaction of having manipulated a difficult machine and orchestrated the coverage of a day's news. But he pays a price. The job is exasperating, exhausting, ulcerating. On a busy day the assignment editor may not have time to eat, and every time he gets halfway to the bathroom he is called back to his desk by a new emergency. I have seen one assignment editor suffer a nervous breakdown. Others have turned into monsters. The best assignment editor I ever worked with developed a green complexion (temporary) and a painful rasp in his voice (permanent) caused by constant hollering over numerous years of fourteen-hour days.

Control Room Macho

In his fine book about television *The Cool Fire,* Bob Shanks describes TV directors as the "fighter pilot personalities" of the TV business. Having spent a year around combat pilots in Vietnam, I relish the comparison. The director sits down at the controls with a lust for action and a bravura confidence that he will face the flak unnerved, hit his targets on the button, react masterfully and even flamboyantly to all unexpected deviations, and wrap up his mission with precision timing and a blaze of glory. Like a fighter pilot, the director often seems like a brash boy playing with an awesome machine, a giant gadget; at other times the director is The Man, the formidable stalwart to whom others turn for command in the face of onrushing chaos.

The producer hands over a show to the director and, with his crew, *the director* puts it on the air. *He* faces the pressure and instant decisions and heart-stopping human and technological screwups; *he* barks orders, blows up, chews out, clowns around, shows off. He is the king of the hill; the studio and control room are *his* domain;

he exercises his power by controlling *the moment,* the immediate, which he unhesitatingly confronts.

He is never challenged from below and infrequently from above. The producer is no longer in the driver's seat, although he continues to be the boss. He is entitled to step in at any time and the director understands that; he might also understand that the producer wants to be in the middle of the fray as his producing effort reaches its culmination.

The producer is probably the only person in the room who would call himself a journalist, and he is journalistically responsible for the show, but he will also be caught up in the highly charged swashbuckling dynamics of the control room. He will assert himself, giving orders with director-style urgency. Some producers meddle outrageously. Others shy away from meddling, which may be just fine with the director but not necessarily in the best interest of the show. The director will ask the producer for decisions and may suggest options, but if the producer is indecisive or slow or busy with other things, the director will take charge. Taking charge is his talent and his personal inclination, as natural to him as skepticism is to the writer. The director is fast and firm, probably more so than anyone else; when the show is on the air his concentration and intensity and surging adrenaline make him nearly always *ahead* of everyone else.

The control room is an exciting arena. Nine times out of ten it is more exciting than the show itself. At any instant something can go wildly wrong and send the show into a hard skid toward the brink of chaos. Sometimes it goes over the brink. At home the viewer sees the production falter and watches with curiosity or amusement, unaware of the pandemonium in the control room where a director is screaming bloody murder to restore order and technicians are frantically searching for the remedy and the producer comes to his feet cursing and shouting over the din. The white-knuckled tautness carries over beyond the crisis, until the director signals that things are back in control. He is likely to do so with the tension-breaking humor of the fighter pilot emerging from a brush with disaster.

The comic relief is so welcome that he can get away with just about anything. A director's control room behavior is the stuff of legends, and he knows it. Often he embroiders his legend with spectacular panache, profanity, physical comedy, stunts, practical jokes. Don Hewitt was evidently the model for antic behavior by directors of news shows, but many sensational performers have followed. My favorite control room tale involves a brilliant network director who chats by telephone with his mother as he directs momentous TV coverage. He seems absorbed in the conversations, which are loud and comical in themselves, but just as people are beginning to worry that he has forgotten about the show, he erupts with directorial instructions, which he shrieks in the most obscene language, without bothering to cover the phone. The punch line is, "No Mom, I didn't mean that *you* are a ————!"

The moment the camera's red light blinks on, the Fundamental Duality tips heavily towards the production side, the director's side. The term *show* is distasteful to serious journalists who prefer the more dignified *broadcast* or *program* but from the control room there is no question that it is a show: its look, smooth flow, and watchability become the prime concerns. People in the control room are thinking television, not journalism.

I've called this section Control Room Macho not only because the atmosphere is rough and rowdy and off-color, along the lines of a men's locker room or a bachelor party. There is also an implicit assumption that this is where The Men take over (even if some of The Men are women), where the doers move in to handle the action, and that *this* action is the core and truth of TV: *it happens here*, not in the newsroom where journalists assemble the pieces, not in the studio where on-camera types behave on cue, not even in the field where reporters do their dance around news events. It happens here, and the people in this room are the Big Guns who make it happen. They make the final decisions, they call the shots, they *control*.

A tenet of Control Room Macho is that instinctive spontaneous decisions made under pressure, decisions made *now*, have more force than earlier-made plans, which pale in the pulsating environment of the control room. The fighter pilot is more than willing to abandon a plan that was crafted with painstaking deliberation in favor of improvising on the fly. An individual item or the whole plan of a show may be thrown out or turned upside-down on a last-minute impulse that catches the momentum of the control room. Spontaneity, virtuosity, impact, pizzazz, cutting and slashing—all control-room values—may crash down like ocean waves on the intricate sand castles built earlier by non-control-room people.

Sometimes this wreaks barbarian havoc on a careful piece of work, a defeat for journalism. But almost as often it adds a vitality that was slipping away or never there, and the journalism is enhanced. Of course, the grumbling, complaining writer would be the last to admit it.

5

Executives

Generalizing about executives causes particular hesitation. Even generalizing about what an executive does is difficult, because there are so many types and levels and functions.

To begin, let's say an executive is anyone who outranks the producer and has responsibilities beyond the daily nuts-and-bolts operation of a news program. The title "executive producer" causes trouble immediately; while this person does have executive functions, the real point of his title is that he is the boss of his show, with lesser producers (including "senior producers") as his deputies.

On the local level, the key executive is the news director (not to be confused with the director in the control room). His superior is the general manager (G.M.) At some stations the G.M. has a subordinate whose title is station manager.

If a station is an affiliate of a network or an O-and-O (owned-and-operated by a network) there are other officials and vice presidents linking the station with the central corporate leadership.

It is widely assumed that local station news departments are under the thumb of network news executives. This is incorrect. In the corporate structure, a network's "stations division" and its network news division are separate entities. Network news and stations might share reporters and reports as well as costs, facilities, and services, but for all practical purposes the local stations are autonomous within the corporation. The future will probably see local stations becoming even more independent as satellite technology allows them to bypass the networks by covering distant events themselves or as part of regional mini-networks.

At the network level, an executive producer is directly in charge of the evening news. He may be a vice president himself, but there are other vice presidents between him and the president of network news. Above that president are other corporate presidents and finally a chairman. These latter officials are exalted and rarely glimpsed;

when they do appear, low-level employees keep a respectful distance and gaze at them with awe and fascination.

Whatever his level, the news executive is concerned not only with the two sides of the Fundamental Duality but also with the *business* of TV news (profits, payroll, personnel, unions, budgets, etc.). Inevitably he is also involved in the *politics* of the business—the external politics of relations with the public and the internal politics of corporate maneuvering.

These aspects are demanding, absorbing, and sometimes obsessive. The executive finds himself in heavy contact with people who never set foot in a newsroom: lawyers, managers, sponsors, budget men, salesmen, publicists, agents, consultants, community leaders, government officials, and higher executives. Sometimes his unique identity as an executive-journalist fades into the commonness of his role as a corporate businessman.

Working journalists tend to think of their news director or executive producer as the top of the news hierarchy, forgetting that he has bosses too. Indeed, he is a middle manager who answers to higher corporate officials, and his answers had better take full cognizance of their value systems.

Two things in particular appeal to the business-minded men who run television: high ratings (which mean high commercial revenues) and low budgets (which mean more profit). They are happy to bask in journalistic prestige, but the bottom line is always expressed in the natural language of business: numbers.

"Bad numbers" are the nightmare of news executives. The news director at a local station is unlikely to lose his job because of insufficient journalism, but he is sure to get the ax if ratings fall or if heavy spending cuts into profits. At the network level it's a bit different, because the corporation is sensitive to the news division as an emblem of the network's prestige. (As Fred Friendly put it bluntly, "The news is the one thing the networks can point to with pride. Everything else is crap and they know it.") Prestige is a key intangible in terms of business success, so the networks will tolerate high spending and even unexciting ratings to keep it.

But there are limits. When a network's news program falls into clear-cut last place, it is interpreted within the TV industry as an indication of mismanagement, helplessness, and downward momentum not only by the news division but by the corporation as a whole. In Big Business such signals can be devastating, and the corporation will not abide them forever. One day there will be a change of command and a bloodbath of firings and a reign of terror until things get better.

While the executive sits in his office worrying about numbers, the journalists are swaggering around the newsroom and not giving a hoot about spending someone else's apparently endless supply of dollars. The pure journalist contemptuously regards *any* consideration of money as an impurity that defiles the temple of journalism.

He may have a similar contempt for ratings. Ratings measure the size of audiences, not the quality of programs, but since they are the *only* numbers they invariably influence subjective judgments on quality. The journalist is offended by every reminder that the verdict on his professional skills is reached by counting the number of viewers tuned in to his station. And he is demoralized by the inescapable suggestion that his journalism is just another commercial product being peddled on television.

In a sense he's correct, but he's also dismissing a reality that cannot be dismissed just because it's impure. TV is a business. Executives are its appointed officers, and the moment a TV newsman rolls down his sleeves and buttons his cuffs to join this corps of officers he begins to absorb its values. Journalism is respected, sure. But ratings and profits are the coins of the realm. As an ambitious junior officer seeking the approval of his seniors, he tries to get in step, putting up only token and sporadic resistance.

He may have started out as a skeptical and independent-minded newsman, but now he becomes a positivist and a True Believer in the company line. His own career becomes a major factor in most of his decisions, and the swaying influence of career considerations is not to be underestimated (it's been said of senior military officers that they will bravely risk their lives for their country, but no amount of patriotism justifies endangering their careers). The aggressiveness he had presumably applied to journalism makes a sudden shift to encompass the new objectives of ratings and profits.

Television is a big-bucks enterprise, and the men who run it do not entrust their expected fortunes to hell-raising firebrands or damn-the-costs idealists. Successful executives tend to be conservatives who have outgrown whatever youthful attachment they had to disturbing-the-peace journalism. The exceptions, and there certainly are some, fight a strong tide and deserve respect. But most are compromised by the realities they had to accept (or didn't mind accepting) as they rose in their careers. It is a common pattern in adult life. It is not immoral, usually, but it is disappointing.

While executives tend to grow increasingly cautious about

journalism, they channel their energies into the other side of the Fundamental Duality—the television side, the Show Biz side, the *appearances* side. Competing stations always seem to cover the same stories in the same way and even run them in the same order, so journalistic content is perceived as about the same wherever you turn the dial. The difference, says the conventional wisdom, is *the show:* its attractiveness and likability, its pace and personality, its "news team." Ratings don't measure quality, so don't pursue higher ratings by upgrading quality. Pursue them by improving *the show.* This, not improving the news coverage, becomes the testing ground for executive creativity.

Instead of spending money on journalism that will get him in trouble or get no attention, the executive spends for cosmetics. It's almost a cliché that his first move is to change the studio set. He buys new theme music or new technical gadgets and control room devices. He fiddles with staging and slogans. If these measures fail he turns to "human sacrifice"—he fires the anchorman or the weatherman and brings in a hotshot from another market. He might also hire consultants, known as "news doctors," to prescribe ways of making his show more popular. They advise cutting stories very short to keep a livelier pace, avoidance of depressing or disturbing "downer" subjects, and hiring warm-seeming reporters in warm-colored outfits.

He pumps up the likability factor, encouraging more chatter and banter among his on-air team. His anchors make a point of complimenting reporters on the air ("Excellent report, Cindy") hoping that viewers will get the message about the station's excellent journalism.

He looks for ways to promote the show. A local station might accept the cost of sending its star reporter to the faraway site of a major national or international story—not because the reporter will add significantly to network coverage of the event or inject a local angle that justifies the expense, but because it creates an aura of big-time journalism that will pay off in advertising campaigns, promotional activity, commercial sales, and perhaps the Emmy awards that TV people give each other with such straight-faced self-interest.

What if all these cosmetic adjustments fail to pull a low-rated news show out of the doldrums? Where does the desperate executive turn to perk up a loser? Show Business supplies an answer, the traditional quick fix known in Show Biz parlance as "T-and-A" ("Tits and Ass").

In TV news, T-and-A means sex stories in the guise of concerned journalism: "investigations" or multi-part series on prostitution, pornography, teen sex, senior citizen sex, sex clinics, sex problems, sex-related diseases, homosexuals, heterosexual singles, the swinging and swapping culture, the nude beach controversy, even rape and breast cancer—anything that might tease viewers with the voyeuristic possibility of glimpsing naked or near-naked flesh or hearing sordid or near-sordid revelations. T-and-A also means tabloid-style coverage (remember, newspapers thought of T-and-A long before TV) of lurid tragedies and blood-and-guts crimes and disasters, but above all it means S-E-X.

What is often forgotten about sensationalist journalism is that it is cheap. Not only cheap in taste and motivation, but cheap in its actual costs. A reporter and crew charge into a massage parlor or sex clinic, get some terrific footage, and wrap it up in forty-five minutes. Or they confront some obvious rip-off artist and come back with scenes of pushing and shoving and threatening—good stuff. The sleazy characters involved in these stories are not likely to bring lawsuits, and in fact they may be thrilled to be on TV.

Covering the sensational story takes little time, little preparation, little research, and no special intelligence; and it has guaranteed impact on the air, especially during ratings "sweeps." It is cost-effective.

It is a mistake to think of sensationalism as bold journalism. It is just the opposite. If bold journalism implies risk, it is much riskier to spend time and money digging into a story that might be very important but not very entertaining on the air. Or a story that might offend powerful people with the resources to fight back. This is where executives get the willies.

Newsroom people observe the sort of executive maneuvers I've been describing with feelings ranging from bemusement to cynicism to despair. Sometimes they find themselves wishing that their bosses would be caught in the act and taken to task by TV critics or public groups. At the local level, it seldom happens.

At the network level, however, things are very different. It is assumed that the whole world is watching (that is, a national audience that includes everyone with power and influence, from the president on down) and that a wrong move will trigger a landslide of negative reactions and repercussions. Decisions are not made casually, though sometimes they have the "you had to be there" quality that's associated with impossible-to-explain funny stories. The local station executive might be irresponsible because he can get away with it; the network executive is acutely conscious of responsibility, partly because he thinks he can't get away with anything less. The difference between network and local executives is probably not a question of who is more noble. More likely it's a matter of playing in different leagues.

The highest executives do not mingle with the troops, but their personalities are pervasive. Network people are always gabbing about the Big Boss; walk into a network office or newsroom and you will hear his name mentioned within minutes. Probably no network news president has been more talked about than Roone Arledge, a man of much mystique. Working for various ABC News programs I've always had the feeling that no conversation was complete without some speculative analysis of his latest deeds or rumored intentions.

On one strange occasion I received an urgent summons to his office. I hurried there certain that something huge was about to happen to me, probably something terrible. Why did Roone (always referred to by first name only) want to see *me?*

A senior producer waiting impatiently outside Roone's office met me and ushered me inside. I was not introduced or invited to sit down—there was no place to sit because the chairs and couches were full with Roone's top subordinates, bunched awkwardly together. Roone sat at his desk, leaning back, puffing a long cigar—a stocky and tough-looking man, unusual in his appearance because of his orange hair and big glasses that seemed to magnify his eyes. And something about the mouth, I'm not sure what. He scared me. He scared just about everyone.

Roone said nothing while one of his executives, surely one of the most accomplished newsmen in America, informed me that I had a writing assignment. He began to explain and several of the others joined in with suggestions; it was clear to me that no one wanted to be seen without an idea or contribution.

I scribbled notes, nodding in acknowledgment of everything I was told. And slowly it dawned on me that what they wanted me to do was . . . *easy*: a thirty-second voice-over for a *20/20* broadcast—something so routine that a bright beginner could have done it in his second week as a professional newswriter.

The senior producer who had ushered me in now ushered me out and led me to a typewriter. As I slipped a sheet of paper into the roller I asked, "Is this all there is? Is there something I don't understand?"

"C'mon, stop dawdling and write it," he said.

It took one minute to write it. The senior producer paced behind me, looking over my shoulder, making noncommital noises as each phrase appeared. I pulled it out of the typewriter, proofread it, crossed out one mistyped word.

"Type it over," said the senior producer. "I want to go in there with a clean copy."

I typed it again, clean.

The senior producer asked, "Do you think this is okay?"

I shrugged.

"I don't know if they'll buy it," he said. We timidly re-entered Roone's office. The senior producer, clutching the paper, read it aloud. As he finished there was a long moment of judgment. I sensed two executives drawing breath, about to speak, no doubt touching off a round of group criticism.

And then Roone blew out some cigar smoke and said casually, "Yeah, that's fine. I like it." The would-be critics sat back in silence. The senior producer pressed me out the door.

I wandered back to my office puzzling over the significance of what had happened. It seemed so inconsequential that I presumed it *had* to be meaningful—if the ambassador to Luxembourg had been urgently summoned to the White House to brief the President and his cabinet on arrangements for the embassy's Fourth of July cocktail party and had been told, "I like it," and then ushered out, he would have felt the same way.

Later, still wondering, I told the story of my visit to Roone's office to a friend I consider wise. And she said, "You know, we're better off not knowing what they talk about in there. We're better off thinking they talk about Very Big matters that we small people couldn't possibly deal with."

6

The Psychology of Talent

Observe the way people encounter a Famous Person: they gape and stare, they move in close, wide-eyed, drawn by some mysterious and powerful fascination, peering into that recognized face and trying to discover something—but what?

I think they are searching for the secret of fame, trying to detect the glow or bone structure or field of force in which fame is manifested physically. But of course it's not physical. It is all in the head—the beholder's and the beheld.

Being seen on TV automatically confers a degree of fame, and fame confers a degree of mystique. For a period of time as brief as a moment or longer than a lifetime, the famous person seems elevated—not necessarily for any reason of quality or achievement, but for the sheer fact of being touched by fame's magic wand. Some TV reporters become local or national superstars while others are barely noticed on the street unless they are conspicuously in action wired to a microphone and camera crew, but all have been touched by the magic wand, and it sets them apart.

My observation is that the presence of a famous person has an unbalancing effect on *any* situation. It unbalances everyone involved, including the famous person himself. It is like a charge of electricity and it jolts things out of kilter. It *changes* things.

Certainly this is observable in the field, where the arrival of a recognized TV newsman and his crew clearly heightens the excitement level. A news event on a city street can become a circus of hyper behavior. A magnetic effect brings gawkers rushing from all directions, surrounding the reporter in a swarm and raptly following his every move, often shouting his name or engaging in wild antics to win his attention. Meanwhile, the news event itself becomes a matter of secondary interest.

In the world outside the newsroom, fame creates a celebrity experience about which most TV reporters are uncomfortably ambivalent. Back in the newsroom, it creates a class distinction that goes against the grain of traditional newsroom egalitarianism. Being an on-camera journalist is like being the Mild Mannered Reporter Clark Kent with everyone knowing you are also Superman; a writer or producer talking with an on-camera person is never certain whether he is addressing a fellow newsman (an equal) or a star (who can at any moment drop the charade of equality and assert his magnitude).

Complicating everything is the built-in clash of values. Fame is difficult enough in an atmosphere that honors it. Journalism *doesn't* honor it. Journalism is anti-fame.

The two sides of the Fundamental Duality are bitterly hostile in this regard. Fame is equated with Show Business and anything that suggests Show Business is anathema to journalists (who conveniently forget how heavily Show Biz considerations affect TV news).

The Pure Journalism Ideology says that anything flashy, phony, promotional, exploitive, manipulative, or egotistic is Show Business. Hype is Show Business. The essence of Show Business is illusion—the absolute opposite of what journalism stands for. Show Biz values debase journalism; stardom corrupts journalists; newsmen are not performers.

In personal terms, most of it comes down to ego. Traditional journalistic teaching insists that the reporter is only a modest observer from the sidelines, a conveyor of facts, an instrument of communication, a servant of truth. The story is the thing; he is only the messenger. His ego may be large and volatile, but the attention he demands is primarily for his story, his product—not for him personally. The Show Biz figure is just the opposite: his purpose is to look good and be looked at. As a newscaster he is the *star* of the news, the featured performer in a news report. The news is his vehicle; "newsman" is only the role that puts him on camera.

Fame was never much of a problem for reporters until TV came along and created the hybrid TV Newsman—part TV creature, part journalism creature. He was unlike all other TV figures because he was a journalist. He was unlike all other journalists because he performed on TV and became famous, whether he embraced it or tried to evade it in the interest of pure journalism.

No one else in news or Show Business shared his in-between identity or had to cope with the never-ending ambiguities and conflicts of being in between. The newsman was never certain whether he was *primarily* a journalist or a TV entity, a performer. Whenever he wandered too far in one direction he was rudely yanked back in the other.

His identity became the rope in the tug-of-war between the opposing values of the Fundamental Duality, and the tugging strained all his professional relationships—with his off-camera colleagues, with his audience, with journalism, and ultimately with himself.

To understand these strains, it helps to become acquainted with a jargon word, *Talent.* Even orally it seems right to use the word with a capital T. It refers individually or in the plural to professional performers, even including performing animals. Anyone who is paid to go out on stage or before the cameras is Talent.

The term derives from the language of Show Business contracts ("Talent will be provided with a full-time hairdresser, a limousine, first-class air accommodations . . ."), but in recent years it has come into fairly common usage in TV news, along with other Show Biz contributions including star systems, agents with more power than producers, and superstar contracts that turn certain performers into wealthy and pampered celebrities and sometimes larger-than-life prima donnas.

One generalization about people described as Talent is that they are uneasy about being called Talent, sensing the daggers of connotation that often lie behind the outward tribute. Only the most naive performers miss the point that the term *does not* imply that Talent is talented. That compliment is withheld as irrelevant. As the term is used and understood by the people who work with Talent, the degree of actual talent hardly matters. Nor does it matter whether Talent is a network anchorman, a sit-com actor, or a pitchman for carrot-slicing devices in commercials that go on in the middle of the night.

The essence of the term is that Talent is Talent: *they are all the same*. They go before the audience and do their act; some do news, some do soap operas; some are gifted, some aren't; some are considerate of the "little people" they work with, others wouldn't care if all the "little people" fell down dead. But in the larger sense they are all the same, members of a single species, members of a tribe—the Talent tribe. What makes them the same is the universality of their reactions to the fame experience.

I am not suggesting that TV newspeople are celebrities who just happen to do news instead of rock videos, but that they experience many of the reactions common to the Talent tribe. It should not be a surprise when, under pressure, an on-camera newsman feels the same pressures and emotions as a Hollywood star and behaves accordingly.

At the crux of it is Performer Ego. By definition, Talent is self-centered (not always obnoxiously) and evaluates everything in the context of self-interest. Further, I think that Talent is driven by a personal need for fame that makes them willing to accept a gamut of bruising lows in return for the highs, a deal that most of us would back away from. Anyone who sustains fame has an ego that demands fame; it makes them formidable and also insatiable. Famous people might have the grace to conceal this hungry need for fame, but never believe anyone who tells you about a famous person who is really easygoing, non-competitive, modest, or selfless.

Also by definition, Talent is insecure, and this insecurity is manifested in behavior that non-performing colleagues would regard as outrageous if indulged in by anyone else. "Talent is having a tantrum over the script." "Talent is sulking in his dressing room." "Talent refuses to work unless someone flies back to Chicago and retrieves his lucky cuff links." (These are not fabricated examples—the first two are common and the third involved a network newsman of meteoric prominence whose insecurity virtually guaranteed his agonizing self-destruction.)

It is implicit that members of the Talent tribe must be treated with velvet gloves because they are so vulnerable—frailty thy name is Talent!—and conversely because they are capable of monstrous explosions that send shrapnel flying everywhere. The implied professional wisdom is to stay low and keep some distance, enduring the headaches they cause for you and other down-to-earth folk who labor off-camera (and have no comparable term for themselves, though they tease each other with Un-Talent or No-Talent).

People who work in entertainment, notably theater, seem to develop an intuitive understanding and worldly tolerance for the frailties of Performer Ego. They realize that facing an audience creates a haunting fear of failure or rejection. Probably this fear would keep all stages empty if not for the countering force of ego. Therefore, the performer's ego must be continually bolstered while his insecurities are indulged and assuaged. It is not only practical but humane to fortify your Talent with huge servings of ego-boosting praise and reassurance (which need not be sincere): you're great, you're terrific whatever you do, they can't get enough of you, everything worked out great, you were dynamite out there!

This is called star treatment.

In the world of Show Business, star treatment is institutionalized, part of the fabric. Not so in TV news, where, except in the cases of the few celebrity newspeople whose presence electrifies any situation, the notions of star treatment, Talent, ego, and insecurity are so unwelcome that newsmen would rather pretend they do not exist.

In the newsroom atmosphere, insensitivity to the frailty of Talent is cultivated as a matter of salty professional pride. Newsmen are supposed to be thick-skinned and accustomed to giving and receiving rough treatment in the real world. They are supposed to face audiences of hundreds of thousands or millions without a flutter of nerves or a gulp of vulnerability. They are supposed to have a personal perspective wider than self-interest. They are supposed to go through the necessary motions of performing but hang up their fame suits the moment the red light goes off. They're supposed to be regular guys whose fame has no effect on their view of themselves or other people. They are supposed to be as ego-less and secure as boulders (and as sensitive as boulders), and if they have a weakness for alcohol, drugs, flattery, lechery, or uncontrolled behavior, or personal lives filled with destructive tumult, it's not supposed to be related to being Talent.

Newsroom people, including writers, tend to be grudging or simply oblivious about the pressures on Talent. However, people in the control room or studio know that when it comes to going before the camera, performer emotions take over. The producer, straddling both sides of the Fundamental Duality, must also be aware of Performer Ego—or face the recurring disasters and eruptions that take place when the performer's insecurities boil over.

These displays dismay the newsroom people, who regard them as unprofessional. And they are, but it is also unprofessional to deny reality. Perhaps TV journalists should be immune to performer emotions, but they're not. Anyone who has ever stepped in front of an audience should have a sense of the naked emotions involved.

Any discussion of the psychology of TV newsmen should make a key wheat-and-chaff distinction: the Talent of TV news includes many good journalists, but it also includes many who are strictly performers and can hardly be called journalists at all.

In this category I would put some but not all anchorpeople—I'm thinking of the old *Mary Tyler Moore Show*'s hilarious satire of the figurehead anchorman, the vain and buffoonish Ted Baxter. I would also include most weathermen and local station sports "reporters," who virtually never contribute anything that hasn't already been carried on the wires. They owe their existence (and salaries higher than everyone's except the main anchors) to production considerations *only;* their subjects are popular, and their presence allows stations to add personality and "mix" to their news team.

Most of all I am talking now about TV reporters who are only pretenders, chosen for their ability to go before cameras and *act* like newsmen. As many movies and comedy skits show, it is an easy and hackneyed role, a matter of imitating a familiar stereotype. A microphone in hand, a well-scrubbed face, an earnest look and furrowed brow, a certain diction—that's enough to masquerade as a TV reporter.

"He's just an actor" is probably the most disparaging thing that can be said about a TV newsman. It says: This person may be going through journalistic motions and playing the role but he is not for real as a newsman. He knows little about the news and has never paid attention to current events. He doesn't understand the traditions and purpose of his profession—let alone the responsibilities. He has little of the journalist's natural skepticism or idealism or curiosity. He has no commitment to the values that guide and motivate a good journalist.

Let's call him a *news-actor.* It should be said that he is not *consciously* pretending when he plays his role. He thinks he is doing what a newsman does: performing on the air. He is oblivious to any more substantial requirement. He is utterly without depth. His perception of his profession has less to do with Edward R. Murrow than with Miss Nebraska of 1983, who radiantly announced to viewers of that year's Miss America Pageant that she looked forward to a career in broadcast journalism "because it's a happy combination of the things I like best, people and performance!"

Hey gang, let's put on a news show!

Miss Nebraska's limited perception of TV news as a show and nothing but a show is shared by the news-actor. To him, appearance and appearances are everything. He thinks about nothing but his "image."

He reads an international story with a gravity that suggests he has spent hours discussing its ramifications with the United Nations secretary-general—rather than ten seconds glancing over wire copy. He panders for approval—at the close of a sad story he shakes his head in woe and says, "Gee, that's tragic!" and bites his lip, showing that he's one hell of a deep and compassionate guy. (In the control room and newsroom there is a round of groans and snickers as the staff marvels once again at his capacity for insincerity. Perhaps someone quotes the great line attributed to George Burns, "Sincerity—if you can fake that, you got it made!")

The essence of the news-actor is that he is not *authentic*. Which raises the question: what *is* authenticity? What makes the difference between a real TV newsman and a news-actor?

The difference is clear enough in concept or comparison (e.g., news-actor vs. Bill Moyers) but in day-to-day journalism the difference can be close to imperceptible. Is authenticity just a matter of writing your own copy? The news-actor can usually handle that— he is verbal and bright enough to master the clichés. Is it a matter of going out on stories? The news-actor can get by in the field, especially with a producer's help. Most stories are routine and a confident performance on-camera tends to avert scrutiny. The news-actor's on-camera abilities may go a long way towards concealing his journalistic deficiency.

What the best TV journalist has in common with the most flagrant news-actor is that both must be able to act on camera, *to play the role of newsman*. The authentic newsman is not excused from the performing requirement: he cannot *not* play his role. He must have on-camera technique, skill, identity, credibility. His performance must be at least as good as the news-actor's.

Over the short term his authenticity is no special asset, because he can't prove it to the camera. The more he tries, the more he finds himself imitating the news-actor in consciously fashioning an "image." If he appears on camera looking and sounding like a real newsman—rumpled, hair uncombed, collar sticking up, talking in off-camera tones and off-camera vernacular—it would only come across as a Real Newsman act. It would be a *pose,* and a bad one. Viewers would reject it. They would not accept his dishevelment as proof of authenticity. On the contrary, they would call him a faker and a slob and send postcards saying, "Why doesn't that bum buy a comb and fix his goddamn collar?"

Authenticity, like fame, is not physically manifested. Sometimes it is maddening that it is not more easily identified and spotted, so you could look at one reporter and say, *Wheat!* and at another and declare, *Chaff!* It comes from within. It is a matter of integrity and, perhaps, faith.

Authenticity means a paramount commitment to the values of journalism.

This may sound like some sort of loyalty oath, something not of the "real world." In fact the opposite is true, because the commitment shapes his taste, judgment, journalistic morality. It helps him through the ambiguities and conflicts of the Fundamental Duality. While he's still Talent, he's spared some of the tribulations of ego and insecurity. He knows who he is; the commitment is his compass. The news-actor has no compass and wanders around playing roles.

The commitment to journalistic values is hardly as easy as it might sound. Indeed, it is heavy baggage—the news-actor travels light, but the bona fide newsman can never shed his burden.

He is forever suspecting himself of succumbing to the very values he distrusts. The pressure on him comes in the form of unrelenting temptation, as explained with thundering simplicity in the famous line from Paddy Chayefsky's *Network*, *"Because you're on television, dummy!"*

Because he's on television he is famous yet he cannot allow himself to "go Show Business," compromising his integrity. Merely planting a toe in this forbidden garden fills him with feelings of fraudulence, self-reproach, and alarm. (David Brinkley: "If I start trying to act, I am lost right away.")

He shares the newsroom's aversion to celebrity and the vanity of performer ego; he struggles to be as hard-nosed as anyone in keeping the vigil against these seductions. (Walter Cronkite: "I don't want to be a personality, a presenter, a Show Biz thing.")

His instincts and self-discipline tell him: pull back, abstain, sacrifice. But it isn't easy. Being recognized, admired, envied, interviewed, complimented, flirted with, regarded as a figure of glamor and stature, feeling important, making a lot of money—this is the stuff that swells an ego. And remember, our reporter probably would not have survived the competition for his coveted position had he not possessed a driving ego from the start.

So he walks a fine line, always tempted to let himself go, to revel in the available celebrity and the release from discipline. And why not? Neither his virtue nor his discipline win him any rewards, at least in the short run.

Besides his own conscience, there is very little to keep him righteous. The public does not deny him the fruits of celebrity unless he abuses them outrageously. His bosses would rather have a star personality who pulls ratings than a self-effacing journalist who makes no impression on the audience. His editorial colleagues in the newsroom are hypercritical behind his back, but they will seldom confront him face to face if he transgresses and will rarely give him more than tentative credit if he is strong. In their innocence they demand constant purity; in their sophistication they consider it naive.

The on-camera journalist gets what often seems like a choice between the fine wine and the diet beverage—indulgence of ego or honorable austerity. Making the choice even more difficult is his nagging suspicion that most viewers don't notice or give a hoot about his authenticity, and that instead of pushing himself to live up to Ed Murrow he might as well relax and enjoy being Ted Baxter.

I do not mean to give the impression that serious TV newsmen are or should be reluctant to appear on television (or to shine on television) or that they spend their days agonizing over moral issues or grilling themselves about their motives and conduct. As for being on television, most of them love it (a few find it nerve-wracking and profess to dislike it, but I don't believe them). It would be absurd to discredit television newsmen because they're on television, or to blame them for being famous, or to indict them for enjoying it. They do enjoy it: they enjoy getting and telling the news, they enjoy their salaries and glamor, they enjoy their recognition, and they enjoy flirting with fame. It would be too much to ask them not to flirt with fame. But it's one thing to flirt and another to be seduced.

In a way, the Fundamental Duality helps keep the TV reporter from losing his bearings. Covering stories forces him out of the cocoon of celebrity. He must grapple with the real world and the ego-bruising indignities that are part of every reporter's day.

He also faces the anti-elitist spirit of the newsroom, and newsroom people traditionally enjoy slamming in the harpoon when a regular fish starts acting like a whale. Superstars will be exempted, but a reporter who gets uppity with the staff is subject to eventual retribution in a process as collaborative as TV news. Abusing underlings in a newsroom is ultimately as unwise as insulting your dentist just as he reaches for the drill.

Contact with the outside world and with the prickly crew in the newsroom usually has the positive effect of bringing reporters back to earth; it keeps them from being sealed off in the fame bubble that often forms around the celestial figure of the on-camera hierarchy, the anchorman.

On the face of it the anchorman job is ideal for feeding a hungry ego. The anchorman is the star, the sun, and everything orbits around him. Publicly the program is identified by his name and image. His face looks down from billboards. Advertising layouts and promotional films portray him as an ace newsman on the run, pounding his typewriter, grabbing the phone, rushing around the newsroom in shirt sleeves, thrusting microphones into the faces of news figures.

These activities probably have less to do with reality than with an advertising firm's concept of what an anchorman does. The truth is that anchormen involve themselves to different degrees (from heavy to nil), but in most situations their off-camera involvement is entirely *optional*.

There are other people to do the typewriter pounding, phone grabbing, shirt-sleeved rushing, and microphone thrusting. The only thing an anchorman *must* do is anchor the show. Except on rare occasions, such as live coverage of breaking stories (when he shows his mettle), he is not called upon to demonstrate journalistic ability or instinct.

News-actors don't resent the glorified-announcer aspect of anchoring, but it is vexing to a good journalist who finds that having done well as a reporter, he is promoted to a job as a performer. Having proved himself with substance, he is now judged primarily by his style and popularity. Having established his credibility as a newsman, he must lend it to others with less credibility.

He introduces reports by others, reads scripts written by others. For this he is handsomely paid, respected, honored by his colleagues and the public, and given star treatment wherever he goes. He is glad to accept these rewards, and often, especially at the network level, he deserves them—for accomplishments that preceded his anchorship. But at the summit of his career, he is nagged by the self-accusation that he is barely practicing journalism. He feels instead like a Show Business commodity, like Talent.

The more he feels like Talent, the more his Performer Ego comes to the fore. When his insecurities flare up, he asserts himself as temperamentally as a movie star. He challenges producers, changes copy, complains peevishly about matters large and small, intrudes on all decisions. Traces of paranoia: "I am the star of this operation and I *carry* it all by myself and get damn little support from all these amateurs around me!"

To reaffirm his journalistic credentials, he might insist on getting out of the studio to cover stories himself or do "special reports." But this is a gamble during a bout of insecurity—to go into the field is to invite comparison with lesser reporters. That could backfire. The sun cannot risk being outshined by the planets.

Off the air, the anchorman is entitled to editorial influence, but only the top network anchors have formal positions in the newsroom hierarchy. While they are nominally subordinate to executive producers, the truth is that the superstar network anchormen have so much power that they can bowl over just about anyone and virtually run the show whenever they feel like it—or to put it another way, whenever their ego requires it.

They have this power because they are star-quality journalists to whom networks have pinned the fortunes of their news divisions and the prestige of the corporations themselves. They have huge salaries, fame, privilege, and most of all they have driving personalities that simply overwhelm all resistance. It seems obvious that they have too much power; on the other hand, the system works well, and no serious abuses have come to light.

For all other anchors it is a different story (though big-name anchors in major local markets probably have as much power as they choose to exercise). Producers will always pay attention to an anchorman's suggestions or complaints—the anchorman cannot be ignored. But it is evident to him that he is superfluous, not essential in the newsroom. The newsroom staff feels it could function a lot more smoothly without his meddling, and he gets the message. This is not a welcome message for a man or woman with an anchorperson-sized ego.

From a newswriter's standpoint, the impact of an anchorman's ego is largely a matter of how he treats or mistreats the writer's writing. Anchormen are always entitled to rewrite their scripts. They might rewrite for editorial reasons or reasons of style or pride or because they're just sitting around with nothing else to do.

Writers naturally dislike changes in their scripts, but few would quarrel with an anchorman's right to take part in the writing or go on the air with a script he can read comfortably.

However, there are several things anchorpeople do that drive writers crazy. Here are four, each related to anchor insecurity. Bear in mind that whatever the power balance between anchor and producer, producers usually yield without a fight on small matters—a category that unfortunately includes doodling with the script.

1. They rewrite capriciously.

Making changes for the sake of change, the anchor does not bother checking wire copy, screening tape, making phone calls, or even consulting with the writer. He simply takes the writer's script and rephrases it. Often he inadvertently introduces errors or connotations the writer may have gone to great lengths to avoid.

Once I worked for an important anchorman who practiced the following ritual. Reading scripts in the newsroom before air time, he would call out compliments to the writer, for everyone in the newsroom to hear. At the same moment he would be rolling a sheet of paper into his typewriter to rewrite the script himself.

When finished he would get the writer's attention and, over the din of the newsroom, read aloud his rewritten version. At this point in the exercise the writer was supposed to exclaim, "Hey, that's much better!" If these obsequious words did not spring naturally to his lips, he faced the dilemma of what to say (with the whole newsroom eavesdropping). To quibble over the anchor's slapdash prose or unmeticulous version of the facts would be to transform the glow of the earlier compliment into a testy and perhaps insubordinate challenge to the star. It was better to play the game as cheerfully as possible—and to keep your eyes down to avoid the sly grins of other people in the room.

2. They damage the story by ad-libbing.

The script was fine and the anchorman accepted it without rewriting, but now, on the air, he impulsively throws in some extra points, a few parenthetical facts or clarifications. Doing so, he gives up the advantage of careful preparation and risks misstatements and confusion.

The writer is incensed: Why do I make the effort to write this stuff if he's just going to wing it? Why do I try to state things precisely if he's going to turn them into imprecise babble? Why do I struggle to keep it short if he's going to double it with his stupid ad-libs?

I've always suspected that ad-libbing was at least partially involuntary. The anchorman feels like a ventriloquist's dummy reading scripts he didn't write, so he asserts himself, irresistibly adding something of his own. To paraphrase Descartes, "I ad-lib, therefore I am!"

3. They "proloompherate."

This word was invented by my former colleague Ed Galorenzo to describe an enormous ad-lib, a wild digression that catches everyone by surprise, possibly including the anchorman himself. Launched by something in the script or perhaps trapped into it by a minor ad-lib that seems to require further ad-libbing, he goes flying off on his own, explaining, jabbering, backing and filling, free-associating.

In the control room people say, "I wonder how he's gonna get out of this." And it's a problem because, having exhausted his imagination and knowledge of the story, the anchorman returns to the script only to find that he has already covered what is there. Ending the story then becomes a test of pure improvisation, a desperation lunge that probably leaves viewers baffled.

It seems incredible that anchors would do this but it does happen, and the fabricated comic verb *proloompherate* (emphasis on the

LOOMPH) catches its essence, suggesting a great and absurd spewing forth: "Uh oh, Tom's proloompherating again."

4. *They steal the credit.*

Good writing makes anchors look good. Most of them appreciate it and make sure the writer's contribution is acknowledged, but now and then an anchorman will want the credit for himself.

The urge to claim authorship can be very strong. I recall being among a half-dozen writers working for an anchorman who told a magazine interviewer, "Nobody writes for me, I write all my own stuff." It was a pure lie, utterly shameless. No one spoke a word about it, embarrassed by the transparency of ego and insecurity.

Vanity, insecurity, fear. The need to be pampered and praised. The nakedness of ego. The writer looks up at the anchorman and suspects none of these frailties. He sees a star, the Number One, the famous and confident face, the guy who's got it made. He forgets how *exposed* that person feels, how dependent he is on support and approval. The anchorman who claimed to do all his own writing was perhaps the most secure on-camera personality I've ever encountered, and yet *he* could not keep himself from boasting to an interviewer and grasping every last crumb of credit.

The aspect of fame that may be the most difficult for non-famous people to understand is the constant appraisal by others. The famous person is always having people coming up and staring at him. He is always being sized up and measured, gushingly flattered to his face and maliciously derided when his back is turned.

He is acutely sensitive to the judgments other people are making on him. It's an endless roller-coaster ride for his ego. If the famous person is a TV journalist, he can seek relief by taking cover behind the news. But if he is well-known, it is a thin shield. He is less vulnerable than, say, a comedian or a singer, but he is still vulnerable.

Writers and others in the newsroom naturally tend to feel eclipsed by Talent. When Talent's insecurities are revealed to them, it is a surprisingly and even touchingly intimate experience. It reminds you that even when a star anchorman outwardly claims you don't exist, you *do* exist to him, and your support and goodwill are desperately important.

My advice on dealing with Talent: be straight, be solid. If you don't have an answer or a solution, don't bull your way through— admit it, and then don't waste a moment providing what they need (or think they need).

Be respectful; don't be starstruck. Let everyone else be starstruck, but not you. From you Talent does not ask mute and fawning admiration. He needs feedback—and he should get it from you rather than depending on what he's told by oddballs who approach him on the street or people he meets at parties. He needs criticism (but be diplomatic). He needs to know that the people who are backing him up share his concern about how he will do out there when everyone is watching and judging him.

This support is more than journalistic. It is a matter of personal trust. Dealing with Talent—a significant skill that off-camera people should cultivate—is fundamentally a matter of achieving this trust. To do so, you must show that you understand the secret of his vulnerability but will not betray it (or even say it out loud). You are on his side, a faithful supporter, and he is in good hands. If he feels otherwise, watch things unravel. Remember, when he goes before the camera, he is afraid. Everyone is.

7

Notes on Reporting

Early in my career as a TV newswriter, word reached me that I was being considered for promotion to on-air reporter. To get the job, I was advised, I would have to do two things: pursue it actively and shave off my beard.

I did neither. I didn't pursue it because I liked being a newswriter and because the prospect of being on television filled me with camera fright. And I firmly refused to compromise myself by shaving. (A few years later someone told me I looked like a bearded rabbi. No wonder they'd wanted me to shave—the "rabbi look" had never been desirable for TV reporters. Nor was it desirable in my off-camera social life. I grabbed a razor.)

I have no regrets about not becoming a TV reporter—I got my fill of reporting in two newspaper jobs. Having never been a TV reporter, I am reluctant to make authoritative statements about what it's like. However, I have been talking to and about reporters for many years, and I don't mind suggesting some points about reporters and reporting that might be useful to TV journalists, whether their jobs are on- or off-camera.

Dreaming of Woodward-Bernstein

The brilliant Watergate investigation by Bob Woodward and Carl Bernstein inspired countless young people to seek careers in journalism and re-inspired many journalists whose careers were already underway. It was instant legend, the realization of a dream that lives in the soul of every reporter. The dream existed long before "Woodstein" and will exist long after them, and it has a romantic appeal that goes beyond the profession.

Here it is: The reporter smells a rat. The whiff of rat leads to a hunch, and the hunch leads to an investigative hunt. The reporter spends long and lonely hours following leads, making calls, studying boring documents, going astray and getting back on track, digging, and doing the unglamorous legwork that is so glamorous in the retelling.

The reporter goes out on a limb with his impatient and skeptical bosses; possibly he puts himself in harm's way, wandering into real physical danger as he probes closer to the core of wrongdoing. Slowly the big story yields before his dogged pursuit, and at last the great scandal is exposed, the colossal revelation is splashed across the front page or the airwaves. And then there are prizes, glory, a niche in the journalistic hall of fame.

It is a wonderful dream, and it actually comes true (though usually on a lesser scale than the Watergate investigation). It could happen a lot more. There is no shortage of wrongdoing and never will be.

But there are problems. One is that a news organization must have reporters with investigative talents. Another is that it must have confidence in its reporters and willingness to back them up when the pressure is on.

Ask a news executive what comes to mind when he hears talk of investigative reporting and he'll probably say: journalistic jackpots, prestige, awards, promotion for the show, and possibly a promotion for himself. If he's honest he'll also say: lawsuits, libel, capricious juries, multi-million-dollar damages if we lose, steep legal fees even if we win. All but the most tough-minded news organizations quiver at the very mention of the word *libel*. And most professional Bad Guys know it. The moment they smell a journalistic investigation, their lawyers are on the phone talking tough to the news director and anyone else who can apply pressure.

The news director's anxieties quickly ripple out in all directions. Everyone starts getting nervous, closing doors, and holding meetings. Some investigations are squelched *in anticipation* of this anxiety. It is tempting to call this cowardice, but it is too easy to accuse others of cowardice, especially when survival seems at stake—as it might to a small station with limited resources being sued for hundreds of thousands or millions of dollars.

What is likely to happen is that all the pressure is allowed to come to bear on the reporter. He is summoned to appear before the powers-that-be of his news department and convince them that he's got all the evidence and is able to make the case, without loose ends and to the satisfaction of the grim-faced lawyers sitting there (getting ready to say what lawyers usually say in this situation: *No!*).

If the reporter cannot give an assurance of airtight safety, he will probably be told that his investigation must be dropped, scaled down, or "put on hold."

Thus the threat of a libel suit exerts what is called a "chilling effect." The odds are that in the scene above, the reporter does not have his investigation wrapped up. He might know there's something fishy about "a third-rate burglary" (as Watergate was first called) but he's very far from bringing down a president.

The nature of journalistic investigation is that public feedback is an integral part of it. The momentum of the story gets the phones ringing with leads, leaks, clues, rumors, new dimensions— material the reporter could never have collected and packaged on his own.

For example, today's story of a landlord ripping off a few tenants brings a call to the newsroom that the same landlord is commiting even worse abuses in three other buildings he owns under hidden ownerships. *That* story brings a call about twelve more buildings he owns with some very shady partners. Another caller wonders why building inspectors never set foot inside the landlord's buildings. And then there is a call about a network of kickbacks up and down the line, with corrupt officials or Organized Crime sharing the booty.

If the story gets attention, and if the news organization seems seriously commited to it, the otherwise unreachable sources and whistle-blowers will come forward; they will sense from the journalism they're seeing that they are not the only ones sticking their necks out. Thus a little story expands into the blockbuster investigation a newsman's dreams are made of—unless the landlord's lawyer calling on Day One managed to nip it in the bud.

Newspapers and magazines share TV's concern about libel, but other problems related to investigative reporting are particular to TV. Five such problems come to mind.

The first is cost. Investigations are expensive. Reporters, field producers, and camera crews must be taken out of general assignment for extended periods of time. They run up all sorts of bills and overtime, and while they are gone substitutes must be brought in and paid for.

A second problem is that it is difficult to catch shadowy behavior with a television camera. TV's bright lights, cameras, microphones, and famous reporters scare away the Bad Guys, who vanish (or call their lawyers) when the TV crew shows up; they also scare the wits out of nervous people who might be cooperative sources. As for hidden cameras or surveillance stakeouts, surveillance is exorbitantly time-consuming, and hidden cameras are tricky to manage and often restricted by privacy laws.

A third problem is finding the right stories, getting that first smell of rat. TV reporters are usually moving too fast to notice the little hints and tips of icebergs that lead to productive hunches. Not many TV reporters cover regular "beats" so they are less likely than print reporters to develop the sources or specialized knowledge that will alert them to suspicious activity.

TV reporters do get occasional anonymous tips by phone or letter, but these tips generally deal with imminent spot news (a police raid, a gang fight, a wildcat strike) rather than investigative subjects. Many tips come from crazy people and are completely useless. The best tips come from malcontents and revenge-seekers—the catch is that they are so unreliable and their situations are so convoluted that it's unpromising to get involved unless the potential is spectacular (e.g., the district attorney's son is running a prostitution ring).

A fourth problem is that an investigation might not pan out. It is probably more likely to be a disappointment than a jackpot that exposes wrongdoing, wins prizes, and attracts big audiences. Considering the costs, there is a temptation to say: Why gamble? Let's only cover sure things, the things everyone else is covering.

A fifth problem is that many potentially significant investigative stories are simply not good television: they do not offer good picture or good action; they are too complicated (budget stories, "white collar crime"); they require too much context (TV is weakest in providing context). They are better told in newspapers, so why not let newspapers make the effort and take the risk? If something big is uncovered, TV news will *then* get into the action, seeking a way to hop aboard the story at the last minute. (Watergate is an example of a journalistic investigation that TV news could not get its teeth into until it became a telegenic spectacle.)

The problems of investigative journalism do not keep TV news from longing for the glamor and fireworks of a red-hot expose. As Jeff Greenfield wrote in his book *Playing to Win: An Insider's Guide to Politics* (New York, 1980), local stations often stoop rather low to capture the thrills without paying the bills.

> The average TV investigative reporter prefers to find a case of horrible wrong-doing on a news wire or police report. The reporter, with a crew, then rushes to the scene of this horrible event, has himself photographed by the news crew racing into some building. (No one asks, by the way, how the

reporter, so anxious to find the blackguard responsible for this outrage, managed to run slowly enough to get himself photographed by his camera crew.) The reporter then pounds on doors and thrusts himself into offices, confronting some civil servant or private underling who, finding himself blinded by lights, demands that the reporter leave the premises, or else flees with the avenging reporter and camera crew in full pursuit. (This footage always makes the newscast, because it is visually exciting and is the closest thing to a car chase that can get on the evening news. It also makes the reporter look good, since flight implies guilt.) (P. 167)

So the TV reporter's dream of doing the classic Woodward-Bernstein investigative story faces discouraging prospects (although there are many other worthwhile investigative stories that lack the cloak-and-dagger sleuthing aspect I've been talking about here). The odds are not hopeless, but success requires a lot of luck and an extraordinary commitment by the reporter and his organization. The organization, of course, has more to lose. A genuine investigative success, particularly in TV news, merits the highest admiration—not only for the result but for the decision to try.

Idealism versus Ideology

Traditionally the best and brightest young journalists arrive at their first posts short on experience of the world but aflame with certitude about the forces that move it. The source of this certitude is not knowledge but a dangerous cousin of idealism: ideology.

In the old days, the most spirited young journalists were blazing Lefties. Their ideology was political and economic in a broad class context. Now, the ideologies tend to be fragmented along minority lines: young journalists are likely to interpret the world in the context of the racial, ethnic, or campus constituencies from which they come and which they feel pressured to represent and champion.

No matter how sympathetic or convincing they may be, they are biased. (Of course they don't see it that way, because human nature insists that it's always *the other guy* who is biased.) Far too often, bosses take a gingerly attitude towards such biases—out of good will, out of fear of seeming to be against the Good Guys, out of aversion to being drawn into ideological brawls in the newsroom. The young journalist misconstrues this silence as approval; actually, it is apprehensiveness.

After a few years, most journalists become skeptical about ideologies, including their own. Unlike most other people—including incensed viewers who phone in with accusations of ideologically motivated plots by "the media"—the newsman is constantly obliged to give fair hearing to both or many sides of issues. This exposure to the infinite complexity of reality puts a terrible strain on the blind and rigid logic of ideology.

"There is no such thing as ideological truth," wrote H. L. Mencken. "Inasmuch as a reporter is a liberal reporter or a Communist reporter or a Republican reporter, to that degree he is no reporter at all."

It is understood among journalists that 100 percent objectivity is impossible, because no reporter can entirely put aside his personal judgments and instinctive reactions. However, a 100 percent effort to be fair and truthful is not only possible but imperative.

The penalty for failure is severe: *loss of credibility,* the kiss of death for a journalist with serious intentions. His colleagues have marked him as a propagandist; they might like and admire him, but they don't trust him, and he never finds a place in the newsroom mainstream. Viewers catch on to him quickly and resent him for misrepresenting himself as objective.

His ideology has led him out on limbs that could not bear the weight of his assumptions; he has taken some painfully embarrassing falls and found no one there to help him up. This is the worst part: he discovers that he has been used by his own ideological heroes. They have exploited him as they would exploit any willing journalist, and his only reward is a ration of solidarity backslaps.

"As age, experience, and wear and tear reduced him physically, they also revealed to him a strong preference for disinterested judgments." So writes Saul Bellow of his journalist-protagonist in *The Dean's December* (New York, 1982). The newsman develops an ornery insistence on unfiltered truth. Anything else is as wearying as it is wayward, and he won't stand for it.

The Do-Good Temptation

It seems that whenever I've seen young TV reporters interviewed (young print reporters are never interviewed), there comes a moment when they declare their uplifting goal of doing stories that "improve the community" or "right some of the wrongs of society." I'm sure these sentiments are uttered with sincerity, but I have learned to flinch at them.

Consider this scenario.

Just a few years out of college, a compassionate young TV reporter does a few stories that have stunning civic impact. The forces of evil are thrown back in (temporary) defeat; some formerly oppressed or victimized people cry tears of joy. The reporter becomes an instant hero, a social champion.

It is a heady, intoxicating experience, and he seeks more of it. He becomes an unleashed savior, a knight on a personal crusade on behalf of Good. He is encouraged by his bosses because his crusades make for excellent television. His reports draw huge and worshipful audiences. He is rewarded over and over again with moral standing ovations.

Driven to even greater heights, he sheds all modesty about his personal wisdom and worth. He knows with righteous certainty what is right and wrong. He brushes aside the contradictions and complexities of the world, which interfere with his vision. He comes to be convinced that the public interest and his personal interest are precisely the same.

His triumphant momentum cannot be permitted to lag; it must be pushed even higher. He senses that the key is emotion; an emotionally affecting story one night creates pressure for a bigger and better emotional wowser the next night. The values of melodrama eclipse the more sober values of journalism. He wrings emotion out of victimized people, exploiting their plight as he dramatizes it and himself.

He needs villains, and they are easy to find. He picks on standard villainous types—easy targets such as landlords, businessmen, bureaucrats, bosses. They are unsympathetic and bad by definition. He convicts them on the air. He catches them in moments of their greatest disadvantage; he employs the notorious "ambush interview" in which he and his crew leap out of nowhere in journalistic assault, confronting them as in Jeff Greenfield's description. His camera zooms in on their guilty squirming or their attempts to repel the camera. If they flee he runs after them with his crew, huffing and puffing into his microphone to add breathlessness to the chase. They can't win, of course. The situation is rigged. The Good Guys will win and the premier Good Guy is the heroic reporter himself.

So he becomes an opportunist and manipulator, a journalistic demagogue. He hints that he is too big for journalism; he talks of running for office. As in Greek tragedy, he becomes a prisoner of his overweening pride, hubris. Once an earnest soldier of Good, he starts to become a monster.

I have seen this happen, from up close. The reporter was Geraldo Rivera, then with WABC in New York. I like and admire him, and I think he has done some courageous journalism. But I also think he has a terrible problem with excessiveness and self-dramatizing crusader zeal. I will never forget answering phone calls from the most wretchedly pathetic people when he proclaimed himself willing to solve the individual problems of all downtrodden souls. The calls came by the thousands, heart-breaking cries for help. Few of them got much help, or even courteous attention. It was a very cruel thing to do. I doubt that the motive was ugly, but the result was ugly indeed.

A TV journalist is given tremendous power. Often, especially on the local level, there are few restraints on him, particularly if he is attracting a big audience. So most of his restraint must be self-imposed. A young journalist might permit himself to waive these restraints on behalf of a good cause. It is the first step toward abuse of power. He is irresponsibly claiming a moral and social authority that only a few journalists have earned—the authority to declare what is right and wrong. Those who have earned it have done so partly by proving over a period of many years that they can be trusted to wield their power with restraint and perspective.

There is a big difference between doing good and being a do-gooder. The latter is self-aggrandizing, and newsmen should recoil from it. Drawing attention to wrongdoing and injustice is a proud function of journalism; it can be a great contribution to your community. Any attempt to achieve a selfish or social purpose beyond that contribution is a violation of journalistic boundaries.

Shut Up and Listen

Talk to official spokesmen, press secretaries, public affairs officers, or people who are regularly in the news—veterans at dealing with reporters—and sooner or later you will hear a familiar note of criticism: *reporters don't listen.* You lay everything out for them, explain everything until they can't possibly get it wrong, and then their report goes on the air or into print and it is full of mistakes and misunderstandings.

Surely there is some hypercritical nit-picking here, and some resentment that reporters often refuse to interpret information the way press spokesmen want it interpreted. And sometimes the spokesmen overestimate their own clarity. But there is still a lot of validity in their complaint.

About not listening: It is too common for journalists—especially TV journalists who feel the camera's impatient pressure—to be planning their next question while giving only scattered attention to what the spokesman or interviewee is saying. Consequently the reporter misses key points or makes incorrect assumptions based on what he has only half heard. It may also happen that the spokesman gives an evasive or misleading answer; instead of following up, the reporter drives ahead with his prepared question.

Anyone who has been a reporter, especially in a competitive group situation (such as a press conference), understands why this happens. News gathering can be a frantic and complicated feat: the reporter must split his concentration between listening, thinking ahead, and probably taking notes. He must struggle to inject his own questions and pursue a chain of thought that other reporters are continually interrupting with divergent questions (invariably there are off-the-wall tangents that distract everyone). He might also be in an awkward physical position, standing up or moving, being jostled by other bodies.

And he is in a rush. The Q-and-A will continue for only a short time; his assignment desk wants a quick call; there is pressure to finish up and get going. Further, the reporter is naturally impatient. Doctors have outlined the traits of the heart attack–prone Type A personality, and these traits are alarmingly common among journalists. For instance: thinking or doing several things at once, hurrying the speech of others, becoming unduly irritated when forced to wait, explosive speech patterns including frequent obscenity, and physical mannerisms indicating tension and stress.

It is called "hurry sickness," and it is very apparent among newsmen covering a story. It is no surprise that they have difficulty listening closely or patiently. Norman Mailer has remarked that reporters become hostile to a story if they cannot understand it *in ten seconds*. They get angry at any hitch in their speedy intake of the facts. I have felt this way, and I have seen groups of reporters start to go wild with exasperation when forced to be patient.

For many reporters it takes a conscious act of self-discipline and willpower to let a story unfold at its own speed, to keep from hurrying it along, jumping to conclusions, or insisting that it conform to preconceived ideas.

Good advice: shut up and listen.

One other point about questions and answers: sometimes it is a wise tactic for an interviewer to keep silent instead of rushing in with new questions. The interviewee may then feel a pressure to fill the silence, to keep going beyond his prefabricated answer. Richard Nixon, for example, always seemed to begin answers with calculated shrewdness, but when he was *not* interrupted he would ramble into disclosures that were probably far more revealing than he intended.

The Niceness Factor

Most of the good reporters I know are nice people, but when they cover stories they are very aggressive. When this aggressiveness shows on the air, reporters don't seem nice. They seem pushy, nosy, bitchy, boorish, fractious, abrasive, loud, belligerent. Even if a viewer understands why reporters behave this way, he might be appalled and alienated when he sees it on television.

TV is a niceness medium. Most people watch it in the sanctuary of their homes. Sometimes they are very upset when the stridency of the outside world erupts in their living rooms. The homescreen impression of reporters in action is far more unattractive than the actuality (which usually amounts to a burst of chaos, raised voices and rowdy behavior, all quickly forgotten), but viewers often react with intense and lasting dislike.

Every time a TV reporter takes an aggressive position—let alone an obnoxiously hostile position—he risks making lifelong enemies in the audience. I've heard viewers complain with stunning rage about the mildest reporters. "I *hate* that *bastard!*" Their loathing is amazingly out of proportion when traced back to the minor flash of unpleasantness that caused it. A handful of TV figures thrive on their hostile personalities (Howard Cosell, Mike Wallace), but they are exceptional; most not-nice TV reporters don't last.

The TV reporter knows that and it worries him. He would rather be liked than scorned—and he would rather have his contract renewed than dropped. The secret is to be aggressive *and civilized,* but some reporters miss the point and commit themselves to all-out amiability. They decide to be likable at all costs, like sportscasters (except Cosell). If there is a choice between being too aggressive or too nice, they will be too nice.

The niceness-minded reporter is easily spotted. He displays a forced and hollow geniality. He grimaces to show you this next story is disturbing to him too, and he wishes people wouldn't be such brutes to each other. In interviews he steers away from sensitive areas, even if they are newsworthy and important. He *apologizes* in advance for a tough question, usually softening the question in the course of the apology. If, despite his non-attack, an interview subject begins to falter or become tangled in clumsy lies, Mr. Nice Guy rushes in suggesting loopholes and evasions. He doesn't want to be seen embarrassing someone.

All newsmen know that people often blame the messenger for the bad news he brings. No newsman feels this more *personally* than the TV anchorman, who sits there vulnerably feeling all that heated emotion coming in *at him.* He might be tempted to deflect it (possibly with an ad-lib showing that he feels the same way you do) or mitigate it by contriving a silver lining or some reason for optimism. The misused word *hopefully* will introduce this gesture, as in "Hopefully the little boy who was trampled by the stampeding elephants will be feeling better and playing happily again real soon."

In the winter of 1981, TV news covered the assasination attempts against President Reagan and Pope John Paul II. The president and the pope—the ultimate shockers in terms of targets for violence. The networks were sensitive to this shock, perhaps *too* sensitive. Correspondents and anchormen seemed to bend over backwards to find hope in every medical bulletin, to accentuate every positive and wish away every negative. It was a human impulse, a very decent impulse, but I thought it was a function more for clergymen than newsmen. In critical times *particularly,* journalists must be rigorous in providing straight and unadulterated reporting and not yielding to the temptation to sugarcoat the news for the audience's emotional consumption.

The Aristocrat-Official

It's often seemed to me that the most treacherous figures reporters deal with are high-level officials who are *not* experienced in dealing with newsmen. In particular, I'm thinking of leaders of important institutions with hierarchical structures—big business, the military, government bureaucracy (excluding elected officials, who are in constant contact with reporters).

These people live in sealed-off worlds where they are treated like royalty, surrounded by sycophants and insulated by highly protective staffs from the general rudeness of the world. They are accustomed to having things their own way and to exerting unquestioned *control* over their inferiors—a category that, in their minds, embraces most of mankind.

It is very difficult for young journalists to comprehend how deeply these people—I will call them "aristocrat-officials"—feel entitled to reverential treatment and how indignant they are when it is not forthcoming. As Walter Lippmann said, "Only the rarest of princes can endure even a little criticism, and *few of them can put up with even a pause in the adulation*" (emphasis added).

The aristocrat-official regards reporters as a distasteful but often unavoidable evil. They must be manipulated to serve his will, yet he looks upon them with an aversion his fine manners can barely conceal. By his standards, reporters are mediocrities who would be automatic washouts in any quality-minded organization. They are disrespectful, ill behaved, even ill clad. (TV reporters are usually better dressed than print reporters; however, the TV reporter always arrives with a scruffy-looking camera crew.) They have minimal attention spans and no grasp of subtlety. And to an aristocrat, subtlety is everything.

Reporters invade aristocratic chambers like barbarian hordes, upsetting the decorum and the secretaries, putting up lights and running cables all over the floor, moving furniture, prying, snooping, wandering around unescorted, using the telephone without asking permission. They are grossly uninformed and full of odd and mistaken notions that cannot be corrected in the impatient rush of questions. The official is exasperated trying to deal with this anarchy, this vulgarity and ignorance. And yet he must court them. *They* can make judgments on *him!* They can make him look bad! It is an outrage that he must be at their mercy.

Up to this point, nothing serious. Just a clash of styles. Things get a lot more serious when the reporters have done their reporting.

The aristocrat-official takes in these reports with a mounting sense of frustration and fury. He doesn't realize that press reports are never 100 percent satisfactory. Sophisticated news sources are pleased with much less; they know that reporters won't see the story from the official viewpoint, and they also know that many reporters are not, shall we say, on the quality level of a Morley Safer. It's ironic that people who so quickly accuse the press of simpleminded stereotyping have such a simpleminded stereotype of "the press" or "the media," expecting a uniformity of talent and responsibility that could not possibly exist. The press is as diverse and motley a group as you could ever find. Some newspeople are strong and fine, some are incompetent, sleazy, or drunk, and there is a broad range in between.

The aristocrat-official doesn't understand these realities. He wants 100 percent. Remember, he is accustomed to absolute control. His own speeches and press releases are drafted over and over again, as he weighs every comma for its calculated and favorable effect.

So now he sees his precious subtleties being mauled before a mass TV audience by a reporter who wouldn't know a fine point if he sat on one and has only thirty-five minutes of education on this particular subject.

The aristocrat-official is aghast. What a disaster! Facts are screwed up, important points are left out, key statistics are ignored, concepts are distorted and condensed beyond recognition. The editing is ridiculous and takes everything out of context. Things are twisted, backwards, confused. And the report is so short—how did the reporter pack so much wrongness into such shortness? How could he do such a poor job? Wasn't he listening? *(Why didn't he do it the way I wanted?)*

Excluding physical violence, I can think of three alternative courses to follow when you don't like the way a reporter has told your story.

The first is to do nothing. Usually this is the wisest course, as expressed in Henry Ford II's advice about dealing with the press: "Don't complain, don't explain." The damage is done, so why risk making it worse?

The second is to risk making it worse by contacting the reporter to set him straight on the issue and let him know you will howl when he blows a story. This approach might lead to a big screaming fight, but frequently it clears the air and reminds both sides that the other guy is human and at least one of you is fallible. Politicians and other news figures constantly carry on this scrimmage with reporters. It is generally healthy and prevents the insulation from reality of the aristocrat-official.

The third course is to go after the reporter maliciously, using your power to inflict punishment on him and possibly to damage his career. Naturally this is the alternative chosen by the aristocrat-official.

Despite his contempt for newsmen, the aristocrat-official has difficulty with the idea that mistakes can be innocent (a mistake is defined as anything he doesn't like about the story). No, the angered aristocrat-official questions *motivations*. He senses *conspiracies*. The reporter has *intentionally* butchered the story. For *sinister* reasons. The reporter should be *investigated*. It is time to place some calls to top people, especially top people in the reporter's organization.

This call could be a complaint or a threat, or something more subtle—one top man offering a fraternal warning to another top man about the Rotten Apple in his organization. "Hell, the news media have a job to do, I know that, and *I* can survive this guy's questionable reporting but I'm not sure *you* can. He's gonna get your outfit in real trouble one of these days. And by the way, let's get together for lunch."

So the seed is planted, and planted by someone representing a power structure that must be taken seriously. What happens next? The top executive might dismiss the complaint, resenting its clearly intimidating purpose. Or he might believe it—not all complaints are groundless. Anything can happen. The reporter might be placed on the Rotten Apple List without even being told about it. Or he might be confronted with a few questions about the incident (the interest in it surprises him—to him the story was boring and forgettable, and what's the difference if some bigwig got huffy about it) and even if his defense is good, the probe from High Up might have a "chilling effect" on him the next time he encounters an aristocrat-official. It is a natural instinct to go easy on someone who is capable of stabbing you in the back.

Going easy might mean "objectivity." Objectivity can be a code of fairness and factuality, but it can also be a cover for timidity: playing it safe and omitting controversial points that might bring complaints from important people. As Tom Wicker has written, "Objective journalism almost always favors Establishment positions and exists not least to avoid offense to them" (*On Press* [New York, 1978], p. 37). This sort of objectivity makes for chickenhearted reporters and smug aristocrat-officials.

When journalists deal with the powerful, they should be aware that they have only one real weapon, and that weapon is the truth. If you present the truth accurately and responsibly, Mr. Big can yelp and call your boss, but he cannot sustain much of a case against you. When you deal with formidable people, you must do your most formidable work. If your work is shoddy, you are vulnerable.

One other thing: I've accused aristocrat-officials of pouncing on Conspiracy Theory to explain behavior they cannot understand. Journalists commonly do the same thing, conjuring up devious plots and strategies without considering possibilities that could be more likely, such as happenstance, bungling, jackassed or half-assed behavior. I've always suspected that a person under intense pressure is more likely to act with stupidity and desperation than with cunning.

8

Print

Print reporters envy the salaries, exposure, and impact of TV reporters, but they think TV journalism is inferior. They regard TV reporters as actors, "empty suits," pretty boys and plastic gals chosen for their on-air attributes rather than their skills as newspeople. They think that TV news could not function without relying on the groundwork done by the real journalists of newspapers and wire services.

There was a time when TV journalists did feel that they worked in an inferior medium and were therefore lesser journalists. This attitude has just about faded away. However, most TV newspeople would have no difficulty agreeing that print reporting is the foundation of news gathering and that no matter how much impact a story has on television, it doesn't seem to be certified as real news until it is recorded in print.

But this doesn't satisfy print people. If a TV journalist goes to a dinner party with a bunch of print people, there will be a time in the evening when they attack him with everything they resent about TV news.

Basically what they resent is the TV side of the Fundamental Duality: the glamor and glitz, the intrusion of technology on the hallowed craft of reporting, the emphasis on appearances and on picture over words, the fluff and chitchat, the eager preference that people in the news generally give to television reporters over individuals bearing only pads and pencils.

In the pursuit of news, print reporters feel like underdogs, leaner and keener but constantly and unfairly overshadowed by the elephant of TV.

As for news images on TV, they might concede that videotape is an advance over the still photos in their publications, but in their hearts they regard all picture as mere illustration—a dispensable supplement to the written word.

As for the impact and immediacy of TV, they regard that as unearned. It's the camera, not the cameraman and certainly not the reporter, that accounts for TV's advantage. And let's add one more point, the print writer's natural bias against TV as the medium for the simpleminded: it is the "boob tube," the "idiot box," gazed at passively by an uncritical and undiscerning audience. Dullards watch TV. Smart people read newspapers.

Having stripped away everything about TV news except the words, they measure the contents of a news script against a newspaper story and rest their case. The print story has far more words, far more facts, far more background, more nuance, more quotes, more reporting, more everything. Indeed, many big-name TV newspeople have come forth and endorsed the cliché that TV news is just a "headline service" that must be complemented by diligent reading of newspapers and magazines.

Having completed this rhetorical bashing of TV, the print people are still in a lather. They are particularly upset that the TV person is *not* upset, does not want to lash back with pent-up grievances against print. It is obvious that he and other TV people do not feel threatened or even especially competitive with print newspeople.

This is unbearably galling to the print people. It needn't be, but they bring it on themselves with their specious reduction of TV news. It doesn't work to dismiss one side of the Fundamental Duality as irrelevant while disparaging the other side as the loser in a data count.

Arguments about glitz, fluff, cosmetics, technology, picture, and even shallow reporters all have some truth (and all can be turned back against print) but these are only parts. What print people refuse to acknowledge is the wholeness imparted to TV journalism by the Fundamental Duality. This is what gives TV news its awesome impact and makes it a primary source of news for two-thirds of our population. The Duality brings the news to life; it adds flesh and blood to the bones of factual reporting. Even the skimpiest TV story reflects the dual aspect of TV news, information *and* experience.

By experience I mean the intuitive, non-factual, non-verbal recognition of what happened. A farmer talks about losing his farm, and his face and voice tell you something about loss that no news copy could describe. You see a videotaped report about a car that crashed into a telephone pole, and you learn something about a few moments of terror, of rupturing metal, shattering glass, stifled cries, brutal concussion, crushed bodies, and wheels spinning in the following stillness. The experience of the event is something more dimensional than the flat print report, "One person was killed and another was critically injured when the car in which they were riding crashed into a telephone pole on Elm Street last night." I would suggest that, in this and many other cases, it is often print that performs the "headline service" function, complementing the fuller coverage of television.

TV's power to convey experience is inherent in the medium (if that makes it unearned, so be it). And when major events take place, TV seizes the experience in a way that rips the rug out from under any belittling contrasts between TV and print. TV news simply brings the event into your living room or office, almost immediately and in full force. The explosion of the space shuttle Challenger was probably seen and *experienced* with horrifying impact by most Americans within an hour after it happened. Live network coverage carried us through the day. We knew just about everything we needed to know before we laid eyes on our next newspaper. Yet in the days and weeks that followed print coverage was excellent. TV news and print both did what they do best.

I have worked for newspapers and for TV, and my conclusion is that print is better at print journalism and TV is better at TV. Apples are better at being apples, and in any competition to be an orange, the orange will win.

Coming Over from Print

People coming to TV from print journalism tend to arrive with a certain smugness, expecting TV news to be child's play. In no time at all they are jolted by the Fundamental Duality. They are bewildered and discombobulated by the throes of TV production—the demands and distractions that seem to be such *obstacles* to the practice of journalism as they know it.

The coming-over journalist has a dizzy and sometimes desperate feeling of dislocation in a strange new universe. The technology and jargon baffle him ("What *language* are these people speaking?" he cries with dismay and derision to his old friends from print). He is not accustomed to the NASA-like coordination and interdependence of the TV news operation. Various people come around asking him production questions, and he hasn't the slightest idea what they're talking about. In the editing room he is mystified and flustered. In the field, where he used to function with only a pad and pencil or perhaps a tape recorder, he is now umbilically attached to a crew of two or three technicians and their equipment; he feels encumbered, almost immobilized, as if he were dragging a piano.

If he is to be an on-camera reporter, he faces a painfully embarrassing initiation. He can't believe how idiotic he looks and sounds. He reads aloud clumsily, he flubs and fluffs and flounders, and it is all that much worse because whatever he does, there is always a crowd of people standing around watching him. Just watching. No one gawks at print reporters, but TV reporters are always being gawked at. The former print reporter has trouble coping with it; it fills him with jitters.

And what about his strengths, reporting and writing? He comes up with some good prose and trenchant lines but finds that they don't work on television. Producers urge him to shave his copy, to flatten the wordsmanship he takes such pride in. And he is frustrated because he is strongly discouraged from saying things for which there is no matching picture.

As for reporting, it turns out to his shock that a large percentage of the facts he gathered for his newspaper stories are unusable in a TV report. There is no room for them or for the other special details that distinguish his reporting effort. He grumbles that TV stories are not journalism at all, only the illusion of journalism.

He likes his big new TV salary, and he may be awed by the reaction to being seen on camera. But he is tempted to quit and get back to print where he belongs, where a newsman is a newsman and doesn't have to deal with the extraneous-seeming frustrations of TV production. Maybe he stays, maybe he goes, but until he stops resisting television realities he will have a tough and very negative time.

My advice to a newsman coming over from print is: don't fight it. Don't be upset by the machines and jargon and complexities of production—they are not so difficult to understand. And don't trouble yourself over whether TV news is inferior to print—the point is that it's different. You might decide later that it's not inferior; for now, you will see that it's not child's play.

The Wire Services

At all hours those wire services machines are clattering and humming in newsrooms everywhere. Because the product arrives by machine, and because most wire stories carry no byline, there is a strong tendency to forget that they are the work of fallible humans. The wires seem omniscient and definitive; they provide the universally accepted version of the news. All journalists know that when their stories agree with what the wires are saying, their bosses breathe easier. A discrepancy casts doubt on *your* story, not the wire service version.

Bosses know better, but they forget. Those all-knowing machines are harder to challenge than the individual journalist who stands there in all his human fallibility insisting that he is right while the anonymous voice of the Journalistic Establishment is wrong. Lower-ranking journalists, especially newswriters, make the same mistake of being intimidated by the wires—if the wire story leads with point A, point A must be the correct lead.

But who says so? *Who?* When you think about it, it is astonishing that so much of the news is originally reported by people whose names are never known to those who publish or broadcast it; the same reporting goes out to many millions of people who have *never even heard of the wire services!*

Yet the wire services are the backbone of daily journalism. Small news organizations could not fill their air or pages without wire reports. The networks depend on them too, despite their large reporting staffs. Network newswriters spend their days tearing off wire copy, poring over it, underlining it, stacking it in ragged piles through which they search frantically when it is time to write.

I think the wire services' bylined writers and beat reporters do a solid job. But consider the general assignment reporters, who operate under killing pressure and at breakneck pace. It's my impression that they are either bright beginners or grizzled veterans (the transition to Grizzled Veteranhood seems to take place very quickly). They have seen so much, so many stories; they seem to arrive at a news event already knowing what it is. They practice grab-it-and-run journalism, just the who-what-when-where-and-how and the dash to the phone. There is little time for probing or poking around. Little time to check facts. Hardly any time to stand back and think things over or do any substantial research.

Just get to the phone—that's where the consummate wire service reporter performs his virtuoso trick, dictating his story without writing a word. He looks through his notes and reels it off. If he is on the other end of the phone call, on rewrite, he can do the same trick, taking called-in notes and composing the story as fast as he can type it. It is a dazzling feat of writing that makes other writers feel like turtles.

How is it done? Well, at the risk of insulting many fine wire service journalists, it is done by formula. Covering a story, the wire reporter recognizes the appropriate formula. He knows exactly what facts he needs to fill in the blanks, and he chases them down single-mindedly, wasting no effort or curiosity on other facets of the story. With his data gathered, he packages it in ready-made phrases, rhythms, and viewpoint. The story writes itself. The process is limiting, but it is efficient and indispensable. Urgency requires it. Uniformity requires it.

A difference between wire reporters and hacks is that wire reporters are *supposed* to work this way, and generally they excel at it. It is a journalistic specialty, tailored to the needs of all the news organizations that depend on wire copy. The formula is both the strength and the weakness of the wire services.

Because of the limitations and imperatives that define the wire services, they are especially vulnerable to manipulation. In his book *The Powers That Be* (New York, 1979), David Halberstam described the technique of a master manipulator, Senator Joseph McCarthy:

> [McCarthy] knew that the key was the wire services, they were uncritical, never judgmental, always in a rush, that they in particular loved those bulletins. . . . He always had fresh meat for them. He knew how to play the wire services off against each other. . . . If AP had something, then UP wanted a little more, and then suddenly it was on both wires at night, coming into the city rooms of a thousand newspapers, that much more legitimate, forcing other newspapers which had their own correspondents to match the stories. . . . (P. 195)

The wire services do their job as well as they can. But the journalism on *your* station is *your* job. Pick up the phone, check out wire stories yourself, and you'll learn soon enough that wire service reporting is not to be taken on faith.

Experience

I came out of college with notions about becoming a novelist, but I put the idea aside on the basis of a perception whose youthful wisdom continues to impress me: I realized I didn't know much about the world. I had probably traveled more than most people my age, but otherwise my life had been middle-class and not exceptionally eventful. I was ready to be an author, but I had little to say. Journalism appealed to me as a traditional (and romantic) way of amassing experience.

It was good thinking, not original but good. However, I think it's an approach that favors newspaper or possibly radio reporting over television; it also favors small-town reporting over the pressurized experience of big-city journalism. A young reporter who operates *on his own* comes into daily and frequently unforgettable human contact with the nitty-gritty of life, which is generally very different from life as portrayed in the news media. He learns things about people, including himself, that he would probably overlook in the hurly-burly of highly competitive journalism, where stories often seem to exist as fodder for newsmen rather than real events in peoples' lives. These encounters in small scale teach him lessons that will serve him well when he is working in a larger scale under conditions that do not allow for learning.

Unless you begin at a very small station, television does not offer the same individual learning experience. Many TV people rarely leave the newsroom. When they do, they're attached to camera crews, which is not the same as being on your own.

And there is something about the presence of a TV camera that de-naturalizes an event, teaching the wrong lessons. When the camera is rolling, even unsophisticated people tend to become performers, acting out the roles they think they're supposed to play. Or they become self-conscious to a degree that can be grotesque: the TV crew arrives at the home of the mother of yesterday's murder victim to find that the woman has just returned from the beauty parlor, is wearing her best dress and jewelry, and has postponed her grieving to prepare her home to be seen on television.

When I switched from newspaper work to television, I was surprised by the relatively narrow experience of people who had entered TV directly from college. They were just as bright as newspaper people, but they had not been around very much, even to journalistic locales such as police stations, hospitals, courthouses, and city halls. They had not served in the military or seen the inner workings of a large corporation. They had never been inside an extravagantly wealthy home or a desperately poor one. They had never talked to a criminal or a movie star or a stripper. They had never bummed around in Europe or toured the houses of government in Washington, D.C. They did not read literature or history or anything else except the newspaper. Often they hardly knew what was in the newspaper.

And what a bad sign that is. A real journalist is a newspaper junkie. Watch him page through the daily paper, pausing over everything—hard news, sports, gossip columns, reviews, cartoons, gardening tips, advice to the lovelorn, quips of the day, sometimes even the stock market page (although he has little money to invest). His knowledge may not be deep, but he vacuums in a vast miscellany of information. Someday it will pay off.

The new things you read, think, do, see, and feel may seem unrelated and, by themselves, unimportant. Like old books in a library they gather dust on the shelves of your mind, forgotten until that moment when you need a spark to activate your thinking or writing, and it is *there*. As Justice Holmes said, "An ounce of experience is worth a pound of logic."

Reading

It's not a mistake to read junk, but it is a mistake to read *only* junk. My advice is to read the best books, by the most respected authors. The quality of the writer is probably more important than the subject or whether it is fiction or nonfiction. If the book is well written, it's worth reading.

As for journalism books, I have found that histories of journalism are surprisingly colorful and sometimes inspiring. Scholarly books dealing with Great Issues Facing Journalism or "the media" may be substantial, but they are heavy going.

Books that reporters write about current events are often lively reading, although they become dated very quickly. Biographies and autobiographies of famous journalists are much more interesting.

My impression is that the first half of a journalist's autobiography is usually better than the second half. In the stories of his early career, the reporter is a central figure in tales of adventure and discovery, a journalistic Huckleberry Finn. But when he recounts the momentous events he covered at the height of his career, he loses his central place; he becomes a celebrated outsider, seeing history from close range but taking no more part in it than a sports reporter takes part in a great World Series game. It is one of journalism's trickiest professional hazards: you forget you are a sideliner and start thinking you are integral to the events you cover. But the book you write exposes the pale and disappointing truth.

Last Is Not Least

Here's a writing tip appropriate to the end of this chapter.

Newspaper stories are written to be cut from the bottom. If they are too long, final paragraphs are chopped off. Therefore it's common for newspaper stories to begin with tightly packed essentials—far more facts per sentence than a TV news listener could digest—and to end by trailing off loosely into low-priority information. Unless a story is a feature that requires a neat conclusion, the newspaper writer does not save punch lines or special facts for the end because he knows that bottom paragraphs are always in jeopardy.

A news story on television is entirely different. It's short, very compact, and its impact is fairly evenly distributed. An anchorman would not read the first half of a story in excited tones and then trail off into an anticlimactic mumble. Indeed, the ending of a TV news story might carry more weight than the beginning.

So don't get into the habit of imitating newspaper style and ending stories by dwindling into non-essentials. I was angered when a local TV news obituary of Peter Sellers ended with "Funeral arrangements are incomplete"—a standard closing detail for newspaper obits, but a cold-sounding last statement on a man's life when spoken aloud. It was also ridiculous in its implications that the reporter would have announced the hour and street address of the funeral even if arrangements were complete or that a large number of local viewers were about to cross the Atlantic for Sellers's funeral *in England*.

PART 2

Newswriting

9

The Doctrine of Picture

This chapter is heresy. It is intended to cause a lasting impurity in your TV news soul by shaking your faith in what I call the Doctrine of Picture.

"Picture" refers primarily to what you see on tape or film, though still photos and graphics are also part of it. The term also covers what you hear when you see picture—either talk or natural sound (crowd noise, street noise, the sounds of things happening). Good picture conveys *experience* more than information. It has visual or emotional impact (or both), and usually it involves large-scale physical action.

Good picture: police fighting rioters, athletes mauling each other in a victory celebration, a spectacular fire, a volcano erupting, animals doing just about anything, a lottery winner crazy with joy, an interviewee squirming under tough questions.*

Bad picture is dry and static: a speech that drones on, a wide-shot of a meeting, a complex explanation, anything that stands still and has no physical or emotional animation. At the top of any list of "picture poor" stories would be (sad to say) anything about the United Nations.

Good picture is TV gold. But the emphasis on good picture often takes TV newsmen off the path of good journalism. It can be an impediment, a distraction, a vulnerability.

The Doctrine of Picture is unwritten, which is appropriate because it is implicitly anti-writing and even anti-words: it deplores

---

*A victim screaming in pain or a bereaved parent collapsed in grief fit the definition of good picture, but more and more it is recognized that showing such picture exposes the broadcaster to charges of tasteless exploitation of horror and heartless invasion of privacy. Undeniably these charges have merit, yet so does the argument for using powerful newsworthy images. It's a dilemma for producers. Probably the best guideline is to make case-by-case judgments and make sure you don't *wallow* in people's tragedies.

talk without visual action, whether it is an anchorman or reporter reading script to the camera or a news subject yapping away without supporting visuals—what TV jargon colorfully calls a "talking head."

The Doctrine says that the importance with which a story is treated—the amount of time it gets and its prominence in the program—is directly related to the quality of its picture. Therefore, weak picture reduces the value of a journalistically important story; exciting picture enhances the value of a story that might have no serious meaning at all.

The Doctrine says that journalistic content must be tailored to picture. If you lack good picture of a key element of a story, or if the picture is technically flawed, there is pressure to shift the story to a tack that suits whatever better picture is available.

The Doctrine says that using picture is always right, that it always adds—it says that if a story is about milk prices, it is reasonable to show pictures of cows. It says picture never distracts or confuses the viewer.

The Doctrine says the audience is held by picture and lost by talk. It says talk is boring.

The Doctrine says your organization has paid for the picture in work, time, and money, so you'd better find a way to use it.

The Doctrine is passed down from seniors to newcomers in a patronizing lecture you will quickly learn to recognize by its opening sentence, "TV is a visual medium. . . ."

You will hear this lecture often. You may feel a nagging desire to argue against it. But how can you argue that TV is *not* a visual medium?

Well, of course it is a visual medium. But what the lecture (and the Doctrine) tends to forget is that it is so much more than visual. TV is also an oral medium, a journalistic medium, an entertainment medium, a nationwide communications medium, a medium that conveys facts and thoughts and emotions as well as the images that fill the screen.

To antagonize the lecturer, you might make a case that even on television the news is *told* more than it is *shown*. (The words are the freight!) Or pose this question: If you needed to get the news and had two TV sets, both partly broken, would you switch on the set that receives only audio (it is basically a radio) or the set that receives only video (it is the pure visual medium)? I think the automatic choice would be the audio-only set; the other set's flow of soundless moving pictures would be frustratingly difficult to decipher, like charades or pantomime. Of course, the clever solution would be to turn on both sets. The result would be: television! Not simply a visual medium.

But the lecturer doesn't want to hear this guff. He believes in the Doctrine. Let's consider some of its cardinal principles.

Weak picture diminishes a story's news value.

One of my earliest and most edifying temper tantrums in a local TV newsroom took place when I wrote a forty-second obituary of Walter Ulbricht. Ulbricht was the leader of East Germany for twenty-one years (1950–71) and a quintessential Soviet puppet. His image was bathed in Communist gray, and he was hardly a household name in the U.S. (I would barely remember him myself if not for this anecdote) but he was notably involved in numerous crises of the Cold War, and he played an important role in one event that shocked the world, the construction of the Berlin Wall.

I thought that was worth forty seconds. I wrote it nicely and sat back to admire it on the air. But I did not admire what I heard: my story had been slashed, rewritten, and knocked off in fifteen seconds.

I exploded and, finding no lesser figures on whom to vent my rage, charged into the office of the news director. I protested furiously; I pointed out that we lived in a city full of German-Americans, Russian-Americans, and European-Americans, as well as all other kinds of Americans who would have been affected by a major war igniting in Ulbricht's domain; I cited our duty as newsmen to remember and help explain the history of our times; I argued that the difference between doing it right and hardly doing it at all had been a mere twenty-five seconds, which we would not hesitate to devote to out-of-town sports scores. The news director listened and nodded in diplomatic agreement. Then he explained why the Ulbricht story had been cut: "We don't have a picture of him."

I was dumbfounded, flabbergasted that an audience exceeding one million people would not be told why Walter Ulbricht was important, because we could not show them what he looked like.

"Oh. No picture, no story, right?"

"We gave it fifteen seconds, didn't we?" said the news director. He shrugged and waved me out of his office.

Standing in the corridor, I lobbed in a few more hand grenades of indignation until I realized I was making a fool of myself. Then I went away.

That was my introduction to the Doctrine of Picture. It was a kindergarten-level learning experience in TV News Arts and Sciences, and the lesson was: when a story's visuals are weak, the story's value plunges, no matter how significant it might be to the world outside the newsroom.

This doesn't necessarily mean that big stories are ignored or shortchanged because the event cannot be shown on tape or film. Under pressure there are always angles to be found. Producers strain their sometimes formidable ingenuity to find ways to inject picture, and usually they succeed.

For instance, in the spring of 1982 television covered a whole war without a picture of it. News cameras were not allowed to enter the combat zone around the Falkland Islands, yet the story was reported prominently on TV every night. In the absence of combat scenes from the Falklands, there was picture from London and Buenos Aires, from Washington and the United Nations and elsewhere. There were telephone calls ("foners") and radio transmissions played over still photos and graphics. The action was plotted on elaborate maps and large tabletop models showing the topography and geography of the Islands. There were computer-generated graphics showing little boats and helicopters zipping all over the screen (Bruce Morton of CBS compared it to PacMan). There were features on the weaponry (including the oft-repeated manufacturer's footage of the French-made Exocet missile) and the ships that were sunk. In addition to the military angles, there were historical, diplomatic, political, economic, journalistic, and psychological angles. And of course there were the last pre-battle images, especially the endlessly recycled footage of the British fleet steaming off to distant warfare.

Near the end, Max Robinson, then anchoring for ABC's *World News Tonight,* introduced seventeen-day-old film from what he called "the war the world couldn't see." Yet we had seen plenty. And just four years later we had indications of a new era in which commercial satellites would provide picture from otherwise inaccessible locations: attack sites in Libya after an American bombing raid and the Chernobyl nuclear power plant in the Soviet Union. Coverage of the Chernobyl accident also included expensively purchased videotape that turned out to be an embarrassing hoax, accentuating TV's overeagerness for picture.

If the picture is very good, it need not be journalistically substantial.

There is nothing wrong with using interesting picture for its own sake. An old favorite, for instance, is the dynamiting of a decrepit bridge or building (you will probably see the demolition at regular speed, then in slow motion and then, for laughs, backwards). However, as TV newsmen make their daily effort to satisfy the Doctrine's lust for picture, they tend to be seduced by splashy visuals. If the picture is very good, producers are lenient about a story's lack of content or the reporter's failure to dig into its substance. The Doctrine encourages the pursuit of images instead of meaning, a journalism of externals and exteriors.

There is no better example than the coverage of political campaigns, which are designed almost exclusively to manipulate television's dependence on good picture. The best example in my memory is the 1980 primary campaign, in which coverage seemed to consist entirely of candidates popping out of airplanes at photogenic arrival ceremonies; a visitor from another planet might have surmised that we choose our leaders on the basis of their ability to disembark. It was perfectly feasible for a candidate to go no farther than the landing area, greet the crowd, say a few quotable words (guaranteed to become twenty-second sound bites on the evening news), reboard the plane with a vigorous step and an expansive wave, and fly off on a short hop to get local coverage in the next market.

Substance made few appearances in all this: the candidates were apparently glad to avoid it, and the TV teams didn't demand it as long as they got their juicy picture of the airport festivities. In their voice-overs, the reporters would dispense a few tidbits parceled out by "sources within the campaign," do some speculating about the candidate's current strategy, and explain with a mixture of sophistication and resignation how journalists were being kept at bay by the media sharpies running the campaign.

The Doctrine of Picture makes TV news terribly vulnerable to manipulation. The secret is out, and everybody knows it. Attention seekers, whether they are professional media advisers, public relations experts, or amateurs hoping to get someone or something on television, understand that assignment editors are trained to select stories with high visual potential and neglect stories that make for dull picture. Thus the publicity stunt, the "photo opportunity," the "pseudo event."

Advice for the few publicists who don't already know: the way to bring out the cameras is to provide something that will make good picture, whether it is a grim-faced politician touring a bombed-out ghetto or girls in bikinis leading leopards on studded leashes. It's also wise to provide food and drink, so the reporters and crews will linger to nibble the freebies instead of packing up after a quick look and rushing off.

Conversely, the way to *discourage* TV attention is to hold a news conference in a drab room and become a talking head, standing still and attempting complicated explanations in an inarticulate mumble. The Iran hostage crisis produced an incomparable practitioner of this art in Robert Armao, a high-priced public relations adviser and spokesman who represented the deposed Shah of Iran. Asked a probing question, Armao seemed to start slipping into a coma. You could barely hear him. You could hardly follow him. He was so slow, so careful, so colorless. He went on and on, world-shaking urgency dissolving into torpor. He did not dodge questions—he made you wish you hadn't asked. It was nearly impossible to extract fifteen seconds of usable tape. The temptation, therefore, was to give minimal attention to the Shah. Which was fine with the Shah and a subtle victory for Armao.

Journalistic content must be tailored to picture.

Words tell. Pictures show. When TV news is at its best, telling and showing complement each other to produce a fullness of coverage that could never be equaled by words or pictures alone. But what happens when the TV journalist wants to tell something he can't show?

A print reporter who becomes a TV reporter encounters this problem in its clearest form. He has the facts, the words, the news, but the producer says to him, "What have you got for picture?" and the reporter goes into a tizzy. The picture requirement is a ball and chain, a drag on his journalistic expression. He may have found out what was said at a top-secret meeting, but how can he match it with picture? Routine solutions, such as file footage or scenes of participants entering and exiting the meeting room, seem unsatisfying and even ludicrous. He feels gagged and hog-tied by the visual requirement.

An experienced TV newsperson would be less distressed. He has learned to think double, to weigh details for journalistic as well as visual merit. If a detail or idea offers little visually, he might instinctively discard it; but if he thinks it is especially important anyway, he *can* finesse it into his story. He squeezes the unpicturable material into his on-camera open or close or into his studio lead-in. Or he works it into his voice-over narrative, knowing that for brief stretches picture need not match narrative so long as there is a semblance of flow.

To use the campaign example, an extra ten to fifteen seconds of the candidate working the crowd (TV people might call this "generic hand-shaking") will occupy the screen while the reporter describes a behind-the-scenes decision or a fund-raising crisis or campaign staff in-fighting—none of which is remotely illustrated by the picture.

This is a workable and common solution, and it's not bad—up to a point. I'm not of the school that says words and picture must complement each other with strict literalness (words functioning as captions for the images), but it's obvious that as sound and picture diverge, the viewer's attention is pulled in different directions, with words and picture competing instead of complementing each other. If you show crowd scenes while discussing staff infighting, how do you control which gets primary attention and which gets background attention?

The answer is that a strong narrative will keep the upper hand, but only for a short time—perhaps enough for two sentences and even less if the picture is especially eye-catching. A good TV writer can cover a lot in, say, fifteen seconds, but have no illusions about comprehensive detail.

The next problem with picture is: What happens when you go into the editing room without the right picture? Given time and re-sources and a high priority, producers can find visuals to back up just about anything. But if it is a late-breaking story, a complex story or a haphazardly covered story—and especially if you are at a local station with limited resources—you may find yourself with a lot of important words and a weak selection of visuals.

What happens then? The Doctrine says that particular aspects of a story become dispensable as soon as you discover that you can't do a good job of illustrating them. Thus, when you don't have picture to illustrate a certain point, you will be tempted to chop out the point rather than create an awkward piece of editing. Of course, this is a setback for journalism.

What is even more frustrating is to be foiled by minor technical imperfections. Let's say you have two sound bites of an official making an important statement. In Sound Bite A he says it well. But a telephone rings in the background, blotting out a few words. Or there is a flash of static "breakup" in the tape. Or a bystander wanders into the picture and momentarily blocks the camera's view. Or the cameraman is jostled, creating a jumpy picture.

Sound Bite B has none of these defects. However, it is less interesting or articulate or less to the point. Perhaps it's about an entirely different aspect of the story.

You have three choices (actually four—I'll explain).

Choice 1 is to insist on using Sound Bite A. Your editor will resist because he cannot bear to edit in such a flawed piece of work. It goes against his grain; it's like asking a writer to commit a blatant grammatical error. You will have to whip him into submission. And then some higher-up will whip *you* into submission: "We can't use *that!* Why the hell did you put *that* in there?"

Choice 2 is to use Sound Bite B. This decision detracts from the journalism, but the piece will flow smoothly, and when something flows smoothly people tend not to notice other deficiencies, such as what might be missing from it. Just as you feel pressure against Choice 1, you will feel pressure in favor of Choice 2.

Choice 3 is to use neither sound bite. Instead, you paraphrase the excised material in your voice-over. Or perhaps you simply drop this aspect of the story. If the story is no good without it, you kill the whole story or, more likely, reduce it to a fifteen-second voice-over. All because of a jostled camera or a ringing telephone.

There is a Choice 4, but instead of illustrating obedience or defiance of the Doctrine it takes a middle course. You play with the better sound bite, salvaging what you can, covering deficient video with other picture, jumping over unusable audio with voice-over connectives (called "bridges"). Choice 4 requires time, effort, finesse, and some luck, but it's a good alternative.

Picture always adds, never distracts.

Objectively considered, illustrating a story on milk prices by showing pictures of cows seems like a comical idea. Certainly it would be peculiar to illustrate a face to face conversation about milk prices by whipping out a photo of a cow. Nevertheless, this principle is practiced on TV news every night. The anchorman reads on-camera for a few seconds and then continues voice-over as you see the cow shots. Or shots of a supermarket dairy case. Or of cashiers ringing up grocery purchases. Possibly numbers showing the price change are superimposed on the picture.

These visuals might set some viewers' minds wandering at the expense of journalistic facts, but this is a simple story that does not demand total concentration. Perhaps the picture has an interest-catching effect, or perhaps its images make the story stick in the mind. Or maybe the picture is only visual popcorn for tube-gazers. Whatever, I doubt if it hurts the story, and I would be in favor of it on grounds of elementary production values: it puts movement and variety on the screen and takes the camera off the anchorman.

But suppose the story is more substantial and complicated. For instance, a story on the economy of Japan. As the voice-over attempts to do justice to this serious but uncaptivating subject, the picture shows red-hot blast furnaces, engines being lowered into cars, assembly lines of computerized industrial robots working with hypnotic efficiency, shots of speeding motorcycles and shelves of stereo equipment and cameras, great cargo-laden ships sailing off to sea at sunset, money-counting machines, busy shopgirls, crowded streets in Tokyo. The editing is tight, the action and variety are constant. Under the reporter's voice track is natural sound: factory whistles, hissing engines, machines groaning, stereos playing, motorcycles revving, etc.

In short, the picture is far more engrossing than the script or substance of the report. The reporter is talking about economics, and no matter how brightly he explains it, he cannot compete with the dynamic visuals. The viewer watches the piece with interest, but is he still listening? Is he learning—or just looking?

The Doctrine does not accept my argument that picture can overwhelm subject matter. It says the more a piece is packed with spectacular visuals, the better it will be. The more watchable it is, the more attention and concentration it will get. If it's slow-moving and dull, people won't listen anyway.

That's a good argument, but it's no excuse for launching a cinematic exercise in the guise of a news story. The problem with the Japanese economy piece (to critique a hypothetical story) is not that the picture is too good and should be made dull, but that the picture is *not journalistic*. How the Japanese make cars is not news, shopgirls at work isn't news, ships at sunset isn't news. This is sheer pretty picture, visually terrific but empty of statement.

The Doctrine is softhearted toward pretty picture, exempting it from the journalistic requirement to say something. Picture of a busy Japanese assembly line intercut with picture of a closed-down American assembly line would be saying something. Picture taken in an American city showing a thriving Toyota showroom across the street from a languishing domestic dealership would be saying something.

Years ago I saw a reel of hilarious scenes captured by news cameras, including a famous sequence that showed, in the foreground, a newsman trying to interview a zoo official. In the background, two huge antlered animals charged in and out of frame until the male mounted the female and they copulated in a frenzy, bucking and snorting as the two humans struggled through their Q-and-A. No one seeing this sequence could ever again doubt the power of visuals to make a farce of editorial content.

Picture holds the audience. Talk without picture bores them.

A news producer works hard to achieve momentum and agonizes when momentum lags. This is bad news for depth. Depth means bogging down in details. Momentum means speeding ahead.

From the most respected newscasts all the way to the trashiest newscasts, there is a rush to picture. Picture is the grabber, the involver, the mover-along—as A. J. Liebling once described sensational headlines, the "eye-smacker." The Doctrine says: Cut the talk and roll the tape.

Fast pace is largely a matter of ever-changing visual activity on your TV screen. It can be intoxicating to producers. News stations that practice the television equivalent of tabloid journalism are positively drunk on it. It is not enough for the pace to be brisk— the desired tempo is cyclone speed.

Cyclonic pace is achieved by creating an impression of breathlessly whizzing from one thing to the next, barely touching down. Even the picture is tightly trimmed, to show only peaks of action. The best action is violent, abrupt, shocking, intense, even repulsive. Corpses. Crashes. Victims. Suspects. Screamers and cursers and sobbers.

Multiple anchorpeople toss the camera's attention back and forth like a hot potato. Much time is spent excitedly hyping or "teasing" what's coming next, lunging forward.

Scripts are written in short melodramatic style. Bursts of information. The word *tonight* is forced into every story to fabricate pulsating immediacy. It's happening now, Now!, NOW!!

Talk is anathema. If an anchorman rambles or stumbles, or if a talking head goes on for more than a sentence or two without covering video, the producer feels his program grinding to a halt, losing its fever pitch, and he is on his feet in the control room shouting, "Cut him! Speed him up! Get him off! Kill him! Shoot him!" He is bored, instantly and intolerably. He rests his head on a control room console and feigns loud snoring, or he pretends to phone the desk to leave a wake-up call.

For a while it can be a kick to work in this kind of circus atmosphere. But it is nothing to take pride in, really. It presumes that viewers are drooling dolts who need wall-to-wall firecrackers to stay awake and that if you don't give it to them, they'll be reaching for the channel selector.

The notion that a viewer's attention is constantly slipping away and must be recaptured each moment is fairly new to TV news. Not too long ago we could watch a deliberately paced newscast without impatience. The great Murrow broadcasts and many great *60 Minutes* stories prove that well-edited talking heads are not boring. But in daily news production, they are certainly in disfavor.

Now, conditioned by fast-paced production, it is probably true that we lose interest sooner and turn the dial quicker. This suggests two dire conclusions: that our attention span is shrinking to infantile dimensions, and that the effort to make the news less boring has created a boredom threshold so sensitive that we could hardly sit still for an important story that takes more than twenty seconds and lacks action-packed picture.

These conclusions are cynical and, I think, wrong. They result from a blurred distinction between the production values of news and escapist entertainment. An escapist TV series heaps on the car chases, shoot-outs, pratfalls, and titillation to jolt the viewer into watching even though there's not a morsel of dramatic substance. A news program that tries the same formula is heading for the same frenetic and hollow result.

The millions of people who watch TV news are not seeking escape. Just the opposite: they are trying to make contact with the substantial things happening outside their own lives. Some talking heads and actionless stories are indeed boring but some are interesting and should not be treated with fear that viewers will go berserk after eight seconds. It is even conceivable that we lose interest quickly because we get *too little* to engage our interest. Like a speeding train, the eight-second talking head goes by before we can climb aboard.

If you have it, use it.

The reason for scaling great mountains is also a reason for using picture of mediocre quality: because it is there.

Shooting a story costs time and money. Even if the result is of marginal quality, there is a great reluctance to throw picture away.

The most common example on local news might be the crime "aftermath" story, showing the street corner where the crime took place many hours earlier. With luck the cameraman finds a splotch of blood on the pavement and studies it from many different angles. Without luck, he finds an ordinary street corner and a small crowd of gawkers who appear to be fascinated by the street corner and its recent history; actually, they are far more fascinated by the TV crew and their prospects of becoming part of the picture.

It adds little to the story. But you shot it, you got it, and you use it. It's picture.

All the above comes under the heading of consciousness-raising. It is unthinkable and unrealistic to suggest turning away from the Doctrine of Picture. Without it, TV news would be televised radio, a throwback to the caveman era when announcers (they were announcers then; "anchormen" came later) divided their eye contact between the script and a single camera, and the visuals consisted of still photos or newsreel-quality silent film.

To make a blanket argument against the Doctrine is to identify yourself with that bygone era and dismiss the leaping progress that has come since. Nightly news on network and local television is now extraordinarily sophisticated. It owes much of its evolution and improvement to the Doctrine of Picture, which created a philosophy of production that channeled the creativity of thousands of TV journalists.

My complaint with the Doctrine is that it is doctrine. It is taught and accepted as an article of faith. It is *enforced*. The journalistic limitations it imposes are generally accepted as unalterable facts of life.

The Doctrine is so much a part of the creed that to suggest a criticism or argue for an occasional breach of Doctrine is to stamp yourself as a subversive maverick or an uncomprehending fool. Newswriters play both roles with innate skill. A challenge to the Doctrine of Picture may be heresy, but it is not punishable by decapitation or boiling in oil. Instead, someone will march over to your desk and begin a tedious lecture with the words, "TV is a visual medium. . . ."

10

Writing for the Ear

Words and phrases written by a newswriter and read aloud on television reach the listener at nearly instantaneous speed. Their physical existence is on an invisible wave of sound. A listener cannot hold on to them, slow them down, or run them by again. They are gone almost as quickly as they are said, landing in the listener's mind and melting as quickly as a snowflake on a wet pavement.

Such is the depressingly short lifespan of a newswriter's work. In the same moment his words are uttered, the process of forgetting them begins. Even if they linger for a moment, newer words come rushing along to crowd them out.

There is only one hope for their survival: that the listener can mentally assemble these receding signals into a linked chain of meaning so that a thought or idea or image remains even when the sounds have faded. Fortunately this miraculous process is accomplished by the human brain with routine efficiency; without it, there would be no such thing as oral communication—a severe blow to broadcast news.

However, the process is fragile. Spoken ideas must be linked together smoothly before they float away; any hitch in that smoothness invites total collapse. The enemy is distraction. If, in midstory, an anchorman rears back and sneezes violently, it is guaranteed that no one will remember what he was saying pre-sneeze. The distraction is like a bomb thrown into the assembly room of the listener's brain. It obliterates the thought under construction. And the distraction need not be as shattering as a sneeze. It can be as subtle as a curiously inappropriate word or an awkward phrase that snags the listener's mind and sends him wandering off on a tangent of free association or confusion.

The writer is absolved of guilt in the case of the sneezing anchorman, but he is clearly at fault when there is a snag in the copy. The reason for such snags might simply be the writer's lack of skill

99

or sensitivity, but more often it is a lapse in his orientation: he has reverted to the original orientation of writers, writing for *readers*. He has forgotten that he is writing for *listeners*. And since TV listeners also happen to be *watchers*, they are vulnerable to visual distractions too, such as an anchorman's gaudy necktie or an "Egypt and Israel" graphic flashing behind him as he reads a story about a fire in Philadelphia. Of course, the writer can do nothing about on-air visual distractions, but he should appreciate the overall distraction potential and make his own contribution to minimizing it.

The eye and the ear have very different powers. To be indifferent or oblivious to the distinction is a major error. Here are some points about writing for the ear.

Backing into the Story

A writing device that works well for readers but causes strain for listeners is "backing in":

Claiming they don't practice what they preach . . .

Eh? Who is claiming? Who is being accused? What is this business about practicing and preaching?

. . . Secretary of State Schultz criticized French foreign policymakers today.

Ah. Schultz is upset because he thinks French policymakers don't practice what they preach. I understand now, but only because I managed to hang on to the practicing-preaching idea long enough to insert it mentally when I found out where it belonged in the building of the thought. A little more distance from practicing-preaching and I wouldn't have hung on.

Here's another example, written by a well-known network correspondent who spent most of his career as a newspaperman:

Unpredictable and unclear. Those two words describe the situation in Africa now that Libya's Colonel Qaddafi is making trouble again.

"Unpredictable and unclear" hit you before you know what he's telling you about, and by the time he's told you they've started to float out of your consciousness and the connection is weakened.

(Also, the viewer is more interested in the situation than in the correspondent's opinion of the best adjectives to describe it.) Wouldn't it be better to say:

> Now that Libya's Colonel Qaddafi is making trouble again, the situation in Africa is unpredictable and unclear.

Here's another one, featuring a chain of thought that, like a bucking bronco, does everything possible to throw you off:

> Vowing to be "totally frank" in discussions aimed at sustaining world opposition to Soviet aggression . . .

Once again an unspecified news figure (the president, it turns out) is doing something, and the listener is going to have to scramble to piece together all the elements: a quotation ("totally frank"), two large concepts (world opposition, Soviet aggression), a news event (discussions), one fancy word (sustaining) and one image-making action verb (vowing). This clause is already loaded with informational signals. The listener is already under strain. He might be able to handle it if he could fit all the data into a context. Unfortunately the context has been withheld. But here it comes. Try to hold on:

> . . . President Carter arrived in Italy today for the start of a summit meeting with the leaders of six Western nations and Japan.

Only now can the listener go to work assembling the story. Don't be surprised if he balks. The story is such an overcrowded mess, he has probably tuned out in annoyance. He will not give you his attention if you abuse it. This is wire copy, not broadcast copy.

A reader controls his own pace and retention and, when necessary, looks back. A listener has no such control. He cannot look back and he cannot be forced to juggle airballs of thought, fact, and image until he is given a place to put them down.

He will have trouble assembling a story frontward if you give it to him backward. The argument against backing in is not an argument against starting with a subordinate word or clause. It's an argument against starting with subordinate information.

Here's the beginning of a story that led a network newscast:

> In a decision with enormous impact for genetic research . . .

This is not a cart-before-the-horse construction. The clause creates a context for the facts about to follow. It gives you a foundation to build on, and a rather exciting one. It is not a case of a writer enticing you with frilly details you will have to cling to and insert later. True, you don't know yet who has made the decision, but you will find out quickly and without interference (unlike the "vowing" example):

> . . . the Supreme Court ruled five-to-four today that . . .

The facts are building: you know that the Supreme Court has made a major decision involving genetics and the decision was very close.

> . . . scientists may patent new forms of life they create in a laboratory.

The story (which was followed by a taped report) is airtight. It takes you directly to the news. It backs in, but the information reaches you in frontward order. The backing in could also have been done via participle ("Ruling today" or "Deciding today").

But why back in at all? How about this:

> The Supreme Court ruled five-to-four today that scientists may patent new forms of life they create in a laboratory. The decision will have an enormous impact on genetic research.

This works, but I think the other version works better because the backing in prepares the listener for the exotic subject coming at him, the patenting of lab-created forms of life. If, however, the Court had announced a widely awaited decision on a matter already understood by the public—for instance, the famous decision forcing President Nixon to turn over the Watergate tapes—it would have been wrong to back in with a preparatory explanation. The hard news would come first, the ramifications afterward.

Delayed Attribution

Another newspaper-derived device for launching a story is the catchy opening quote or paraphrase, with attribution to follow.

> Anyone who opposes prayer in public schools is an atheist and a downright Communist.

Huh? When those words come at you from your trusty anchorman, what are you supposed to think? Has he thrown editorial neutrality to the winds and uncorked a shockingly vehement personal statement? It catches your attention, no doubt about it. But what is it? Is it a quote? You don't know—you can't *hear* quotation marks.

. . . Those were the words of evangelist Elmer T. Johnson.

Oh. But you had an alarming moment there. The distraction will take a moment to subside.

Opponents of prayer in public schools are atheists and downright Communists, according to evangelist Elmer T. Johnson.

This paraphrased version sounds a lot better. At least the sentence doesn't end until you are given the attribution. But the attribution is tacked on, the anchorman is running out of breath, and what you're hearing is a read-aloud newspaper story.

Opening with quotes or paraphrased quotes grabs for attention but risks confusion. The listener doesn't know what he's hearing or where it's coming from. And I think it's unnatural to oral communication. If you were telling a friend about this story, you would not "open" with an out-of-the-blue quotation. The general rule for broadcast writing is that the attribution comes first.

Direct Quotation

Since the listener cannot hear quotation marks, you must point out explicitly when you are quoting. There are several tried-and-true ways of doing this:

The mayor said today—in his words—"Enough is enough."

The mayor said QUOTE Enough is enough UNQUOTE.

The mayor expressed his opinion in three words: "Enough is enough."

The mayor said the city could not bear another tax increase. As he put it, "Enough is enough."

These devices, though sometimes required, quickly become grating. Use them sparingly. Don't feel obliged to force them into your copy when the language is commonplace and the effort of turning it into a quotation creates an effect so bland it sounds absurd:

He said he would QUOTE appeal the decision UNQUOTE.

He said a goal would be—in his words—"to hire more nurses."

He said the explosion was—as he put it—"loud."

Homonyms and Homophones

As an avid Yankee fan rooting for my team during a pennant race, I was distressed to hear the following:

The Yankees won tonight, but the Orioles won *two*.

Or maybe it was:

The Yankees won tonight, but the Orioles won *too*.

Whether the Orioles had won two or too made a critical difference. It was maddening to be left in doubt.

The use of homonyms and homophones is a surefire way to confuse your listeners. This is an important lessen in righting for people two hear—you must knot do the same thing to their ear that I'm now doing too your reeder's aye. A listener cannot tell weather you are telling him about a miner or a minor (could the miner have been Henry K. Glotz's sun, the air to the Glotz fortune?). When you are reading you can look back to figure out these false signals in your own thyme. But the listener has only a fleeting moment to recognize a word; if he is puzzled by it, he may lose the chain of thought and never ketchup.

Homonyms are words with the same sound and spelling but different meanings: a *pole* is a stick or a point on a compass or, with an unhearable uppercase letter, a citizen of Poland. Homophones have the same sound but different meanings and spellings: an opinion survey in Warsaw would be a *poll* of *Poles*. Homophones are more likely to cause you trouble, because their written appearance is so different that it does not occur to you that they are identical to the ear.

There is no foolproof safeguard against the homonym-homophone problem, except for your own alertness and sensitivity to it.

My advice is that if you notice even the possibility of confusion of this sort, you should steer away from it immediately and find another way of saying what must be said. Don't try to convince yourself that it won't cause a snag for the listener.

This is an important point in oral writing. Or aural writing.

This Way, That Way

One of the most subtle devices of writing for print works out negatively in writing for broadcast.

President Reagan's speech was not without humor.

Governor Morton was less than thrilled by the city's response.

The exhausted Bradshaw was not ungraceful as he accepted defeat.

Condon was pleased if not jubilant at the turnout.

The listener must work quickly to decode these constructions and grasp their intended subtlety. In the Reagan example, the listener feels guided in one direction by the "not" and then forced to scramble back in the other direction when it becomes "not without." As the Morton story comes at him, the first signal indicates a negative ("less") but the onrushing second signal seems like a positive ("thrilled").

The Bradshaw story takes a moment to figure out, even in print. The Condon story, using the "if not" device I associate with newsmagazines, is mystifying: was Condon pleased to the point of jubilation, or was he just barely pleased and nowhere near jubilant?

These constructions make trouble for the listener. Sometimes they also indicate that the writer is not confident or clear about what he wants to say and is hiding his uncertainty in exquisite equivocation. He may be impressed with his literary finesse, but *oral communication is not literary.* Few thoughts are too subtle to be expressed in plain language.

President Reagan's speech had moments of humor.

Governor Morton was critical of the city's response.

Bradshaw was tired and dejected but had words of praise for the team that defeated him.

Condon was [whatever he was].

Upward-Downward

This is This Way, That Way involving quantities. It is technically correct (or should I say, "not incorrect"?), but it causes trouble because it suggests contradictory directions of thought, upward-downward or positive-negative.

> Unemployment is up.

This sounds like a positive ("up") but in fact it's negative (more people are out of work).

> Unemployment dropped last month.

Here are two signals of downwardness ("un-" and "dropped"), which make the statement sound like a negative when in fact it's a positive.

In both cases, the thought is simple, and most listeners could figure it out in a moment. But why force them to figure out what you mean? When you give listeners little puzzles, some will get the wrong answer, some will not bother trying, and some, temporarily diverted, will miss the next few sentences or more. So, let ideas travel in only one direction at a time:

> Unemployment has gotten worse.

Or

> More people brought home paychecks last month.

Here are some more examples of direction reversers—downs that go up, negatives that are positive, etc.

> The trade deficit rose.
> Joblessness improved.
> The Kremlin is slowing down its spending increases.
> He added that reductions are needed.

And put this one in the This Way, That Way, Upward-Downward Hall of Fame:

> The increase in the international value of the dollar has played a not insignificant role in the decline of America's net exports.

Not

Not is a critical word in journalism. It has huge meaning, but it is a tiny word that tends to get lost. You omit it while typing or the anchorman's eye skips over it on the air. Or he reads it but with too little emphasis. The results misspeak for themselves. Imagine the "not" dropped or unheard in these sentences:

> Jones said he was [not] a homosexual but sympathized with the gay rights movement.
>
> Jones said he thanked God that he was [not] killed in the explosion.
>
> Jones said he had renewed faith in American justice because the jury found him [not] guilty.

Some newsrooms make it a standard practice in court stories to substitute "innocent" for "not guilty," rather than risk missing a "not."

If you're concerned that a particular "not" may be overlooked, take the precaution of underlining or capitalizing it for extra emphasis.

Repeatophobia

One of the basic rules drummed into all writing students is: Don't repeat. At almost any cost, do not repeat. If you use the same word twice your teacher will circle the offending words in red ink and blast you with the marginal notation "REPETITION!!!" The result is lifelong repeatophobia.

Well, repetition is not that bad. Not that it's good. It creates an instant monotony that grates on the ear and exasperates your listeners. For instance:

> In Chicago today, a fire at the Chicago Board of Trade took the lives of sixteen Chicago men including four Chicago firemen. Chicago Mayor Harold Washington said the fire was one of the worst fires in Chicago's recent history.

Yes, that's terrible. But consider the death-before-repetition approach:

> A fire today at the Chicago Board of Trade took the lives of sixteen local residents including four municipal firefighters.

Windy City Mayor Harold Washington called the blaze one of the worst tragedies in the recent history of the Illinois metropolis.

Both are terrible (and both, of course, are exaggerated to show the extremes caused by the repetition problem). My feeling is that Example 1, crude as it is, leaves no doubt about what has happened. But in Example 2 telling what's happened seems secondary to the writer's primary goal of avoiding repetition. Thus the listener is forced to deal with "Chicago," "local," "municipal," "Windy City," and "Illinois metropolis"—all meaning the same thing. ("Windy City" and "Illinois metropolis" are junky journalese, and a writer who uses either should be tortured.)

Repeating is preferable to ridiculous stretching to avoid repeating. If the story is about snow, don't reach for a ludicrous alternative like "the white stuff" unless you are willing to call rain "the wet stuff" and sunshine "the warm and bright stuff." If only one word is correct, don't sacrifice precision by selecting an inexact synonym. Remember that an anchorman can take some of the monotony out of repeated words by varying his inflection. Most anchormen do so instinctively.

Huh? Who? What Was That?

The problems of writing for the ear are compounded by human nature: most of the time, people only half-listen.

Say the news is on and you're watching it while looking through a magazine or eating or talking on the phone. Suddenly you're hearing the obituary of someone famous and important. But you didn't catch the name. *"Who died?"* you demand of your TV set, and it replies, "He was sixty-seven years old." Then a commercial begins. You will have to get the answer elsewhere.

Writers can't always conquer inattention, but they should be aware of it and do what they can to lessen viewer frustration. In this case the writer might argue in self-defense: "Yes, but I *do* give the [deceased's] name! The story *starts* with his name!" True, but if the viewer misses it, the story fails. Don't lean too heavily on the assumption that *because you said it, he heard it.* Instead of challenging the viewer to pay attention, help him catch up with you. Keep repeating the name, especially at the end of the story.

Also to be avoided in obituaries is the long and tantalizing identifying clause inserted (in wire service style) between the name and the verb:

George Washington, who commanded the Revolutionary Army, presided over the constitutional convention . . .

"Oh my God," cries the viewer, recognizing what might be a death announcement.

. . . and became our first president, serving two terms in office . . .

The viewer waits in riveted suspense. Is Washington dead? Or has he assumed some great new responsibility?

. . . and will undoubtedly be remembered forever as the Father of our country . . .

The viewer's shock is turning to impatience.

. . . died today.

It is ridiculous and tasteless to torment the audience with this device. Write: George Washington died today. He was . . . .

The "Tell 'em" Rule

One of the venerable rules of thumb for broadcast writing is: "Tell 'em what you're gonna tell 'em, tell 'em, and tell 'em what you've told 'em." For example:

(Tell 'em what you're gonna tell 'em)	There was another decrease today in the prime interest rate. . . .
(Tell 'em)	Major banks lowered the "prime" by a half-point, to 12 percent. . . .
(Tell 'em what you've told 'em)	The prime rate has now fallen eight points since April, when it reached a record high of 20 percent.

The "Tell 'em" rule imposes a monotonous rhythm, heavy redundancy, and a narrow, formula approach to newswriting. It feels, uneasily, like spoon-feeding the listener. But it is perfectly suited to the ear. It's a useful guideline when a story is getting too complicated. (The "Tell 'em" rule is generally attributed to Paul White, who, as the first news director for CBS Radio in the 1930s and early 1940s, was one of the founding fathers of broadcast journalism.)

Writer's Ear

Before you turn in copy, read it to yourself and try to hear how it will sound. Often this will alert you to problems the eye does not detect, such as overlong sentences, sounds that mush together, inadvertant tongue twisters.

Some newswriters actually read their copy aloud, sitting there mumbling to themselves in whispery newscaster cadences. If this works for you, fine. But remember that your reading style may be different from your anchorman's, and that he will not be as intimately familiar with the copy as you are—shades of emphasis and meaning that are obvious to you might be missed by him.

After a while, however, you will develop an intuitive "ear" for his style. You'll write it naturally, and when you read over a piece of copy you will hear in your mind how it will sound on the air.

11

The Cliché

John O'Hara nicely described the place of the cliché in writing news in a short story about a plodding but dutiful smalltown newspaperman, "Claude Emerson, Reporter" (in *The Cape Cod Lighter* [New York, 1962], p. 54).

Claude Emerson had never pretended to be a writer. He learned early that there was a set journalistic phrase for nearly every detail of every event that made a news item, and when he had acquired them all he saw no reason to originate another batch.

That paragraph describes many newswriters. They acquire the clichés early and think they are equipped for a lifetime. I recall, in the first week of my first newspaper job, wrestling with a story about a bank robbery committed by three men. In many references I called them alternately "the three men," "the three robbers," and "the three." It felt clumsy and repetitious, and I strained to think of something else to call them. Nothing came to me. But later in the day, comparing my story with a wire service report, I discovered the elusive variation: the trio.

Eureka! The *trio*. Oh, how I could have used that word! The moment I saw it there in that wire copy I sensed with a feeling of exhilarating progress that it would be imprinted forever in my journalistic vocabulary. Whenever a story involved three of anything, I would be quick on the draw with my new word, *trio*. No matter that the word is commonly used and understood to mean a three-member musical group; no matter that it would never be used otherwise in natural speech ("Well, this trio of robbers came into the bank . . ."). No, unless the bank robbers were armed with guitars, banjos, and tambourines and sang as they robbed, this was not a trio. But in my pleasure at acquiring a new "set journalistic phrase," I did not question it.

An embarrassingly long period went by before it occurred to me that I had been enthusiastically training myself to write like a hack. *Trio* is a hack's word, and the many other clichés I'd adopted so proudly had put me in the company of young Claude Emerson.

I had learned that a fire was also a "blaze"—who but a newsman would call a fire a blaze? Under severe synonym-seeking distress, the newsman-hack might escalate the blaze to a "conflagration." I had learned that a blaze takes place in a burning structure called an "inferno" or perhaps a "fiery shell"; that flames "leap" or "spit" from the windows of an inferno; that a conflagration leaves a fiery shell "gutted," with "homeless residents" (*homeless residents?*) "huddled in grim clusters." And of course the fire is "labeled suspicious," so investigators "sift the charred remains" for signs of arson and police go about "apprehending the alleged perpetrator." But the writer shuns this last one; having recycled so many clichés of journalism, he cracks down on the pearl of police clichés, changing "apprehending the alleged perpetrator" to something else and congratulating himself on being a vigilant soldier in the war against jargon.

Claude Emerson may have been dull-witted, but his early insight was correct: there *is* a "set journalistic phrase" for nearly everything. The clichés of newswriting are a language unto themselves. It is called "journalese." It's conceivable that journalese could be programmed into computers and that computer-newswriters disgorging high-speed printout scripts could replace and outperform a fair number of human newswriters—not the ones who are good or struggling to improve but certainly the Deadwood Claudes who never even try to break away from that original batch of hack words and phrases.

Few of the clichés of journalese jump out at you with the identifiable, laughable badness of "apprehending the alleged perpetrator." Most of them are barely noticed, humdrum, faded and gray like old laundry. We impose the dreariest language on lively stories and get away with it because everyone is so attuned to hack newswriting that they mistake it for slick professionalism—the mistake I made with *trio*.

What this means is that the conscientious writer must detect and root out clichés as a personal mission. Others in the newsroom aren't thinking this way; they may be dismayed when you declare that a golden-oldie cliché like *blaze* has lost its power to evoke the crackling heat and ferocity of a fire and is only a used-up synonym.

Say this much for the cliché: it is handy and economical and wouldn't have lasted long enough to become a cliché if it had not been serviceable from the start. Some clichés inflict themselves with a kind of inevitability—how can you write a fire story without fire clichés? Most journalists are indebted to the cliché because it has come to the rescue in many critical writing situations when there is not enough time to struggle for a fresher alternative. Better a tried-and-true "set journalistic phrase" than paralysis at the typewriter or some awkward new construction whose only virtue is that it isn't familiar.

But familiarity is not the prime flaw of the cliché. News events repeat themselves and so do the words that describe them best; it would be futile to stretch for new variations every day. The prime flaw of the cliché is not overuse so much as *indifferent* use. Every burning building is automatically an inferno; every new widow is automatically grief-stricken; every disaster is tragic; every murder is a brutal slaying; every tax or rate increase is whopping; every contrast is marked or stark. The clichés are hauled out without care; the writer presses levers to swing different cliché-units into place. It is writing by rote, by formula, by fill-in-the-blanks. It denies the individuality of every event; by denying individuality, it denies the *news* of an event.

The cliché is not just a writing problem. It's also a thinking problem. Thinking in clichés is a professional hazard for newsmen who've been around for a long time (and sometimes their younger colleagues pick up the same bad habit). They regard the news itself as a succession of clichés. They force their clichés onto every event; they see only what they have seen so many times before, and anything that does not conform to their clichéd expectations is treated with irritation, cynicism, even outright denial.

Which brings me to a favorite story, which, like the trio incident, took place in my early days as a newspaper reporter for the *Providence Journal-Bulletin*.

I was covering a town council meeting in a very small town in Rhode Island. In the council chamber that night were four or five councilmen, a scattering of townspeople, and two reporters, me and the local Claude Emerson. There was also a janitor named Frank.

The council's debate, on a controversial subject I cannot remember, was mired in confusion and acrimony. Each councilman took his turn rising to dispense oratory that was incoherent in terms of the issue but effective in terms of righteous posturing and colorful insults. As I tried to follow the arguments (reporters cannot sit back and enjoy this sort of spectacle, they must earnestly try to follow it) I noticed that Frank the janitor was mopping his way toward the front of the chamber and showing attentive interest in the debate.

As he mopped into the vicinity of the council table he began, not at all abruptly and to the evident surprise of no one, to become engaged in the discussion. His comments were sensible and cool-headed, and in an effortless transition he sat down at the council table, still holding his mop as he became, indeed, the moderator of the debate.

I was incredulous. I whispered to the Claude Emerson, "Frank is running the debate!"

The Claude Emerson turned to me with a patronizing glance and said, "Don't be silly. Frank is the *janitor!*"

Right. The janitor could not be running the town council. But he *was*. The debate ended when Frank advised the chairman to call for a vote. Frank observed the voting with interest (he did not vote himself) and then got up from the council table and resumed his mopping.

To this day I rue my failure to feature Frank in my story. But while Frank didn't enter my story, he didn't even enter the consciousness of the Claude Emerson, who presumably had seen Frank intervene many times before and had routinely edited him out of reality—to protect the dignity of the council but also to protect the cliché of the town council meeting. The cliché-buster had literally walked into the story and sat down in the middle of it, but the insistent weight of the cliché had declared Frank invisible, non-existent, null and void.

When you find yourself on the verge of thinking in clichés or using them in your copy, slam on the brakes and ask: "What's happening here? What does this really mean?" The cliché creates an illusion of meaning, but when you give it a moment's thought, little or nothing is there. For instance:

City residents braced today for a major transit strike.

This sounds active and even exciting. But you must ask yourself: Are people in fact *bracing?* What does bracing mean? Are people really doing anything along the lines of a citywide mobilization, as the cliché suggests, or is the bracing simply an invention from the mind of the newswriter?

Perhaps the people are doing something. Perhaps they are preparing for a transit strike by arranging car pools, reserving hotel rooms in the city, repairing their bicycles, or shopping for hiking boots. To my mind none of these activities constitutes bracing, but if true, they are good solid facts. So drop the empty dramatics about bracing and go right to them. However, if you cannot be sure that these preparations are being made, you have no basis for any assertion, general or specific, about what a whole population is doing. It could be that no one is doing anything to prepare for the strike, an annoying challenge to the newsman's clichéd concept of how things should be.

I know of no comprehensive list of broadcast clichés and bad usages that have become clichés. But here is my own personal list, along with some points of advice and short bursts of peeve.

Never use the word *hopefully.* You will probably misuse it (it means "having hope," not "it is to be hoped," so "Hopefully the cold weather will end by the weekend" is incorrect), but even if you get it right, a newsman has no business injecting his personal hopes into a story, no matter how goody-goody they may be. The same goes for *thankfully.*

Massive and *crucial* and *bizarre* are fine words, but they have been overused to the point of meaninglessness.

Above I mentioned *bracing.* Another thing that populations are supposed to do when havoc approaches is to *gird themselves.*

The words *posh, plush,* and *fashionable* are terribly overused and seem to have a disapproving connotation, a reverse snobbery that probably dates back to the days when the press played the role of the spunky "little guy" sneering at the over-privileged rich.

Never describe anything as *in-depth,* because it probably won't be.

Think twice about *brutally,* as in "brutally murdered" or "brutally raped." Violent crimes are brutal by definition. If a crime is exceptionally ghastly, and you want to tell why, specific details are better than horrified adjectives and adverbs: "She was hacked to pieces by a killer who used a machete and a saw," or "She was forced to watch thirty-nine episodes of a certain situation-comedy." The same goes for *savagely, viciously,* etc.

Slay is a newspaper word, ideal for short headlines, but old-fashioned and unnatural in common speech unless you are describing the killing of dragons. Use *kill* or *murder.*

Beward of words and phrases with gross sexual connotations: don't use *beat off* to mean repel, *eat out* to mean go to a restaurant, or *hung* to describe a man who was hanged.

Gay was a lovely word until it meant homosexual. Be very

careful with it. Don't write, "Last night President and Mrs. Reagan attended a gay ball in Washington."

Young people are young people, teenagers, fourteen-year-olds, children, or even kids, but don't call them *youths*. It is a newspaper word, and a silly one that no one uses in common speech ("Bobby and his friends are nice youths"). Above all, don't link a definite with an indefinite: "a fourteen-year-old youth."

Boy and *girl* are innocent words, but except in a sports context, both should be used with special sensitivity. Black males have good reason to resent *boy;* I would not use it to describe a black male much older than ten or twelve. *Girl* and *gal* are offensive to many adult women, although some people think it's cute to call elderly ladies girls. Somewhere around high school age a girl becomes a "young woman"; a few years later you drop the "young."

I realize that *whopping* is an emphasizer, but I've always found it meaningless and dopey. "Prices will go up a whopping ten percent." Is someone whopping the prices? Are consumers being whopped? The word also brings to mind the ethnic slur *wop* and echoes unattractively in stories about Italian-Americans: "Senator D'Amato has a whopping campaign war chest."

Like *whopping, literally* is often used as an emphasizer. *Whopping* is bad because it's meaningless, but *literally* is worse because it's wrong; it means exactly the opposite of what it's often used to mean. It means to the letter, exactly, actually, no exaggeration. On the eve of the American hostages' release from Iran, the normally impeccable Roger Mudd led the evening news with an almost out-of-control sentence misusing *literally* and mixing up his pronouns— he declared, "All of Washington is literally holding their breath for the hostages." If that had been literally true, all of Washington would have died in a few minutes. The right word is *figuratively,* but it is so right that it puts a damper on the thought. The best solution is to avoid both words.

Super- seems to have become a prefix used to hype a dull adjective. In a single night of TV watching I heard the weather described as "supercold" and pre-teenagers described as "super-young." When something is less than super, an equally bad prefix is available, *semi-*. Semi-cold? Semi-young?

I associate the word *myself* with dumb-athlete talk, as in "Speaking for myself personally, a good clean-up hitter would take a lot of pressure off myself." I think people use *myself* when they're unsure of *me,* as in "between him and myself."

Military precision entered journalese in that long-gone era when reporters revered the military and glamorized it shamelessly. Hearing the phrase now, you can't be sure whether the speaker is using it in the old hero-worshipping sense (and is therefore duped by the military myth) or with a kind of hip sarcasm (thus needlessly insulting the military). Either way it leaves a bad taste.

Learn the difference between *imply* and *infer.* Let the *f* from infer remind you of *from*. I imply something, you infer (from) what I said.

Media might be tempting as a collective term—and how handy such terms can be—but I advise forsaking it whenever possible. It is a plural word that often comes out in the singular, an error of grammar influenced by an error of connotation: the notion of a big bad media monolith. The problem with the word is that its meaning varies with the mind-set of the user or hearer, including many who are inclined to sinister interpretation. My experience is that anyone who displays a particular attachment to the word will ultimately expose a view of reality that is uninformed, deluded, or otherwise suspect.

These days almost always signals a mush-minded generalization that the writer has invented on the spot, trying to write his way into or out of an abortive construction.

Whether or not can usually be shortened to whether. Occasionally you might want to retain the "or not" to emphasize the alternative, but in most cases you can drop it.

You can center on something but it's impossible to *center around.* A center can't be around, it can only be in the center.

Don't use the ignoramus redundancy *exact-same* or *same-exact.*

Restaurateur is spelled with no *n.* But don't use it. Say restaurant owner.

Go very light on foreign or foreign-sounding words like *macabre, passé, chic, de facto, apropos,* and *vis-à-vis.*

Messrs. (from *monsieurs*) is the plural abbreviation of *Mr.* Said aloud it sounds like "messers." Most men would rather not be grouped with a bunch of messers. Don't use it.

False titles soon become meaningless clichés. Consumer Advocate Ralph Nader. Fugitive Financier Robert Vesco. Avowed Communist Angela Davis. NFL Czar Pete Rozelle. Former Yippie Abbie Hoffman. These labels in particular are so much a part of the names that changing them would be tantamount to tinkering with the names themselves. But with less ingrained identifiers, the word *the* will make the label more digestible: "The noted heart surgeon Michael DeBakey" or "Renee Richards, the transsexual tennis player."

Newsmen are always declaring things *labeled,* as in "The city's hospitals were labeled inadequate." I think there is always a better way to say what you mean, without this contrived process of labeling.

All of these words are followed by singular verbs: *each, either, neither, nobody, no one, everyone, everybody, someone, somebody.* Mistakes are most likely with either, neither, and each.

Words ending in the suffix *-ize* tend to be jargon or manufactured fad words. Common words using *-ize* are not so bad, but using newer ones (finalize, verbalize) is a confession of inarticulateness, as if I were to tell you not to cliché-ize your copy.

Some dreadful colloquialisms add the needless word *up,* as in *head up, serve up, chair up, offer up.* More venerable constructions seem less offensive, such as sign up, stand up, wake up, give up, hand up (The direction in which a grand jury hands an indictment is up, not down).

It remains to be seen is often the beginning of a reporter's tag, as he speculates earnestly on the consequences of what he's just reported. I'm not against the speculation, but I think reporters should be required to find a better way to launch it, something less trite than I.R.T.B.S. or its close cousin O.T.W.T. (*Only time will tell*).

This is only a small and random list. If you are serious about writing, you should develop a relationship with some of the many good books on word usage and the fine points of American English. *The Elements of Style* is the most helpful handbook you'll ever find. I'm a fan of Theodore Bernstein's books, especially *The Careful Writer. The Associated Press Stylebook,* available in bookstores or from the AP, is the handiest, especially for succinct reminders of the differences between affect and effect and other commonly confused words.

12

Natural Style

It was said of the great movie actor Spencer Tracy that you never caught him acting. The mechanics of his performance never showed through; there were no embellishments, no false notes. He seemed so natural you forgot that he was acting.

TV newswriting aims at the same naturalness. You should never be caught writing. The rule is: *If it sounds written, it's wrong.*

Yet students who are told to "write like you talk" (it should be "Write *as* you talk," but that wouldn't really be the way we talk) tend to get the wrong message, and it's about as useless as "dance like you walk." For one thing, people don't really know how they talk. When they try to guess, and put it on paper, the result is usually a strange, self-conscious exaggeration of their sloppiest or quirkiest speaking habits. Mixing such language into a broadcast script produces the inconsistent sound of amateurish writing, a very *un*natural sound.

For another thing, "write like you talk" is an impossible order because the writing process takes away the body language that's so much a part of oral expression. A good talker uses his voice, his face, his hands, his eyes, and even his eyebrows. He does some acting. Writing negates these physical gestures and inflections and leaves nothing but the verbal skeleton. If you've ever read a transcript of a recorded conversation, you've seen how embarrassingly it exposes the verbal deficiencies of natural speech. There is no hint of the fullness of communication that seemed to exist as the conversation took place. By written-word standards, it is a jumbled and primitive mess. And reading it aloud does not bring it back to life— its naturalness was not only in the words themselves but in their spontaneous delivery, and once the words are on paper they can never be spontaneous again.

A well-written news story is a simulation of naturalness, achieved by imposing form and discipline on natural speech. The rules of newswriting are based not on how people actually talk but on how they *ought* to talk (or how they like to think they talk). The oral language gives the writer plenty to work with—it can be muscular and effective. What "write like you talk" *means* to say is: stay with the muscular and effective equipment of the oral language.

The converse of trying to achieve naturalness by writing sloppily or hyper-colloquially is trying to improve on naturalness by borrowing from print. This is what upsets the write-like-you-talk contingent, and with good reason: stylistically, the newswriter's cardinal sin is to become *writery.*

By "writery" I mean that the writing shows through. *If it sounds written, it's wrong,* and print language makes oral copy sound written. It suggests the presence of the writer and the effort behind the phrasing, both of which undermine the illusion of naturalness.

"Writery" might also mean that the writer is hiding behind abstract or affected language, possibly without even realizing it. Once, writing an introduction for a movie star guest appearing on *Good Morning America,* I described the guest's latest movie as "compelling." David Hartman, the host of the program and a man with an eagle eye for detecting writery pretension, asked me what I meant.

I began my reply with a confidence that was quickly overtaken by a realization that I had only a vague idea of what I'd meant to say. When I tried to articulate it—"The movie really makes you want to, uh, keep watching it"—the thought crumbled from the sophistication of "compelling" to the cloddishness of "It sure was good!" (Compelling does mean more than "sure was good." It means calling for thought, demanding attention, convincing forcefully. But if I'd intended any of these meanings I should have articulated them instead of strutting—and tripping over—my unexamined film jargon.)

Print journalists who have come over to TV news often experience a feeling of panic about confronting the typewriter without the writery devices that sustained them when they turned out copy for newspapers or magazines. They find they cannot fall back on nimble wordsmanship to write their way past weak spots. Broadcast writing exposes a writer's uncertainty; it doesn't tolerate groping towards the point. It forces the writer to go directly to the center of the thought rather than circling in on it.

James Wooten, an author and *New York Times* reporter who became a TV correspondent for ABC News, wrote an article for the late and lamented *Panorama Magazine* about his difficulties adapting to television, making this confession about his first story on the air:

The writing was wildly complicated, baroque and labyrinthine; I'd employed irony, similes, metaphors, and even a bit of Agnewesque alliteration. I doubt if more than a half-dozen viewers in the entire country had any idea what I'd been driving at in the story.

And he added this:

A TV script, I have learned, is a thing of beauty when it's well done. The TV reporter can rarely use any of the techniques available to the newspaper writer . . . and because he cannot, his writing is all the more difficult. (*Panorama Magazine,* October 1980, pp. 79, 82)

Yes, it is all the more difficult. Many talented writers can never get the hang of it. The broadcast style strips away the devices Wooten mentioned and more; to the degree that these devices are writery flab, it's a big plus for newswriting. No flab allowed, just bare bones. Just the nitty-gritty, the basics. Spencer Tracy, or Ernest Hemingway in his most vigorous writing, showed how expressive the boiled-down basics can be.

In discussions of newswriting, it's often implied that writery-sounding language is wrong because it's too good, too fancy for broadcast, too literary. Sometimes that's true but we may be flattering ourselves that our writing is too elegant or advanced for this mundane medium. More often, the language newswriters borrow from print is only the latest thing in journalese, the latest fad words or jargon. Journalists deplore jargon in principle, but in practice they like it as much as everyone else and for the same reason: they think it makes them sound sophisticated.

Natural style requires the writer to reduce his writing to the irreducible and trim away everything else. When you find the needle you can throw away the haystack.

In Praise of Rule 16

Rule 16 of Strunk and White's masterpiece on writing, *The Elements of Style,* is: "Use definite, specific, concrete language" (3d ed., p. 21; in previous editions the same rule appears as Rule 12).

It's a perfect rule for newswriters. No TV writer mindful of its strictures could describe a movie as "compelling."

Here's an example of a writery violation of Rule 16. I noted it in a network report during the primary campaign of 1980 when President Carter was successfully practicing his "Rose Garden strategy," remaining in the White House to deal with the Iran hostage crisis instead of taking part in political campaigning:

> With three victories under his belt so far, the president has managed to stay out of the political arena but very much in the public eye.

Now that doesn't seem so bad. You think you get the point. But notice that, except for "three victories," nothing here is definite, specific, or concrete. "Under his belt," "political arena," and "public eye" are all figurative. They are journalistic code language. The viewer is expected to understand them without definition. But what *is* the political arena? What *is* the public eye? (And why bother with "under his belt"?)

The listener must translate these phrases into their literal meanings, and there's no guarantee that he'll bother or that he'll translate them as the writer intended—the looser the phrase, the looser the translation. Indeed, the writer has not even translated for himself, or he would have seen other problems in this sentence. The president had won three primaries, which hardly constitutes staying out of the political arena—"off the campaign trail" would have been a more accurate cliché. Also, the implied cause-and-effect that links the two clauses is illusory: the president was not staying out of the political arena or in the public eye *because* he'd won three primaries. The sentence turns out to have very little meaning.

A Rule 16 approach would force the writer to think more literally about what he is trying to say. He would translate "three victories under his belt" into "has now won three primaries." "Political arena" would become "campaigning." By "public eye" he is trying to indicate "dominating voter attention."

> President Carter has now won three primaries without campaigning, dominating voter attention by dealing with the crisis in Iran.

This version is more definite, specific, and concrete. It's more economical—seven words shorter with the Iran crisis mentioned as a bonus. It's more modest—a straightforward statement with none of the windbag tone of political analysis. It's clear and fully translated from the figurative. The cause-and-effect is not perfect (winning the primaries entailed more than dominating voter attention) but it's a foundation for a fuller explanation.

And, it sounds natural. An anchorman could read it aloud without self-consciousness and without reminding viewers that he is reading from a script. An important reason for natural style is to save your anchorman from looking like a puppet, saying words put into his mouth by someone else.

Broadcast language is best when it seems born of the moment, not born in a typewriter (or word processor). Say you're washing your car, and a neighbor stops by to pass the time of day:

> *Neighbor:* You're in the news business, whaddaya think of these primaries?
> *Newswriter:* Well, with three primary victories under his belt so far, the president has managed to stay out of the political arena but very much in the public eye.
> *Neighbor:* Uh, yeah . . . see ya later.

The neighbor is disconcerted by the stilted and unnatural sound of this writery language. It could have been worse. Suppose the neighbor had asked about that tornado in the Midwest and you'd replied, "Yes, that killer tornado carved a path of death and destruction, leaving a devastated town reeling in the aftermath of the twister's whirling fury."

The Rose Garden story is weak by the standard of Rule 16, but it got on the air. Let's now consider a story that could never get on the air, an example of writery and un-concrete newswriting at its worst. It was written as part of a writing test by a candidate for a network newswriting job:

> Conscience doth get the best of us all, sayeth Shakespeare, and so sayeth the managers of the Waldorf-Astoria. Seems that former guests are sending back silverware they swiped from the world-famous New York City hotel. Latest to come back are four demitasse spoons. The reverse rush of stolen silverware began some two months ago, and there doesn't seem to be a reason why, except conscience. The Waldorf people are welcoming back all wandering silver, no questions asked.

The young man who wrote this was not a professional, writing tests are very awkward (as I discuss elsewhere), and the toughest stories for newswriters are feeble features like this one—it's not funny, it's barely interesting, and there's no reason to bother with it except to fill a few seconds. Also, it is incomplete, at no fault of the writer: there is no solid explanation of why the silverware is suddenly being returned, so the writer can only speculate. So much for mercy.

He begins with maximum writeriness, the Shakespeare line. He puts these words, including a "doth" and two "sayeths," into the mouths of the Waldorf-Astoria's managers. This is a terrible opening sentence, because instead of getting the story started or even stimulating interest, it delays the start of the story and probably discourages interest. It makes the listener more aware of the writing than the story itself. And the writing is bad.

When the story does get started, the writer switches from high-brow Shakespeare to, yarn-spinning folksiness: "Seems that," "Latest to come back are. . . ." Then two very writery combinations, "reverse rush" and "wandering silver." "Reverse rush" is alliterative wordplay suggesting an unsubstantiated image: four spoons is not a rush. "Wandering silver" is even more uncontrolled: the silver didn't wander, it was stolen. "There doesn't seem to be a reason why, except conscience" is redundant after the Shakespearean much ado about conscience. It's also inarticulate; what he means is, "Conscience seems to be the only explanation."

Try to read this story aloud without feeling foolish. It is unnatural and contrived—writery. It's writery because it's not concrete. (And it's very difficult to read without stumbling over the lisping sound of "Conscience doth . . . sayeth Shakespeare . . . so sayeth" mingled with the tongue-twisting sibilance of "*s*ending back the *s*ilverware they *s*wiped.") All we learn concretely is that in two months four spoons have been returned to the Waldorf.

Four spoons? Is that all? No! A look at the four-paragraph Associated Press copy from which the story was written tells us the number of silverware pieces returned to the hotel in two months: *thirty-three,* including a champagne bucket, two candlesticks, a silver oyster fork, and the demitasse spoons. The spoons are sixty-five years old and were stolen from the original Waldorf-Astoria, which stood at a different site—they were stolen before the current Waldorf existed! And now they're being returned. This is almost interesting!

How could the writer omit these details? The answer, I think, is that he'd used up too much time and space showing off with his silly Shakespearean opening. Something had to go, so he chose to part with information instead of prose.

How would you write this story concretely?

First, I think, you must establish the Waldorf-Astoria at the very beginning of the story. Not just a hotel, but a place likely to have fine and tempting silverware. Second, the suspected motivation for stealing the silverware. Third, the dimensions of the story, the thirty-three pieces. Fourth, something about why the silverware is being returned—you don't have the answer, but you must somehow deal with the question. Finally, you have to wrap it up.

> New York City's Waldorf-Astoria Hotel has always been a symbol of luxury. Over the years, hotel guests have taken some of that luxury home—stolen souvenirs, including valuable silverware. However, in the last two months some of this long-missing silverware has been anonymously sent back—a champagne bucket, two candlesticks, four spoons stolen from the *old* Waldorf before the *current* Waldorf was even built, and twenty-six other pieces. The Waldorf doesn't know what caused this apparent wave of guilty conscience. But it's hoping for more.

This is eight words longer (about three seconds on air)—soft features require more time than hard news—but at least it's factual and unembarrassing. There is nothing marvelous about it, but there is nothing forced or fabricated about it either. To make more of the point that the silver is being returned after a very long absence, the writer could have phoned the Waldorf to find out when the current building was opened and deduced from the answer (1931) that the returned spoons were stolen "more than half a century ago." Concrete detail, not writery overkill, is the only way to make this kind of story succeed.

Rule 16 is the key to a natural style of newswriting. If you learn to stay away from writery blabber and shopworn phrases that obscure facts instead of revealing them, you'll always be solid. To paraphrase Yossarian in *Catch-22*, "That's some rule, that Rule 16."

The Action Verb

> Racial violence *tore* through Miami last night.

> *Packing* 120-mile winds, Hurricane Allen *roared* ashore in Texas tonight.

> Mayor Johnson *lashed out* today at critics of his proposed city budget, *ripping into* their charges that he. . . .

The action verb is the beloved heavy artillery of journalese. Here's part of a definition of journalese, from Wilson Follett's *Modern American Usage* (New York, 1970):

> The tone of journalese is the tone of contrived excitement. When the facts by themselves do not make the reader's pulse beat faster, the journalist thinks it is his duty to apply the spur and whip of breathless words and phrases. Since these exist only in finite numbers they get repeated, and repetition begets their weakening, their descent into journalese. (P. 190)

The beginner should be aware, as Follett indicates, that the biggest guns in the Action Verb Arsenal have passed their prime and exhausted most of their impact. And they are terminally writery on the air. They still appear in tabloids and wire-service copy (many of the bad habits of TV newswriters are attributable to their steady diet of wire copy), but they need not be passed on to broadcast audiences.

If the heavyweight action verbs are to be taken out of action, what is left? What is the writer to do without his rippings, roarings, rackings, lashings, tearings, and other interchangeable action synonyms?

Rule 16 comes to the rescue: use definite, specific, concrete *facts*. Instead of unleashing a hail of verbs, unleash the power of *facts:*

> A race riot in a black section of Miami last night left two people dead and twelve injured in street fighting that lasted until early this morning. Police made thirty arrests. Dozens of stores were looted. A half-dozen stores were burned to the ground.

> Hurricane Allen hit the Texas coast tonight with heavy rain driven by 120-mile-per-hour winds.

> Mayor Johnson said today that critics of his proposed city budget were "shameless and irresponsible fatheads.'

The verb is the strongest part of speech, but the fact is mightier than the verb. The excitement created by facts is authentic. Excitement imposed by the writer is artificial and hollow. Violence "ripping" through a city is a figurative notion, the creation of a writer. It is not factually true. It is hype.

To grasp the right verb the writer should make a mental effort to dig into a story, to visualize it and find the essence of it. For instance, did someone "flee" or "elude pursuers" or "run away"? Or "disappear"? Or "skedaddle"? In the Waldorf silverware story the writer chose an interesting verb, *swipe,* which suggested something less seriously criminal than stealing. Yes, that's exactly what the hotel guests had done: they had *swiped* the silverware.

This doesn't mean the writer should always look for offbeat verbs like *swipe.* Familiar verbs are always realiable; there's little danger of a wrong connotation if you stick with words that are familiar to everyone. Less familiar verbs are worth considering, but they are chancy because they jump out at the listener, which can be good or bad—good if the word perfectly captures the thought and deserves the extra notice it will attract, bad if it is so exotic or cute or conversationally unnatural that it calls attention to itself at the expense of the story.

Once you've got a clear idea of the essence of what you want to say, it's obvious that vivid and forceful verbs are better than summary language. "He banged on the table and shouted" is better than "he emphasized." "He crumpled to the floor" is better than "he collapsed." "He shot back" is better than "he returned fire" or "he replied quickly." "Stock prices went up today" is more active than "Stock prices increased today."

Trying too hard to come up with that colorful verb offers several dangers. One is the temptation to run amok. "In sports, the Bulls gored the Pacers, John McEnroe nuked Ivan Lendl, the Giants made midgets out of the Eagles, and the Indians scalped the Blue Jays with a wing-clipping attack in the ninth inning." Almost every student-newswriter writes a few excruciating stories like this and thinks he's really writing up a storm—until someone else reads it and bursts out laughing.

A more serious form of verb abuse involves editorializing. *Time Magazine,* in its long era of opinionated slanting of the news, seized upon the action verb as an instrument of propaganda. A news figure admired by the magazine would "stride" while an enemy would "waddle," "plod," or "mince." It was character assasination by thesaurus, deliberate and nasty. But it can also happen with innocent motives: trying to write colorfully, the writer adds a bit too much color; the result is not description but unintended characterization. It's a plus for television that film and tape usually take the characterizing weapon away from the writer and leave the judgment to viewers. If you write voice-over copy describing a walk as a "sashay," you had better be certain that an overwhelming percentage of viewers will see it as you did. In the words of Othello, "Be sure of it; give me ocular proof."

Adjectives and Adverbs

No discussion of newswriting style would be respectable without a stern injunction against adjectives and adverbs. If your verbs and nouns are strong, why add weak modifiers? Adjectives and adverbs are extraneous clutter. They are writery embellishments. They reflect the writer's opinion rather than fact. So don't use them.

Yet there are times when you can hardly do without them. Facts can be expressed in spartan verbs and nouns, but explaining and interpreting usually require adjectives. Try an economics or diplomatic story without adjectives. Try a weather report without adjectives. In these cases adjectives (and adverbs to a lesser extent) are acceptable because they are necessary.

When a modifier is minor, squeezing it in is a small minus, unlike the small plus it might be in print style. But when the modifier is important enough to use, don't sneak it in—feature it prominently and give it emphasis. "The unprecedented decision surprised legal experts" is print style, with the adjective "unprecedented" less strongly accented than in "Legal experts were surprised by the unprecedented decision" or "The decision was unprecedented. Legal experts were surprised."

As for the adjective *unprecedented,* the late Turner Catledge, in an interview after his retirement as executive editor of the *New York Times,* was asked what advice he would give to young journalists, and he replied, "Play it straight, keep it short, and never use the word 'unprecedented.' "

Short Sentences

Short sentences impose vigor and self-discipline. Your thinking and writing become crisper (make sure they don't become simple-minded). There's no room for writery flab. You don't get into trouble with complex constructions. If you use an adjective it stands out strongly rather than disappearing in verbal foliage.

Like a boxer's jab or a tennis player's sharp volley, the short sentence has punch. The Russian author Isaac Babel wrote, "No iron can pierce the heart with such force as a period put at just the right place."

Questions

Questions are difficult to read aloud. The question mark at the end of a sentence seems to function like a hook, yanking up the voice to a pitch that might be uncomfortable. Questions also require a bit of performing, and that too is uncomfortable. Read aloud: "Have you ever wondered what it's like to prospect for lost treasure?" or "Whatever happened to the American dream of a nice home in the suburbs?"

Chances are that you heard your voice go thin as you approached the question mark and that your face somehow took on an actor's expression, a phony expression. It takes an especially good voice and a good on-air reader to handle a question naturally; most anchormen are not up to it.

The argument in favor of questions is that they involve the listener, draw him in personally, get him thinking about the subject ("What would *you* do if a mugger put a gun in your ribs and demanded your wedding ring?") Maybe. But you must be careful about making demands on your audience. Posing a question can be like issuing an order, saying in effect, "Give me your undivided attention." Viewers may be inclined to respond with defiant disobedience.

The First Draft

Whatever its flaws, the first draft is often your most naturally written attempt at a story. Refining the story in subsequent drafts, you risk adding devices that will make it writery and the unnecessary details and qualifications that may overload it with complexity. As you rewrite, it becomes increasingly difficult to preserve the natural fluency of the first draft.

Hemingway's advice—"Get it down, then get it right"—is certainly solid, and I am not discouraging rewriting. But keep that original draft and compare it with your final effort; you may see that you've lost something that might be worth trying to recover. Most good news scripts are written in a single draft, though it may take some experience before this will happen for you.

A suggestion: news scripts are short enough that it makes sense when rewriting to run *the whole thing* through your typewriter, instead of tinkering with just one sentence or isolated words. If you rewrite the whole instead of the parts, you're less likely to lose the rhythm and unity of the story. And you may hit on new and better ideas.

Chronic rewriters will see a bit of themselves in a description of Chopin written by his lover, the novelist Aurore Dudevant (better known by her pen name, George Sand).

His creative power was spontaneous, miraculous. It came to him without effort or warning. . . . But then began the most heartrending labor I have ever witnessed. It was a series of attempts, of fits of irresolution and impatience to recover certain details. He would shut himself in his room for days, pacing up and down, breaking his pens, repeating and modifying one bar a hundred times. . . . He would spend six weeks over a page, only to end by writing it out finally, just as he had sketched it in the original draft. (Quoted in Joseph Machlis, *The Enjoyment of Music* [New York, 1977], p. 87)

13

More on Natural Style

Natural style means stripped-down language. Stripped-down language tends to enforce concrete thinking; it cuts through the haziness that often comes over a story when the writer strays from the straight and narrow of Rule 16.

Surveys constantly discover that the TV news audience comprehends an alarmingly small percentage of the information in a newscast. News business insiders shrug and scratch their heads and worry that the audience isn't very smart or isn't paying attention.

But assuming that the surveys are accurate (the more you find out about how a survey was done the more difficult it is to make this assumption), it doesn't surprise me that viewers often miss the point. The reason it doesn't surprise me is that I too often miss the point when I am watching newscasts: I find myself watching with eyes glazed over, hearing a stream of narration and staring at dancing picture, yet taking in very little of it.

Having failed to understand a professional-seeming story, I tend to blame myself for failing to concentrate. Most viewers who miss the points of a story probably assume (if they bother to wonder about it) that it was their fault. Sometimes it is, of course. But frequently it isn't.

Consider, for example, the basic network "stand-upper." A correspondent stands there intoning authoritatively from the White House lawn or State Department lobby. His script is concise, seemingly well written, and sophisticated. It is read aloud with impressive cadence and apparent perfection. Key words are heavily stressed and there are corresponding physical gestures, head tilts, and cocked brows. It seems immaculate. You could not point out a flaw.

Except that it doesn't work. It bounces right off your consciousness. It has the effect of double-talk:

. . . And so . . . from the State Department . . . the *alternatives* seem *clear.* If there is to be a *choice* . . . between abject *appeasement* . . . and thermo*nuclear war* . . . the United States will not *lean* towards the *former* . . . without paying serious *heed* to the potentially *grim consequences* . . . that *hang* . . . as one senior diplomat here says, "like the *sword of Damocles*" . . . over the *latter.* It remains to be seen . . . if and *when* . . . that *sword* . . . will *fall.*

This sort of writing is easy to satirize—indeed, it satirizes itself. No listener is to blame for missing the point. The writer is to blame for not making a point, or for obscuring it with his writery bombast.

If it sounds written, it's wrong. The rule applies not only to overly literary writing and journalese, but also to the opposite extreme of cutely or colloquially "writing down" to the audience.

Eloquence

William Jennings Bryan was a former newspaper editor who became the Democratic nominee for president in 1896, 1900, and 1908. En route to his three defeats he found a place in history as the great-granddaddy of flamboyant political orators. For decades the question would be asked of any speaker who poured on the high-flying rhetoric: "Who does he think he is? William Jennings Bryan?"

Eloquence was Bryan's trademark, and he eloquently described it as "thought on fire." Thought on fire does not work in the emotionally cool confines of television, and modern politicians have learned this lesson. The Jimmy Carters and Ronald Reagans express their rhetoric in low-key, conversational tones. They do not try to be flamboyant; they would rather be genial. The style of William Jennings Bryan was right for vast arenas and open-air gatherings, but it would have bombed on the home TV screen. Imagine William Jennings Bryan declaiming under the close-up scrutiny of the TV camera, sweating and straining and, well, *overdoing it* as he bellowed flaming oratory at you from point-blank range. It would be like screaming into a telephone. Too much. Too hot. You'd jump up and switch to another channel looking for something cooler, something that didn't assault you in your own living room.

Television has a way of forcing things to fit its size. It shrinks big things and magnifies small things. An epic drama or opera loses its grandeur when it is squeezed into a TV screen, while a flat and breezy little situation-comedy seems to take on a dimension that far exceeds its substance. As TV news learned this lesson, it started toning down its on-air talent: the heavyset Authority Figure anchorman with the booming radio voice was replaced by milder types with normal voices, normal physiques, and a more modest and natural style.

Writing style changed too, as the better TV writers began to understand that lavish language seemed bloated when read on television. Even a moderately florid phrase—for instance, "the twister's whirling furry"—seems to short-circuit on the small screen. The anchorman who must read it appears stricken with self-consciousness, as if he'd been forced to recite a particularly gooey poem. The only eloquence that works on television is eloquent simplicity, subdued eloquence, which holds its quality on TV because it *lacks* the self-conscious and scalding fever of thought on fire.

It may seem that I am making a case against colorful or expressive writing in favor of something more austere. But austerity is not the point. The newswriter has plenty of latitude, because television magnifies deft writing. The perfectly chosen word has real impact—as Mark Twain wrote, "Whenever we come upon one of those intensely right words . . . the resulting effect is physical as well as spiritual, and electrically prompt."

The finest examples of TV newswriting seem unexceptional and even unimpressive in print. They are controlled, played down, lean, underwritten. Like perfect photographs, they keep their focus when enlarged, they get better in their magnification. TV newswriting is the skill of working in miniature.

"Less is better than more" is a good guideline for writers, especially newswriters. I recall a session of a college creative writing class in which a wonderful teacher named Nancy Packer read aloud two short stories written by class members. In both stories, characters had been made to express emotional distress in the traditionally excessive manner of undergraduate fiction: sudden eruptions of vomiting.

Looking up from the second manuscript just as its protagonist began the second retch scene of the hour, Mrs. Packer complained with visceral distaste, "Does everyone have to *vomit?* Can't they just *cry* a little?"

Metaphors, Similes, Analogies, Imagery, etc.

These are luxury items for writers. They promise to elevate your prose, awaken the imagination of your audience, and win you praise as a stylist. But beware. Figurative language is tricky. By its nature it is the opposite of Strunk and White's Rule 16: it is not definite, not specific, not concrete. Not journalistic.

The problem is that figurative language tends to be substituted not only for literal expression but for literal thinking. A figure of speech pops into our minds, seems right, and we launch it on the airwaves without pausing to ask *What is this really saying?* Too often an appealing phrase turns out to mean something else, usually something less, than the writer intended.

I would lay down this rule: allow yourself no figurative language unless you can also articulate your point concretely. The figurative should complement the concrete rather than substitute for it.

Here's an example of a vivid image and concrete expression working well together, in a story about the creation of the World Bank:

> Wealthy countries were persuaded by President Kennedy's argument that a rising tide lifts all boats—that more prosperity in the world would benefit not only poor countries but rich ones too.

Test that metaphor, scrutinize that simile. Peel back the poetry and take a hard look at what's underneath. If it stands up under examination, fine. But if you've just written something berserk, like, "The Wall Street bull had a tiger in its tank today," you'll know what to do: drop it and scamper back to Rule 16.

Showing Verbally Off

An especially annoying form of writeriness involves the use of supposedly fancy wordplay not only to dress up a drab phrase but to flaunt your refinement. I'm thinking of the writing device that brings us such language as "swept under the diplomatic carpet," "hardly a drop in the geological bucket," "flirting with fiscal Armageddon."

These are only garden-variety examples, all of them taken from network newscasts (I identify them with network style, which does not always eschew pretentious writing). Now and then you catch a real trophy winner: "The weapons system is not yet out of the developmental woods" or "The Administration is trying to get its arms control house in order." The adjectives make absurdities of the images and illustrate nothing except the writer's ego. And they are unnecessary. In each example, the statement would be stronger standing alone. Deleting the adjectives would also expose the lameness of the images and prod the writer into trying for something better.

Armageddon, by the way, is probably the unlikeliest word in the vocabulary of journalese. It is a biblical giant of a word, meaning a final conflict between good and evil, an annihilating war marked by slaughter and destruction so decisive as to make renewed conflict impossible. Only in the most overheated journalism do occasions of this magnitude arrive on a weekly or daily basis. Furthermore, if such an Armageddon did come along, there would be no need to puff it up with a dry little adjective like *fiscal.* And it would certainly not be something that would encourage *flirting.*

Something Akin to Straight Talk

In September 1983, Peter Jennings became sole anchor of ABC's *World News Tonight.* I was one of two people writing for him. It was a brief free-lance stint in which I experienced my first failure to establish working relations with an anchor. Part of the problem was incompatible writing styles.

The broadcast style I advocate in these pages is very American. It is straightforward and shuns adornment.

Jennings, who is Canadian and strongly influenced by British aristocratic style, prefers indirection and verbal twirls that would stand out as raised-pinky Englishy if not for his dashingly masculine appearance and star-quality delivery on the air. He makes an impression, but listen:

> World leaders regard the situation with something akin to horror.
>
> The situation is, to say the least, controversial.
>
> It would not be too difficult to believe the situation is . . .
>
> Efforts to resolve the situation were intense, some would say frantic.
>
> Their assessment of the situation has been far from complimentary.
>
> The situation is something of a diplomatic disaster.

These phrases seem so knowing and elegant. But ask the question, *"What is he trying to say?"* and they are exposed as hedged and bland.

Something akin to horror: He is afraid to make the strong statement about horror, so he pulls back and hints instead about some undesignated relative of horror.

To say the least: Why say the least? What would it be to say the most? The only reason for this phrase is to conceal the blandness of "This situation is controversial." If it is more than controversial, isn't it the writer's duty to find the word that expresses that meaning?

It would not be too difficult to believe: This is roundabout, an eight-word circling-in on a thought that begins with "The situation is . . .".

Intense, some would say frantic: He is shirking responsibility for "frantic," pinning it on "some" people who might say it.

Far from complimentary: Does he lack the nerve or vocabulary to articulate this thought? Instead of telling us what the assessment is far from, why not tell us what it is close to. "Uncomplimentary" would have been more direct. Something like "Their assessment was negative [critical/insulting/devastating/pessimistic/ruthless]" would have been much better.

Something of a: This is either sophisticated understatement or sophisticated overstatement. Basically it's just a fancy way to say "sort of."

Why is it that in these examples plain talk is something along the lines of what certain people might not be reluctant to call, to say the opposite of the least, something akin to anathema?

The Whom Rule

I've titled this rule myself, but the principle has always been around: if you must choose between a grammatically correct but awkward-sounding construction and a grammatically incorrect but better-sounding construction, choose neither. Write it another way.

Whom is fine in print, but said aloud it catches the ear because it is a funny-sounding word (HOOM) and because it seems to call self-conscious attention to its correctness. However, the writer's obligation to honor and protect the language forbids using *who* when he knows *whom* is correct. The best solution is to avoid it.

The president has not yet decided whom to appoint.

The president has not yet made his choice for the job.

The subjunctive causes a similar problem. It often sounds wrong even when it's right:

He said if he were chosen for the job . . .

You could write around it, but a better solution is the present tense:

He said if he is chosen for the job . . .

The present tense is always the freshest and most natural-sounding way to say things. Use it whenever you can, unless it falsely hypes something as a currently unfolding development. "Unemployment is up tonight" probably does not mean that thousands of people were fired after dinner—it means the government's monthly unemployment statistics were released *this morning* showing that unemployment increased *last month.*

Eight "Englishy" Words

Shall
Perhaps
Rather
Somewhat
Quite
Virtually
Remarkable
Considerable

These words are beloved by writers but alien to non-writers. They belong in print; you will seldom hear them in conversation—at least in American conversation. They seem literary and suggest putting on airs. They detract from vigor. They are, well, wimpy.

Shall and *perhaps* are the worst. They are full of literary affectation and both seem prissy, though I am mindful of General Douglas MacArthur's stirring wartime vow, "I shall return." When you're a towering military hero, you don't worry about sounding prissy. General MacArthur was as flowery as they come and knew how to construct a lasting quotation. "I'll be back" just wouldn't have had the same historical zing. But for lesser mortals, especially on TV, historical zing is not the objective.

Rather and *somewhat* tend to be hedge words, used when a writer loses confidence in his chosen adjective and intentionally weakens it. Sometimes this is called for, but hedging is a bad habit. *Quite* and *virtually,* though stronger, are in the same category. Whenever you're about to use one of these four words, ask yourself whether it's really needed.

Considerable and *remarkable* rarely venture out of their homey place in print. When I was a Navy information officer aboard an aircraft carrier during the Vietnam War, I was summoned by the captain, who was seething over a newspaper story written by a reporter who had visited our ship and quoted an anonymous junior officer as saying there was "considerable use of marijuana" among the crew.

"I want to know the identity of the officer who said that," demanded the captain.

"Nobody said it, sir," I replied nervously.

"Whaddaya mean, *nobody* said it?"

"People don't say *considerable* when they talk. It's a reporter's word. The reporter made up the quote. I'd guess that someone told him there was *probably some* use of marijuana—with five thousand sailors aboard there is probably some of anything. But *probably some* wasn't impressive enough for the reporter's story so he changed it to *considerable*."

The captain looked me over for a long withering moment. No doubt in his long naval career he had heard his share of nutty explanations, but my semantic approach was a new one and it got in under his radar. With a shrug he dropped the offending clipping into a wastebasket and the matter was closed.

I backed out of his cabin relieved that I had avoided naming the guilty officer. *I* was the guilty officer. But I'd told the truth, sort of: I had not used *considerable* when the reporter asked me about marijuana.

Also in the bookish or putting-on-airs category are phrases like "as it were" and "if you will." And don't use *one* when you mean people in general: one doesn't use *one* in TV news. You use *you*.

People Talk

It may seem that the alternative to writery language is language that was emphatically *not* born in a typewriter—language that is not only un-writery but *anti*-writery. I first encountered this notion under a newsroom regime that preached a doctrine called People Talk, a glossy label that seemed to herald a conceptual breakthrough in newswriting.

The concept was that writers and most reporters are over-educated snobs who could not write or even speak in the language of common folk (known as "real people"). People Talk insisted on a Lowest Common Denominator writing level. Articulateness and other writing virtues were regarded as vices, as signs of smarty-pants showing off.

The People Talk idea was supposedly egalitarian in its embrace of average speech. Actually, it was elitist in its patronizing estimation of the average viewer's intelligence. It was not "write like you talk" but "write like *they* talk," and the way *they* talked was presumed to be proudly inarticulate. The doctrine implied that people are bewildered by articulateness because it is not their language, and they are hostile to it because it makes them feel inferior to the speaker. If a writer were to actually meet and talk with a Real People, the People would punch the writer in his upturned nose for being so hoity-toity.

People Talk, of course, had nothing to do with journalism. It was a system of pandering for affection. People Talkers aim to be well liked rather than well spoken. The ultimate People Talker is the TV sports reporter, who spends so much time in the juvenile anti-education atmosphere of locker rooms that he becomes finely attuned to the stigma that attaches to any visitor who dares to speak good (not well).

The sports reporter keys himself to an audience of vigilant snob-detectors. He dreads respect for his intelligence, though he prides himself on common sense. His main asset is hearty and unthreatening likability. He compensates for the limpness of what he is saying with sheer physical vigor: broad gestures, winks, head fakes, body English, and fraternity-man shoulder punches directed at the camera. He is a gung-ho booster. And he is loud. This may be related to the experience of doing play-by-play announcing in noisy arenas. It may also be related to being a Good Guy. A Good Guy is an uncomplicated soul, an outgoing hale fellow who brings cheer into your living room—not like those gloomy types who are always telling you to be concerned about the latest undecipherable crisis in the Middle East.

In People Talk doctrine, the sports reporter more than anyone talks to the Real People. The epitome of Real People is the sports fan, the stereotyped dim-witted slob with his six-packs and four-letter-word vocabulary. Therefore, says the doctrine, address the news audience as you would address the sports audience.

My introduction to formalized People Talk came from a newly arrived news director who regarded writers as symbols of the uppity sophistication that alienated Real People. He subjected the writing staff to nasty individual criticism in group sessions and followed up with even nastier private memos (delivered by an assistant who was later made the scapegoat in the backlash against the reign of humiliation and bullying). His criticism was punishing but not instructive. He could not explain *how* to write People Talk. The writers understood the complaint against writeriness but could not learn the anti-writing alternative of "writing down" to viewers.

Later I realized why. It is very difficult for a writer to simulate inarticulate talk and yet convey anything of meaning—it's a challenge for the finest playwrights and novelists, and it's generally beyond journalists. Journalists are capable of sloppiness and banality but not *communicative* sloppiness and banality.

The ultimate flaw of People Talk is its assumption that people understand and prefer inarticulate language because it is their native tongue. This is like saying they prefer bad singers because they sing badly themselves. Dumb writing is no favor to dumb people. Whether it is oversimplified to the point of baby talk or glib conversational blather, it cheats them. The advantage smart viewers have over dumb viewers is that the smart ones are better able to figure out what you mean when you write it badly. The not-so-bright viewers need the most precise and most concrete language or they will be left once again in the dark. In TV news the very best writing is not fancy or dazzling but straight, unembellished, and natural, like Spencer Tracy's acting.

14

Dealing with Numbers

Newsmen place their faith in numbers, which seem so concrete in a world of elusive meanings. Numbers provide at least the illusion of defining things that resist defining. The newsman defines a battle by counting the bodies. He defines an earthquake by its score on the Richter scale. The number gives him a foothold, a tangible starting point, a news peg. It saves him from the dreaded muddle of abstractions. The respected New York newspaper columnist Murray Kempton, who can handle abstractions as well as anyone but occasionally seeks relief by writing about sports, has said of athletes, "You know what I like about them? They have *statistics!*"

A newsman presented with a bunch of numbers enters a kind of craftsman's heaven, working with good, hard facts. But numbers are deceivers, even heart-breakers. Time and again the journalist will be taught this rule about numbers: *The closer you get to them, the less you trust them.*

The problem is not so much with the numbers as with the overeagerness of the beholders. We are suckers for facts and figures that seem to rise up from the disorderly gamut of human experience to capture a truth in just a few nifty digits.

Because of our illusions about numbers, we keep making the same mistakes. Here are four.

1. We treat numbers as superior facts.

Newsmen forget what professional numbers people take for granted: that statistics must always be understood in the context of their limitations. This is a science in itself, and there is a whole literature on data problems—problems of research, availability and processing of data, verification, definitions, criteria, sampling, margins of error, quirks, qualifying conditions, etc.

If I were to announce a gleaming new statistic on the number of numbers in the news—a figure you should instinctively greet with sneering skepticism—it might turn out that the magic number did not include numbers from radio broadcasts because the scripts were thrown away, that it used only estimates of numbers in foreign-language journalism because the researchers knew no foreign languages, and that a 7-3 sports score was counted as two numbers while a 17-3 score was counted as three numbers because of its three digits.

"Well then, it's wrong!" bellows the newsman, discovering all these catches. But the number probably isn't wrong; it measures exactly what it says it measures within its own specified limits. The problem is with the newsman who put his faith in some superior factuality that disappointed him by failing to exist.

2. We equate the numbers with truth.

Disraeli said, "There are three kinds of lies: lies, damned lies, and statistics." It is a cliché that figures can be made to say or prove just about anything. We all know that, yet we are susceptible to the force of the opposite cliché, "numbers don't lie."

Somehow we think of numbers as moral beings; we debate whether they are liars or solid citizens. What we overlook is that for just about every number in the news there are human beings shaping or trying to shape its meaning. Journalists must vigilantly consider the motives and particularly the *self-interest* of these numbers-shapers. Whether it is a public relations spokesman doing his job of putting figures in the most favorable light or a demagogue like Hitler or McCarthy spouting Big Lies, numbers are constantly being manipulated.

This manipulating is not always villainous or immoral, not always deliberate, not always clever. But it is *constant*. When a TV weatherman says there is a 60 percent chance of rain, he is manipulating: he is exploiting the illusion of precise meaning, as if a weather forecast could be calibrated down to percentage points of probability. Saying 60 percent makes him sound like a scientist, whereas saying "There's a fair chance of rain" would make him sound like just anybody.

3. The more we're frightened or baffled about what things mean, the more we pile on the numbers.

We attack our fear of the unknown by measuring everything and hoping the measurements will ultimately make things knowable. Even when this fails, it gives a comforting feeling that the subject can be dealt with rationally and that there is no reason to panic.

A good example of a subject too horrifying to imagine but perfect to quantify is nuclear weapons. Say there is a new bid or bluff in the great poker game of strategic arms negotiations. TV producers drag out the statistics of annihilation and create *Star Wars* computerized graphics comparing this number of warheads versus that number of launchers, submarines versus bombers, missiles here versus missiles there, air-launched these versus ground-based those.

We ponder these unfathomable equations as a monkey might ponder a dinner menu. Then the screen erupts with graphic symbols zapping each other in global warfare, and, even with the most solemn journalistic intentions, the subject loses its impact, dissolving into a video game. What a relief!

Perhaps newsmen perform a social service with this numbers ritual, reassuring viewers that complex or threatening subjects are under measurable control. This might be desirable as public therapy, but it is not desirable journalism when obsession with the parts obscures the meaning of the whole.

4. In TV journalism, the more we pile on the numbers, the more we risk blurring the meaning.

Here we encounter a major difference between print and TV. A reader can deal with lots of numbers, but a listener cannot. When it comes to absorbing numbers, the ear lets us down dramatically. If I gave you a few numbers to add in your head, you might find them fading off your mental blackboard even before you started adding them. If I asked you after a newscast to recall a single numerical fact, you would probably come up blank.

Somehow, numbers must be visualized or conceptualized before they will stick in your mind. This process favors the eye over the ear. A professor of statistics at Yale, Edward R. Tufte, points out that editors underestimate the capacity of interested *readers* to digest a vast amount of numbers—for instance, a sports fan mentally photographing a page of sports statistics, or an investor who scans the closing stock prices in his newspaper and seems to have computer-like recall of every last fraction. I would suggest that these numbers stick because they have intense personal meaning and because they are frozen in print where a reader can grip them in his own way and at his own speed.

TV, of course, is different. A TV *viewer* has no control over numbers coming at him, and most numbers in the news do not have intense personal interest to him unless it is skillfully created by the writer. The ear contributes little in this process; indeed, it interferes by permitting more sounds to rush in as he is trying to concentrate.

TV graphics can be helpful (they can also distract and over-complicate), but I think the most important thing is to present numbers with an awareness of the difficulty your audience will have with them. Therefore:

Use few numbers. Students learning print journalism are taught that every number collected by a reporter is like captured prey, a reward for the reporter's skill and diligence as a fact-hunter. To discard such a prize would be unthinkable; the print journalist takes pride in squeezing in *all* the numbers. Then he moves over to broadcast journalism and tries the same approach, wedging a number into every vacant space between words. It looks good on the page. However, viewers don't get to see the page. Try to rid yourself of the delusion that viewers will take in all the numbers your journalistic heart desires to launch at them.

Emphasize meanings rather than quantities. If you report a 13 percent increase, viewers might not be sure if that's a lot or a little, so the number dies in uncertainty. But if you report "a stunning 13 percent increase," they will understand that a major increase is coming. The best choice is to avoid the facile characterizing of "stunning" or other adjectives (be tough when "whopping" or "hefty" come around begging for a place in your copy) and make the point with facts—"the biggest increase since 1981: *thirteen* percent." If you fail to establish a context, don't be surprised if most numbers fly past listeners meaninglessly, as in the old sportscaster joke, "Here are tonight's scores: 5-1, 8-6, 4-2."

Round off and personalize (sometimes). Don't write that the power company wants a 4.88 percent rate increase to raise its revenues by $31,830,720. This degree of precision belongs in print, not TV. Rounded-off numbers are much easier to digest. But use common sense: you would not round off the number of people killed in an accident or any number that is newsworthy only because of its specificity, such as a record temperature or an uptick in a key economic indicator.

Another valuable device, too often forgotten, is to emphasize figures that make incomprehensibly big numbers understandable by reducing them to personalized or individual proportions: the power company wants to charge consumers an average of eighty-five cents more in each monthly bill to increase its revenues by about $32 million.

Two cautions are in order about personalizing. One is to be careful about doing your own arithmetic. Journalists are notoriously unreliable at arithmetic (and should always seek out someone good at numbers to confirm their figurings), but even if they have decent math skills, they simply cannot be aware of all the statistical complexities involved in most newsworthy numbers stories—don't think you can figure out a power company's rate structure in just a few moments of clear-minded reasoning and tapping on an office calculator. However, the personalized figure is worth seeking out. If it's not announced or published, call some authoritative source and try to get it. Then be sure to include attribution when you use it.

The other hazard about personalizing is getting yourself involved in manipulating numbers. For example, in the fall of 1983 the controversy over creating a national holiday honoring Martin Luther King, Jr., came to a head. One of the more respectable arguments against the holiday was that it would cost too much to give millions of workers a day off.

President Reagan had endorsed this argument, and whether its motivation was primarily economic, racial, or political, it deserved fair attention. It then fell to the reporters to clarify how much the holiday would cost. The government said the loss in goods and services that would have been produced on a normal working day was $7.5 billion.

So the opponents of the holiday had the big number they wanted. Meanwhile, the other side went to work on it, dividing it first by the U.S. population (about 230 million) and then by the number of weeks in a year and then by the number of days in a week, coming up with the figure of *nine cents* per day per American.

So, depending on your feeling about the holiday, its cost was either $7.5 billion or nine cents a day. While I suspect that the large number wouldn't stand up to examination—*the closer you get to numbers, the less you trust them*—the personalized figure derived from it is only a step away from nullifying travesty. (If a holiday cost only 9 cents a day, you could multiply it by 365 days to prove that for only $32.85 per American we could make *every* day of the year a national holiday, even though the economy would be entirely shut down and destroyed.)

Apples and Oranges

How many numbers does it take to short-circuit a TV news story? What is the maximum?

The journalism student clamors for a hard and fast answer, getting into the habit of demanding a number to make the indefinite definite. I don't know the answer, but I will risk a guess: for a "tell" or "reader" story I would try to stop at two numbers and wouldn't go beyond four, even with the best graphics.

However, I think the problem with numbers has less to do with quantity than with clarity and simplicity. Bear in mind that you have put much more time into preparing this story than the viewer will have to understand it on the air. Information that has become clear to you may be new and out of the blue when it suddenly reaches him. So, think hard about presenting it in a way that causes no hitches; if there is straightening out to be done, *you* do it. Don't mix apples and oranges.

> It used to be that 22 percent survived the operation for 12 to 18 months, but now that figure is 74 percent.

If the percentages are apples and the numbers of months are oranges, the story presents its numbers as apple-orange-orange-apple. It's like saying, "She bought five size seven dresses and then looked at size eight shoes and bought a half dozen." *Huh?*

The problem is the "12 to 18" jammed between the 22 and the 74, interfering with the intended contrast between the percentages. Improvement 1 is to get rid of the "12 to 18" by translating it into non-numerical language, trading a degree of precision for an improvement in comprehension:

> It used to be that only 22 percent survived this operation for more than a year, but now that figure is 74 percent.

Improvement 2 brings the percentage figures side-by-side to highlight the contrast:

> The percentage of patients surviving this operation for more than a year has gone from 22 to 74 percent.

(Don't worry about the redundancy of "percentage" and "percent." Technically you could drop the "percent," but listeners probably need it, so leave it in.)
Improvement 3 spells out the point even more:

> The percentage of patients surviving the operation for over a year has more than tripled—from 22 to 74 percent.

Or, sacrificing statistical specificity, you could drop the percentages entirely and personalize the story:

Your chances of surviving the operation for over a year are more than three times as good as they used to be.

Graphics can be a great aid in numbers stories, but only if the graphics are perfectly tailored to the copy. Professor Tufte, author of *The Visual Display of Quantitative Information,* notes that editorial-minded people are usually much more sophisticated about data than illustration-minded people. So make sure that whoever is doing the graphics understands exactly what to show.

To my mind, it's incontestable that print is superior to TV in handling a large volume of data, particularly numbers. Recognizing its limits, TV should be content to focus its journalistic powers on the forest instead of the trees, the meanings instead of the fine details.

Most TV people would agree with this idea in principle, much as they dislike conceding any superiority to print. But then a big numbers story moves on the wires, and all bets are off and we go after numbers as if they were spilled pearls bouncing on a hardwood floor. We hate the idea that we can't find some way to deal with those numbers. Out of vanity, but also out of responsibility, we insist that we can handle numbers journalism as well as the print competition. As for selectivity, writing for the ear, and the reasonable limits of detail in TV news stories—these ideas ebb and flow with the tides. All you can do is be aware and do your best.

Economics

Economics provides a feast of statistics. The menu is abundant and unending. Every day the wires serve us new numbers. Every day we try to cope with them, hoping they don't bring out the worst in us: our impatience (insisting on a newsmaking analysis of every blip and flicker), our willingness to be seduced by important-sounding data and jargon, our shallow knowledge about this subject that is so significant and yet so boring.

Few of the people I've known in TV news are confident with economics stories. Most are intimidated. A good friend who wrote for Walter Cronkite told me of his dread that Cronkite would ask him to expand on an economics story, even the daily stock market report. When I related this story to another writer at CBS he insisted that *he,* not the first writer, had revealed this fear to me. Perhaps there is something in the journalistic soul that shakes at the very mention of economics.

Economics stories present a double problem for TV journalists: understanding them is *sometimes* difficult; explaining them with the simplicity and brevity required by television is *always* difficult. Awareness of these difficulties should foster caution and humility, and this is good: better you should hug the shore than venture out to waters where the economics whirlpool will pull you under.

Humility is also advisable as you begin to think you understand economics. The more you get into its depths, the more difficult it is to return to the surface and simplify it, which is your job. Also, beware the arrogance of newfound expertise: when you finally understand something that had seemed daunting, there is a tendency to flaunt it, to show off, even to take pleasure in baffling viewers with your arcane knowledge.

Economics stories were once left to newspapers and magazines on the grounds of bad picture. Now, with the advent of video graphics, it is popular among insiders to declare that TV is equipped to illustrate and explain the most complicated subjects.

Certainly the results are watchable and imaginative. Yet there is a difference between illustration and illumination. A spectacular approach to unspectacular subjects might succeed in getting attention, but I'm not sure it gets through to the minds of viewers. I have the dreary feeling that economics is a hard subject that can only be taught and learned by hard work. Explaining it must be done with patience, concentration, and other values that have more to do with good teaching than with good television. I suspect that viewers who already understand economics learn little from TV reports, while viewers who don't understand are taught another lesson in frustration.

Patronizing as it sounds, it might be wise when writing an economics story to think how you would address it to children.

You would select only key numbers.

The telling would be uncluttered.

The illustrations would be simple and without dazzling distractions.

You would not show off because you would not be trying to be impressive.

You would not require the child to have special knowledge or sophistication or to make logical connections you don't explain.

Instinctively you would heed the advice of Dr. Seuss (Theodor Geisel) who said, "When you write for kids, if you don't write more clearly and concisely and cut out all the mumbo-jumbo, you lose your audience" (*Time Magazine,* 12 March 1984, p. 67).

And you might discover that this process of eliminating mumbo jumbo, focusing on meanings, and empathizing with viewers actually raises the level of your writing and reporting. If this is patronizing, then patronize.

Polls

Poll results, once scoffed at, are now too often treated as proven facts, which is not what they are. Polling has come a long way, and the best polls are impressive, even uncanny, but you must remember the human factor. And it is healthy to remember Walter Mondale's reaction when asked about polls that showed him trailing Gary Hart in the 1984 Democratic primary campaign: "I have a very high opinion of polls—you can stuff 'em."

Since most polls are privately financed and conducted (by more than a thousand polling firms, which obviously suggests a range of quality and standards), you must question whether the methodology is state-of-the-art, cheap-and-dirty, or something in between. And since polls can be designed to produce whatever findings a pollster's client desires, you must also consider the integrity and reputation of both client and pollster.

In addition to knowing who paid for the poll and who conducted it, it would be nice to know the how, the when, and the where. And it would be nice to know about the size and makeup of the sample. And what the questions were and whether they were asked by phone or questionnaire or in person. And so on.

Unfortunately, journalists (TV journalists in particular) seldom have the time to evaluate a poll or to mention all the qualifiers in their reports. This is probably a fact of life. To be realistic, all you can do in most cases is to be mindful of the *closer you get* rule and remember that while there is much that you're *not* told, you can be tough-minded about what you *are* told.

Be very careful about language—about exactly what a poll says it measured and exactly what it found. Guard against unwarranted implications or loose interpretation. If you have time, make a phone call to the pollster and ask for clarification of what the poll does or doesn't show.

If necessary, step in to guide viewers away from predictable but mistaken assumptions. For instance, if it is reported that 39 percent of the public thinks the president is doing a bad job, there is a tendency to assume that all 39 percent disapprove for the same reason (probably the same reason *you* disapprove). If a poll says 43 percent of voters would vote for a woman candidate for president, that doesn't mean that a *particular* woman candidate would get 43 percent of the vote. If 58 percent of the public thinks solar heating is the answer to the energy problem, that doesn't mean that there is a vast movement to convert to solar—or that there ever will be.

Journalists are attracted to polls for the same reasons they're attracted to numbers in general, but the attraction is most intense when it comes to politics. Caught up in horse-race-style campaign coverage, newsmen demand that polls serve as scoreboards telling who's winning and who's losing. This might sound harmless, but in fact it tends to affect the flow of campaign contributions, volunteer workers, media attention, and Old Mo (Mo-mentum) in general.

The excitement creates a stampede in which reporters or pollsters who try to be meticulous about poll results are often trampled underfoot. Many colleges are now teaching polling methodology in journalism departments. The increased awareness should have some positive restraining effect, causing newsmen to pause briefly for sober appraisal before they give in to their instincts and charge screaming into the fray.

Estimates, Records, Superlatives

There are times when the newsman absolutely *must* get the numbers, times when he must drop all reservations and nit-picking and scramble for numbers because the story cannot be told without them—whether it is a cataclysm forcing an emergency style of coverage that overrides all fine points or, at the other extreme, an event so shapeless and *factless* that there is almost nothing to say about it unless you've got it quantified in every direction.

In either case, the pursuit of numbers is more desperate than discriminating. When "hard" numbers are unavailable, we settle for estimates. In the absence of informed estimates, we either plead with news figures to take guesses or we round up some sort of approximation by consensus ("Observers believe . . ."). When we cannot come up with a respectable guess, we pick at rumors.

At the scene of a major disaster, newsmen clamor for numbers, which are unknown and might not be accurately compiled for days, weeks, or months—an intolerable delay. Newsmen create a fierce pressure in situations like this, and it is fiercest at scenes of chaos and carnage when the urgent need for numbers overwhelms any consideration of the realities of numbers-gathering.

Say a plane crashes into a town. Police and firefighters are everywhere; ambulances are rushing people off in all directions. No one knows how many bodies are missing in the wreckage. Some bodies are counted twice—or not at all. Some survivors can't be found and are erroneously listed as missing. Bystanders and workers who are injured in the rescue effort are listed as if they were passengers. Unauthorized people give out incorrect information; authorized people are inundated with demands and bog down. Revised numbers are repeatedly re-revised, and no one is sure which revision is the latest.

Fact-checking is close to impossible. Phone lines are overloaded. Hospitals and police stations are madhouses. Families arrive in hysterics, gawkers clog traffic, news crews push in everywhere with their blinding lights and in-your-face microphones that create a giddy media awareness. Then the mayor and governor come on the scene, making statements on their own, using facts no one has heard of, pulling important officials away from their duties to confer or pose with the honchos. Their aides squabble, rumors fly, and a feeling of surrealistic comedy invades the tragic reality of the situation. This is the atmosphere in which our holy numbers are born.

Yet reporters covering the story cannot afford much skepticism. They must accept a distinction between numbers that are convincingly accurate and numbers that are accurate enough *for now,* even if they are tentative and unconfirmed, even if they are just guesses squeezed out of harrassed and distracted officials.

Meanwhile, in newsrooms far removed from the chaos of the crash scene, there is an uncompromising demand for all the big numbers *now.* There is zero tolerance for any delay in getting these needed facts or for fretting over their reliability. The insistent pressure newsrooms put on reporters in the field reinforces the pressure the reporters put on disaster officials. Finally, all this pressure is too intense to be denied, and the numbers flow, good or bad, right or wildly wrong. And guess what? Everyone is happy.

No reporter is immune from the pressure to get the numbers. But whether he is the producer in the control room or the reporter in the field, he will function more wisely if he is mindful of the true conditions from which the numbers come. This plus a little skepticism and a sense of the human comedy might serve him well when numbers frenzy strikes.

The opposite of the big story that demands numbers because of their importance is the little blob of a story that has no bones and demands numbers for its journalistic skeleton. We cover such stories every day (especially in local news), feverishly measuring everything measurable so we will have something to say, something firm to *build* with even if our numbers tell little about the real nature of the event.

For instance, as a beginning newspaper reporter in Rhode Island I was sent to cover an outdoor concert on a very slow summer Sunday afternoon. The crowd was fairly large, the weather was pleasant, the music was nice, and I was lulled by it until I realized that my pad was blank.

I had no facts! A few names and the location, but that was all. "The crowd was fairly large, the weather was pleasant, and the music was nice" was a passable lead sentence (and indeed it was all that needed saying about the event, leaving only trivial details), but *then* what would I write?

I started scurrying around, hunting for facts to note in my pad, and a moderate panic was welling up when journalistic instinct came to my rescue: *get the numbers!* So I rushed around counting things: number of musicians, number of songs, number of people in the crowd. I found out how much money the concert had made and how much it made the previous year. Later I called the weather bureau and found out the precise temperature.

With a little more zeal I would have recorded the height and weight of the band leader, the age of the tuba player, the average income of the folks in the crowd. I wrote a numbers story about a summer concert and felt pleased by my demonstration of how a real newsman digs out facts. But what I had proven was my inadequacy: I dug out everything *except* the essence of the event.

I particularly recall my crowd estimate, 750. When I mentioned this figure to the concert's publicist, she was aghast and proceeded to prove to me that the number of seats, most of them occupied, was more that *3,000*. My estimate was about one-fourth the true number.

It amazed me that I could be so tremendously wrong. And if I could be so wrong, so could the next guy. What I learned about estimating was: it's very easy to be very wrong. Never again would I accept an estimate (mine or anyone else's) without skeptical examination.

Several years later, covering my first story in San Francisco, I went along on a drug bust at a diet doctor's office. The police confiscated millions of amphetamine pills packed into huge multi-gallon jars. The raiding officers made a grand show of lugging these jars out of the doctor's office, and the senior cop took me aside and told me this was the biggest drug bust in history. And there I was covering it, on my first day on the job. *Wow!*

Something that might be even more difficult than estimating the size of a crowd is estimating the number of drug busts that have been called the biggest in history. It's an impressive superlative, but even if you narrow it down by type of drug, street value, by nation or state or city, by different law enforcement agencies, by diet doctor cases, by drug busts covered by gullible reporters (I came to my senses a few minutes later), you must then ask, who keeps these records? (No one reliable.) Who certifies them, arbitrates them, and does so without self-interest? (No one at all.) What do these records signify? (Not much.)

So why are record-breakings and superlatives and biggest-evers so enticing? The answer, of course, is their high energy; they transform an ordinary story into a story that seizes your attention. The transformation is artificial but also beneficial: the reporter is happy because this extraordinary story is his and the record-claimer is happy because he gets credit for outdoing his competition.

Sometimes others benefit too, such as the victims of a big robbery or disaster who sense the possibility of a bonanza recovery through insurance or lawsuits and therefore claim gigantic losses.

The lesson is that numerical estimates in the news are likely to be *inflated*. Claims of records and superlatives are probably stretched. Numbers-boosting is usually in the self-interest of some or all of the story's principal participants, and journalists are sorely tempted to find it in their self-interest as well.

They should resist. They should be careful to stress that estimates are estimates, more guesswork than precision fact-finding. (Don't be surprised by pressure to do the opposite, because it's felt that confessing to untrusted facts will be taken as a sign of weak reporting.) They should stress attribution, making it clear who is responsible for a particular number. That person, when interviewed, should get the face-to-face message that the newsman does not intend to be a winking conspirator in exaggeration.

Common sense should restrain you when there is an obvious impulse to keep a number rising, such as the money damage caused by a hurricane or the number of people killed by a new disease or by a heat wave. (If you'd check out these individual numbers I'd bet the *closer you get* rule applies: for example, is it a heat wave death if someone dies in an auto accident while taking an air conditioner to a repair shop?)

Such numbers are not only of dubious accuracy, they are also grotesque in their morbid glee to report ever more suffering and tragedy. To me, the most offensive is the holiday weekend tally of highway fatalities, in which there is a barely suppressed rooting for a record-breaking number of deaths.

Finally we come to wars, which produce numbers galore. Few of them are reliable. Aristotle said, "In war, truth is the first casualty," and he wasn't kidding. In fact, the first casualty in conveying battlefield reports is caused by the word *casualty,* whose meaning is widely misunderstood. It refers not only to deaths but to all persons removed from combat because of wounds, injuries, accidents, capture, or other causes. But since many viewers think "casualties" means deaths, I would say, consider it jargon and don't use it. Instead of saying 100 casualties, say 40 dead, 60 wounded.

A word about international news. Most of the nations of the world, particularly those with dictatorial or strong-arm leadership, do not share our idealism about the free flow of information—at least of accurate information. It is also true that many nations lack the sophisticated information apparatus we take for granted. Whether the explanation is propaganda or just helplessness, extravagant numbers arriving from such sources should be taken with extra caution and framed accordingly in your reports.

Crime Statistics

Crime is a journalistic staple. It's an arouser—always has been, always will be. And because the subject of crime has such impact, it requires a special discipline to cling to the distinction between the reality of crime and the different reality of crime statistics.

We might be better off without crime figures. At the very least, we should always remember and stress that they are statistical tools of most value to those who understand their statistical limits. This excludes most viewers.

It also excludes many journalists, who may be inclined to force unwarranted inferences. *New York Times* reporter David Burnham, whose eight-page pamphlet "Crime Statistics: How Not To Be Abused" (Columbia, Mo., 1977) is the best guide I've seen on this subject, tells of writing a story inferring from an increase in narcotics arrests that narcotics activity had leaped dramatically.

Later, to his chagrin, he learned that the statistical leap was caused not by more narcotics activity but by police making more arrests. The size of the narcotics division had been doubled by a mayor anxious to be seen combating a surge in crime. But the surge was in arrests, not crime.

"Almost always, changes in the number of arrests are the result of changes in police department policy" (rather than criminal activity), writes Burnham. Police policy might or might not be intended to influence statistics, but inevitably it does. And while policy influences numbers, numbers also influence policy. Accurate or not, they are the *only* numbers and are therefore the basis for policy-making, budget allocations, patrol assignments, etc.

Most crime statistics that are not based on arrests are based on reported crimes. But you must bear in mind that a significant number of crimes are not reported to police. Victimization studies show that the main reason for not reporting a crime is a feeling that there is nothing the police can do about it.

But there are other reasons too: Women are ashamed to report being raped, men are mortified to have been conquered by a mugger, ghetto people distrust or fear police. Some people plan private revenge. Others are simply intimidated by the questioning and paperwork that go into reporting a crime.

The most accurate reporting probably involves the most serious crimes. Murders are reported because there are bodies to be dealt with. Rapes are more likely to be reported when there is injury. Property crimes such as robbery are more likely to be reported when the loss or damage is extensive, because the victims are thinking about insurance and taxes.

The fact that many crimes are unreported is a well-established flaw of almost all crime statistics. It is a limitation that should hover like a blazing asterisk over any crime numbers we announce on the air—*"this figure does not include the many crimes that people don't report to police."* What we're really saying is, "Understand that this is a statistic, not necessarily a truth." But does the audience understand that? I don't know.

Another statistical problem involves categorizing. Federal, state, and local agencies have differing crime terminology and reporting practices. Another consideration is the interviewing talent and report-writing skill of individual police officers, not to mention the reliability of victims, eyewitnesses, and newly arrested criminals.

Getting accurate figures is difficult enough given the statistical problems, which by themselves should trigger a five-alarm warning under the *closer you get* rule. But then consider the *politics* of crime-related statistics.

There was a time when crime statistics were notoriously unreliable because of outright falsifying as well as poor methodology. Things are better now, but have no illusions that across-the-board purity has come to crime statistics.

Ask whether public officials are above gamesmanship on an issue as volatile as crime. Think about all the votes and careers and funding that ride on findings about crime and law enforcement. Think of all the *power* at stake. Then think about the journalistic reflex by which these numbers are tossed into broadcasts without a moment of critical thought or a qualifying phrase on the air.

Going hog-wild over a sensational crime story might be justified by the community's gut interest in it, even if this interest is morbid and unattractive. But when it comes to broad statements on a subject that touches deep emotions and vulnerabilities, we should exert some self-discipline. We should rein in the hog-wild impulse and tell a numbers story as a numbers story instead of exploiting it as an emotional grabber. (Crime is down so get happy! Crime is up so get a Doberman!)

Don't expect to talk producers out of using crime statistics. But perhaps you can talk them into using a phrase or sentence suggesting that such numbers need not be regarded as eternal verities. Go for that small victory.

Six More Points about Numbers

1. "Eight injured in explosion" versus "Explosion injures eight."

Numbers have a kind of interchangeability until you focus on their content. To hear "Eight people were injured today in . . ." could just as well be 80 people or 180 people until you know what this story is about. *Then* it becomes important. If you were telling the story to a friend on the street you would say, "There was a big explosion at the factory—eight people got hurt," instinctively establishing the context before you supplied the powerful detail.

2. Especially with numbers, use the active voice and state positively.

Don't say, "The measure was disapproved of by 42 percent of the voters." Say, "42 percent of the voters were against the measure."

3. The "Tell 'em" rule is particularly useful in numbers stories.

"Local electricity rates are going up about four percent. The higher rate takes effect next month. The additional four percent will mean a monthly increase of about three dollars on the average electricity bill." (Tell 'em what you're gonna tell 'em, tell 'em, and tell 'em what you told 'em.)

4. "As many."

I've never understood what attracts writers to phrases like

"twice in as many weeks" or "four times in as many games." Say twice in two weeks, four times in four games.

5. Guard against confusing millions and billions.

This is an it-can't-happen-to-me mistake—but it will. I recall turning in a script warning that the population of China was heading for a million. Very embarrassing. The way to prevent it is to get into the habit of underlining the *m* or the *b* as a way of asking yourself if you have made a typographical or mental error.

6. $26,500 . . . 26-thousand 5-hundred dollars . . . Twenty-six thousand five-hundred dollars . . . and so on.

Some teachers, anchors, and news departments are fussy about how numbers are written in a script. Some aren't fussy at all. The virtue of the number itself is that it is easily recognized; the argument for writing it out is that it permits an easier measurement (by counting words or lines) of how much time will be consumed saying it on the air. I think this is a case where style is less important than consistency.

15

Dealing with Humor

It's an average news day, and there is a rich selection of wars in which humans are maiming and slaughtering each other for reasons which, from a distance, can hardly be taken seriously. There is mayhem in the streets; knives are unsheathed in fatal duels over parking spaces. An auto company is forced to admit that the car you are driving might have a slight tendency to explode if hit at any angle by an oncoming bicycle. A porno theater is opening near your home, the Russians are building missiles bigger than skyscrapers, racial violence is brewing, and a strike by sanitation men is leaving heaps of rat-infested garbage on every street corner. Your elected officials once again prove themselves to be fakers or crooks or morons. Your favorite TV series has been canceled; your favorite athlete is injured and out for the season. Every river, lake, and raindrop is contaminated with chemical poison, and researchers have found some new causes of cancer. No one cares about old people, narcotics-crazed teenagers are running wild, and a storm will ruin your Saturday plans. And tonight we begin a five-part series on incest.

Every evening our souls are assaulted with such stories, the evening litany of atrocities and stupidities, disasters and disasters to come. Periodically, viewer protests swell up against newscasts that seem so determinedly grim, so barren of happy items. It's an understandable criticism, but of course it is more emotional than sensible: journalistic judgments and story selection should not be based on cheerfulness or lack of it. And yet there is something obviously misguided about a definition of news in which the only legitimate stories are those which are horrible, menacing, or depressing.

Many things happen in the world that are rip-roaringly funny, all the more funny because of the gloom they dispel and because of a truth about humor: nothing is really funny unless it is somehow really serious. It may be minor in its historic or global significance, but there must be something humanly serious in it. President Ford's famous pratfalls had no significance by normal journalistic standards, yet they were hilarious because of his serious mantle as president and the seriously intended occasions he shattered—tumbling down airplane ramps as welcoming ceremonies unfolded and bands played "Hail to the Chief"—and because of the personal embarrassment he must have seriously felt as a human being making a buffoon of himself in public.

When it works, humor in a newscast is pure champagne. It is a treat for viewers and a high for the Talent, because making people laugh is always an exhilarating experience. Producers and news executives relish the sparkle it gives their program. And it is one of the rare occasions when the finesse of the writer is noticed and appreciated. It is as if he has pulled off a little piece of writer magic.

And he has. Humor is magical, and writing it seems to be more a matter of inspiration than of conscious skill. Given the large number of writers with rich senses of humor, it's remarkable how few of them can write anything funny. The moment they sit down at the typewriter their humor becomes inaccessible. They stiffen, they become mannered or heavy-handed or coy or literary. Sometimes they slam into the great wall of Writer's Block and can't finish a sentence. The onset of self-consciousness seems to shut off whatever valve it is that allows humor to flow.

I will not present examples of stories I consider models of newswriting humor, simply because they would lose their funniness under the microscope. As E. B. White has written,

> Humor can be dissected, as a frog can, but the thing dies in the process and the innards are discouraging to any but the pure scientific mind. . . . [Humor] has a certain fragility, an evasiveness, which one had best respect. Essentially, it is a complete mystery. (*The Second Tree from the Corner* [New York, 1978], p. 165)

One general guideline about humor in TV news is that the humor should be in the picture, the on-screen images. When the humor is in the video, the writing only sets it up. This is a modest function and it's important to restrain yourself from trying to compete with the funniness of the picture; let the picture get the laugh, and don't try to horn in with your own hambone lines. And that's about all there is to say about humor in the picture. It is not always in the picture. Sometimes it's in the script, read by an anchorperson without video support. Writing humor stories for this purpose is what this chapter is about.

I cannot tell you in anything but the most general terms how to write successful humor stories. But I think I can give you some ideas about *how not* to do it. It also helps to give some thought to the risk you take by putting humor into a newscast: it may be champagne when it works, but it's dishwater when it flops. The on-camera person suffers egg-on-the-face mortification, the producer is chagrined, and the writer goes to the doghouse.

My theory is that TV news viewers are generally not critical, but an attempt at humor jars awake their critical sense; it forces them to respond, rather than passively receive. While forcing a response may not seem like a huge imposition, consider how rapidly you become ill at ease when someone makes you listen to an unfunny joke or how you turn against an unfunny comedian or situation-comedy with an almost violent impatience. Yet you will sit through a boring newscast or predictable TV drama with nary a complaint—they ask nothing of you, but humor demands a response and if the payoff isn't a good laugh, you resent being forced to participate.

It is remarkable how intense this resentment can be. Comedians live in dread of it, describing their failures in images of annihilation: "I bombed" or "I really died out there." Johnny Carson's durability as TV's consummate stand-up comedian is undoubtedly related to his deftness in surviving jokes that don't work. A former *Tonight Show* writer tells me that a Carson script includes "savers" along with almost every gag: if the gag fails, Carson is ready with a funny crack about it that deflects the resentment, like a matador deflecting a charging bull. Thus he "saves" himself.

Humor in a newscast is a gamble. Seeking the sweet reward of laughter and brightness, you risk annoying the audience—and you don't have an anchorman with the skills of Johnny Carson to get you off the hook if things go wrong.

Because humor is a gamble it should be undertaken only when the odds are strongly in your favor: if you don't have a winning hand, don't play. It need not be a boffo, sidesplitting belly-laugher, but my feeling is that a humor story that isn't genuinely funny is not worth the risk. No one will notice if you leave it out—a newscast is not expected to be funny—but viewers will definitely notice and make judgments if you leave it in.

On the other hand, if you *do* have a funny story, don't waffle, don't back off. The fear of bombing creates a strong impulse to water it down and play it safe. But the decision to gamble on a humor story is a decision *not* to play it safe. Indeed, boldness is the only way to present humor; tentativeness only calls attention to your vulnerability.

Even if your material is unquestionably hilarious, it will not work unless your anchorman is confident that he will succeed with it and will not embarrass himself. You must be sensitive to his concern. If he is at all hesitant or nervous about the story, drop it like a hot potato—it is the worst mistake to push him in front of the camera with a humor story he has doubts about. That impulse to pull back to safer ground will seize him just as he becomes committed to barreling forward—like a high diver having second thoughts the instant his toes leave the diving board. You will see a display of dissolving composure as he hedges and squirms, dilutes the story with nonsensical ad-libs, tries to explain it, fights an urge to apologize for it, and of course, muffs the punch line. Back in the newsroom the writer seethes at the butchering of his finely crafted story; he is not likely to empathize with the anchorman who made himself vulnerable by asking for a laugh but received no human feedback, only the wilting stare of the TV camera's thick glass eye. It takes a lot of confidence to tell a joke to a lens.

An anchorman's lack of confidence in his ability to deliver a funny story (especially if it is justified by a lack of talent) is one good reason to abstain from humor. And there are other reasons.

Success at humor seems to invite an assumption that a person or program is not serious, not credible. It is clearly a wrong idea that serious people do not have senses of humor (it might be that *not* having a sense of humor is a bad sign about anyone regarded as serious). But the reality is that revealing too much humor in public is simply not wise. It casts doubt, plants a suspicion of frivolousness. It betrays the Cronkite Ideal. When a truly serious story takes place, people will not want to hear it from a joker. Since credibility and seriousness are the foundations of journalism, it's not too much to ask newsmen to keep somewhat private the comic sense that many of them abundantly possess.

Also, humor is often rough and unkind to the people or groups who are the butt of it. Perhaps they fully merit being laughed at, but TV news is not a good vehicle for ridicule, because it is just too big and too powerful to be trusted with the role of deciding who or what should be made fun of.

Further, what is funny in private conversation is often intolerably offensive in a public medium. An innocent jest brings on a deluge of angry phone calls. The milder calls threaten to boycott your station and your sponsors' products; other callers threaten to wait for you in the parking lot and make certain structural changes in your anatomy. Once I worked for an anchorman who took special amusement in mentioning Mafia nicknames on the air—until a nationally prominent gangster known as "the Snake" phoned him at home and said something like, "I never liked dat name and I don't never wanna hear you call me dat no more, unnastan?" This took the fun out of the snake jokes, which ceased. What didn't occur to any of us until much later was that the Snake had a reasonable complaint about being gratuitously ridiculed on TV.

If ridicule is out, it's no great loss, because humor that is hostile or negative doesn't go down well on television anyway. American television has never produced a sardonic destroyer like H. L. Mencken; satire has never worked consistently on U.S. TV; angry comedians like Mort Sahl have burned out quickly; an insult artist like Don Rickles must make a great effort to display the warm heart beneath the slashing exterior; a Joan Rivers must openly wallow in her own deficiencies before turning her outrageous cattiness on other victims.

The raw emotion that underlies hostile humor is just too much for television, too hot for the "cool" medium. The TV camera detects it ruthlessly and brings it into a viewer's living room with a bristling, upsetting impact. If it is derisive or malicious, it will almost certainly backfire; it will seem mean or, to use an inelegant but appropriate word, snotty.

I would say that humor in TV news doesn't work unless it is fundamentally good-hearted and fair (and a bit surprising). It need not be toothlessly bland and it need not be confined to sugary tales of kiddies or doggies. ("Oh, isn't that adorable!" is not a reaction to be sought in a humor story.) But avoid the souring effect of put-down humor. It might work in wisecracking sit-coms, but it doesn't work in news.

The warning against not-niceness also extends to wittiness. Wittiness is sometimes taken as a higher level of humor, so high that it need not be funny. When a humor story fails to be funny, the writer tells himself it was witty. If it's not convincingly witty, he will accept "dry" or "wry" or "ironic" or perhaps even "droll." In the conservative quarters of network news, the humor is frequently so formal and cautious that it seems strangely constipated. I have had the experience of inquiring about a peculiar network story only to find out that it was regarded as a rollicking humor piece. Oh. Did insiders actually think it was funny? Yes, but probably only because it was such a relatively giddy departure from the usual solemn constraints.

The problem with wittiness, even at its best, is that it calls attention to itself instead of the story. It creates a pressure to admire the writer's cleverness. This is probably why puns are invariably followed by groans—open disapproval for something that strikes Americans as showing off or being that one thing that Americans hold in unanimous contempt, "pseudo-intellectual."

It's also a reason why newsmen should never indulge themselves by writing stories in their own dreadful verse and fractured meter:

'Twas the usual crowd for Christmas at Macy's
With long lines of little Freddies and Eddies and Stacys
Awaiting their moment atop Santa's knee
To tell St. Nick what they wished for under their tree.

Certain occasions, like Christmas, seem to bring out the doggerel in every newshound. There's nothing wrong with the poetic impulse but there's no excuse for giving in to it and reading aloud to a TV audience something you would be embarrassed to read face-to-face to a single eleven-year-old child. The only way to get by with rhyming narrative in journalism is to be Charles Osgood of CBS. So here's a rule about rhyming news stories: do it *only* if you are Charles Osgood.

A close relative of unfunny wittiness and junk poetry is flippant wordplay. This is the downfall of broadcast newswriters, a temptation to which they easily succumb. Samples:

That swarm of bees that *bugged* workers in the downtown federal building is gone now. The Fire Department had a *honey* of an idea and *stung* the yellowjacketed pests with high-powered hoses. Everyone was glad to see those bees *buzz off.*

Basketball star Joe Doaks *dribbled* into court today—not a *basketball* court but a court of law, where he faced drug possession charges. The judge called a *foul*—and *slam-dunked* Doaks into a jail cell.

Joe Doaks has been trying to set a record for most hours on the Coney Island roller coaster, but he's really been having his *ups and downs.* . . .

This sort of thing—called a "brite" in newsroom jargon—was once considered the official way to write broadcast humor. And it keeps popping up, often introduced with apologetic announcements of impending trivia: "And on a lighter note. . . ." The anchorman swings into a sudden mood of artificial gaiety, puts a chuckle in his voice and a twinkle in his eye, and takes off on a wing and a prayer.

It's hard for me to believe that lukewarm wordplay like this ever brought laughter from anyone, except of course the person who wrote it. It's simply writer doodle, and very dreary doodle at that. And it violates the rule of naturalness: in a face-to-face conversation you would never allow yourself to tell someone about "the honey of an idea that made the bees *buzz off.*"

By now it may seem that I've ruled out much and left little: ridicule is out, cutesy is out, wittiness and rhymes and puns and flippant wordplay are out. They all have one negative thing in common: instead of letting the *story* be funny, the *writer* tries to be funny.

The three stories I've given as samples of wordplay illustrate the giant blah that follows when the writer tries to pump synthetic levity into an unfunny story. Nothing in the actual situations these stories describe gives a hint of anything that might actually make people laugh. This is a good signal that the story should not be treated as funny. However, the writer often has no choice; he is at the mercy of the ingrained newsroom habit of mistaking insipid stories for humor stories. The thinking is: if it's not serious, it must be humorous.

Which brings me to another staple of broadcast news humor, known as the "geek piece" or "folk tune." Some jerk is trying to set a record for singing in the bathtub, or he is crusading for the civil rights of poultry by going around in a chicken costume. Writers love these stories. I was no exception, but after a while I realized that they were drivel. There was no differentiation between stories that were funny and stories that were just stupid. They were put on the air because program formats slotted in humor pieces, or "kickers," regardless of quality.

Another flaw is that many of these stories are at least partly bogus. Some literary license is tacitly permitted when humor stories are involved; the normal rules against embellishing are relaxed. The culprits are usually the reporters at the source, usually in remote locations, often local reporters or stringers who are working on their own, who know their story has to be fairly good to make the wires and correctly assume that no one will want to spoil a gem of a humor story by checking out its details.

Related to geek humor is bad taste humor, which is most often sexual. Mae West pointed out that "it's hard to be funny when you have to be clean," and there is some truth to that; but there is no truth to the notion that anything that's suggestively dirty is funny. Sex humor in local TV news (you'll see it mainly on the late news, not the dinner-hour news) tends to consist of titillating mention or near-mention of taboo body parts or dirty words. I recall writing a story about the mysterious disappearance of a shipment of bull se- men—it got a big sniggering laugh because it used the word *semen* on television. This was considered to be oh-so-naughty. I wrote it knowing I would get credit for writing a funny story, a credit I en- joyed. But later I felt soiled by it.

On the other hand, I remember a wonderful story about a naked man and woman who in the course of an adulterous and inexplicable sexual frolic became handcuffed to a chandelier, with the keys out of reach. They dangled there for a considerable time, as lust waned and awareness of their plight set in. At last one of them managed to use a foot to reach a phone and dial the operator, which led to the arrival of police. The cops, turning out in large numbers as they always do when nudity is involved, had to break down the door, crashing into the room where the poor man and woman hung stark naked and handcuffed, exposed in their morti- fying foolishness. No doubt the cops roared with laughter and took their time about restoring the couple's dignity.

The story was racy, but it did not leave a bad taste. It was classically comical and hilariously human; you could empathize, sympathize, and enjoy the variety and the wages of sin. It had sex, justice, and blundering. It was rich with images and emotions. It had a good beginning, middle, and end. The facts rang true and were in the public record. Telling the story on TV wasn't cruel because it happened in Florida, and I was writing for a local audience in New York. And no names were used.

Two points: Point 1 is that the humor was there in the story, not contrived by the writer. I didn't try, when I wrote it, to inject the humor through my cleverness. I let the story tell itself. All I did was to highlight the images and emotions I thought were funny, so the audience would see them the same way. I didn't save my script, but I remember the story vividly because of its strong images. That is Point 2: *show* what's funny. If the humor is not in the videotape, create the image in words. Funniness is not always physical or visual, but you can show the scene that frames the inward comedy. Find the right viewpoint and the right details, then get yourself out of the way.

So, if the story is President Ford falling down at an airport arrival ceremony, the writer might zero in on the schoolchildren who were turned out for their first brush with the pomp and splendor of the presidency; or on the welcoming party of local dignitaries who waited nervously to bow and scrape but instead watched in horror as the president arrived in a headfirst plunge and had to be helped to his feet; or on Mr. Ford himself, keyed up to reap the honors of his office and make points with the electorate but blowing it all in a single klutzy misstep.

During the coverage of the 1980 Winter Olympics at Lake Placid, I took note of a humor piece that seemed to be a textbook example of failing to capitalize on a story with genuine comic potential. The correspondent was a woman I have worked with and respect in some ways, but not for her sense of humor. Her style is to signal a joke by slapping your knee or socking you in the shoulder. Unable to manhandle a television audience, she is deprived of her primary humor weapon.

But she gave it a try, explaining that Olympic medals would be engraved with all the names of winning team members, that the engraving would be done in "the language" of the winning team, and that it would have to be finished very quickly in the interval between the victory and the medal ceremony:

> so for example, if the Russian hockey team wins, the engraver might have only two hours to engrave fourteen different names on fourteen different medals. That's one job I'm glad that I don't have.

Thus a fairly promising story ended with a disappointing clunk. I felt that she had vaguely sensed what was funny about the story but hadn't been able to close in on it. Consider: first, Russian names tend to be multi-syllabic jawbreakers, meaning lots of work per name; second, medals for Russian athletes would have to be engraved in their "language," meaning Cyrillic lettering; third, the engraver was evidently an American from the Lake Placid area who would be miserably unfamiliar with Russian names *and* Cyrillic lettering.

For sure this man would be rooting against the Russians (in fact the American team won) rather than star in a scene of real-life situation-comedy worthy of Lucille Ball or Jackie Gleason or even Laverne and Shirley: a desperate engraver racing the clock to inscribe Cyrillic spellings of long and exotic Russian names (a telephone call to the Olympic Press Center would have gotten her some examples, the best of which was Zinetulla Bilyaletdinov). Fourteen names on fourteen medals—196 Russian names in two hours. With some anxious official leaning into the work room every ten minutes asking, "Hey Fred, you almost done?"

This approach would have created a picture showing what was funny about the engraver's dilemma. Instead she gave up, fizzling out with an unimaginative and lame wrap-up line ("That's one job I'm glad that I don't have") that would have been superflous if the story had succeeded in *showing* why the job could have been such a bad dream. The fizzle-out wrap-up line is the curse of the humor story.

Writing humor requires special ability. It can't be well taught, but it can be learned. It's worth a serious try. It will make you a better writer. Network news has little time or tolerance for humor, but much longer local programs have plenty of time to fill and welcome the personality and change of pace that humor brings. The only drawback, if you do well writing it, is that every wacko story in the world will find its way to your desk, and you will have to put up a fight against the sillier ones. But it's still a good bargain. Instead of dodging humor stories, you will enjoy writing them. It's a pleasant change from writing about fires and crimes and catastrophes.

One last caution about humor. Many stations are becoming more permissive now about two big humor subjects that used to be strictly out of bounds, sex and politics. And some light teasing about race or ethnic origin might be acceptable here and there. But never, *never* joke about rape, religion, serious illness, or death.

16

"All Else"

In the division of labor among the three newswriters at CBS evening news, there is a writer assigned to foreign news, another to national news, and a third to "all else," which includes economics, accidents and natural disasters, features and human interest, and miscellaneous overflow.* It's a fitting name for this chapter of miscellaneous overflow about newswriting.

Look Out the Window

Common Sense Rule 1 in broadcast newswriting is: Before you make statements about the weather, look out the window. Check your copy with the skies.

Young people, advised of this rule, tend to laugh nervously—it's so *obvious,* ha ha, who could ever make a blunder like getting the current weather wrong? But sometime later, working in a windowless newsroom, they forget to check with the skies. They write "partly sunny" when it is raining torrentially. The phones light up. Many callers can hardly wait to express their low opinion of journalism in general and especially of *you.* This is a want-to-die moment.

Look out the window—consider it a principle with applications whenever anything seems so obvious that you don't have to do it, check it, or even think twice about it.

Concentration

You cannot write well if you cannot concentrate, and it can be very difficult to concentrate in the bedlam of a newsroom. You must learn

---

*ABC followed this system in the 1970s but no longer divides the work by specialties. NBC took the no-specialties route for many years but in the mid-1980s switched to a CBS-like system in which the designations are domestic, foreign, and politics.

to shut out all the distractions. When it's time to write, pretend you're a submarine and dive for the bottom.

As you write, you will be interrupted frequently. Some interruptions are justified but many are not. When you are struggling to nail down a phrase, it is no time to be hit in the ear by a paper airplane or asked if you have change for a ten dollar bill.

I think it's important to discourage unnecessary interruptions, and it's ideal to do so without temper tantrums. So I recommend the Zombie Routine. Your concentration has put you in a kind of professional trance. You'll be glad to fight your way out of this trance to cooperate with the interrupter, but it may take you longer than he wants to wait. The process is visibly agonizing as well as slow. Even when you break out of the trance, you may have difficulty focusing on what he wants from you.

If you do a good Zombie, he'll be embarrassed and exasperated and probably reluctant to bother you again.

Typing

Little is asked of writers in the way of manual skills. But a newswriter who types poorly cannot call himself a professional. Learn to type well.

I have always felt that typing ability can be a factor in writing ability. Four reasons why.

First, if you type quickly you'll be able to get your thoughts down quickly. Often a story's most natural form pops into your mind spontaneously, and you want to capture it before it floats away. In *The Elements of Style,* Strunk and White speak of marksman-like wing shots "bringing down the bird of thought as it flashes by."

Second, if you type easily you'll be less lazy about rewriting. As an editor I often asked writers to rewrite a sentence or two and then watched as they laboriously attempted an easy fix by pencil rather than returning to the typewriter. Frequently they had to return to the typewriter anyway, after making an awful mess full of arrows and carets and smudgy erasures.

Third, if the page is a mess, it's a good bet that the thinking it reflects is also a mess. My teachers in elementary school tried to drum this into me, and twenty years later I started to believe it.

Fourth, even though things do get hectic and disorderly in the minutes before or during air time, it is outrageous to send a person before the cameras with a script that doesn't do everything possible to minimize the possibility of fumbling on the air. Even if the script is retyped for prompting machines (prompter typists working in a rush will introduce mistakes of their own, not to mention the problems they'll have if your script is illegible) the anchorman's fallback copy is the sheaf of pages on the desk before him. Don't let him fall back into a mess of cross-outs and scribbles.

Remember also that the director and the entire on-air production staff work from the script in which your typing appears. Camera calls, roll cues, timings, and other critical production details are largely keyed to what they see on paper. They don't care about spelling or literary grace, but they'd better be able to read what you've written.

I haven't said much in this book about writing speed. There isn't much to say about it. My favorite quotation on the subject is A. J. Liebling's boast that he could "write better than anyone who could write faster, and faster than anyone who could write better."

Obviously, writing speed should be developed, which includes developing your typing skill. When the chips are down, a slow newswriter is about as valuable as a slow gunslinger.

Using the Telephone

If possible, don't get on the phone with a news source until you've jotted down some notes to remind yourself of the things you absolutely need to find out. Using the phone is one of the arts of the journalist; it's embarrassing to be so unartistic at it that you finish a phone interview only to realize you forgot a central question or were smoothly diverted from something you should have pursued. You have to call again—and nine times out of ten you won't be able to get your source back on the phone. Either he's avoiding the question he knows you should have asked, or his line is busy for the next hour, or he's gone home.

Prepare. Have a strategy. A common strategy is to get the minor information you need before getting to the tough questions that make him think you're out to get him, at which point you may encounter a freeze-out or an abrupt end of conversation. Listen to his tone—if you hear impatience, go right to the main point.

The opposite approach, unattractive but often successful, is to shock him into believing that a disaster is guaranteed unless he stops in his tracks and tells you absolutely everything. To achieve this intimidating effect, you give the impression that your mind is just about made up against him and only a vigorous defense will make you reconsider. Or that you are so reckless and mixed up that your story will be a horror. Of course, this strategy is a gamble. Instead of opening up, he might slam the door in your face, leaving you empty-handed and without recourse—also with a damaged relationship that might hurt you if you ever have to call him again.

About asking questions: don't be self-conscious, and don't worry about sounding impressive or showing how smart you are. Many journalists try to show off with esoteric questions (to which they often get esoteric and therefore useless answers). They are playing a vain and time-wasting game. Don't be intimidated by it. A simple and even naive question is frequently more disarming and effective than a sophisticated "insider" question—the interviewee is not prepared for it, and it may force him to reply without his customary artifice.

Not Seen Here

When writing voice-over copy that will be read *live,* don't gamble on specific picture coming up in perfect timing with your script. That is, don't write "this man" or "as you see here" or "the woman on the left" or "these numbers show."

Using such phrases tempts fate to play pranks on you, and fate can be a devilish jokester. The tape rolls a few seconds too early or too late, so when the copy says, "Arrested today and charged with child molesting was this man, Joe Doaks," the image on the screen is a cutaway shot of a dog. Or a building. Or an innocent bystander. The innocent bystander turns out to be a prominent clergyman. His brother is a top libel lawyer. *Ouch!*

This warning applies only to a live voice-over. When the voice-over is prerecorded, the tape editor will make sure it matches perfectly with the picture.

Also, remember that 10 percent of the audience is watching on black-and-white sets, so don't identify things by color. I recall writing a voice-over about an exciting Olympic speed skating race in which I identified the skaters by the colors of their uniforms, one red and one green. Unfortunately, they were shades of red and green that look exactly alike on a black-and-white set. It was a network program; I had annoyed viewers from coast to coast.

Jawbreakers

When you're dealing with impossible names, do your anchorman two favors: give a phonetic pronunciation (and give it again each time the name is used) and use the name as few times as possible. Otherwise, the anchorman and audience will be in for bad times when the story begins, "Polish transport minister Mieczyslaw Zajfryd arrived today in Wroclaw. . . ."

Unanswered Questions

It's not fair to tantalize viewers by raising questions you don't answer. If you make a point of a company's becoming the second biggest oil producer, don't make the viewer wonder which company is number one and which company was displaced as number two. If you say that a player has broken into the top three of golf, make sure your story names the other two top players.

If your copy raises a question that can't be answered, don't leave it hanging. You must find a way to deal with it: "Economists can't agree on what's caused the new round of inflation." "Officials haven't decided when the rained-out game will be replayed."

In the old days, reporters would say that anything they couldn't find out "remains a mystery," hiding behind the suggestion of exotic forces concealing the answer. I think it's better to tell the truth: you don't know the answer because officials are not saying, or because a spokesman did not return phone calls, or simply because people simply don't know.

Edit They Will

In most newsrooms, a writer's script is given a cursory screening by the producer or associate producer—neither of whom has the time or temperament for editorial nit-picking—and then passed on to the anchorman, who may choose to re-rewrite it. Some larger newsrooms have an editor or writing specialist of some other title whose primary job is scrutinizing copy. He has the options of sending copy through untouched or with minor changes, or having the writer rewrite it, or rewriting it himself.

As a matter of principle, I think it is best for the writer to do the rewriting. It is his job and the source of his satisfaction; he should be the one to finish a script, even if he is not thrilled by what the editor has told him to do. A writer who is consistently denied the satisfaction of finishing his scripts will lose motivation and come to regard his scripts as rough drafts that might as well be written sloppily.

However, the editor will often find that there is insufficient time to go through cycles of sending back and resending back an individual script. He may also have difficulty communicating to the writer how he wants the script changed, and sometimes the writer will exaggerate his difficulty comprehending the editor's instructions or writing it the way the editor wants. Anticipating this problem, the editor might do the rewrite himself rather than begin an unproductive go-round with a resisting writer. I have been on both sides in this kind of situation, and it can become an unpleasant and childish battle of egos.

A fact of life about editors: editing is their job, and edit they will. They feel delinquent if they don't make *some* change in copy, however minor; they are reluctant to keep hands off. I worked under one editor who seemed to start scrawling changes while the copy was still in the air on the way to his desk. His attitude was that the copy was raw material that *he* would mold into a final product.

I didn't like that, although I had to admit he did an excellent job. I also confess that I was frequently tempted to pad my copy with blatantly extraneous words or sentences for him to delete—he would have the satisfaction of editing, and I would have the satisfaction of seeing the final script the way I wanted it. I don't remember whether I succumbed to that unprofessional temptation; I hope not.

Transition Mania

Possibly because it gives them a chance to display their ad-libbing prowess or the dexterity of their anchoring, some anchormen seem to be obsessed with on-air transitions between stories, no matter how contrived or awkward.

> Military expenditures are going up but so is the temperature and here's Phil with the weather.

> Thanks, Phil, and as hot as it gets tomorrow, Police Chief Duffy was just as hot under the collar today when protestors demonstrated outside the police station.

The appeal of transitions is that they create at least the semblance of continuity or *flow.* Producers always seem to be entranced by continuity, which has a surprising effect on the selection of news stories. One fire might not make the news, but two fires suggests a thematic link that somehow enlarges the newsworthiness of both of them. A local fire of marginal interest might be covered *if* there was a big fire a thousand miles away. The producer jumps at the chance to slot the distant fire story into the lead-in to the local fire tape story, making a package.

It is rarely questioned whether such groupings are helpful to viewers. I'm skeptical. Tell two or more similar stories in a row, and see if the details don't blur —this fire here, that fire there, a bomb in Beirut and a blast in Belfast. It's smooth production but probably not good *telling*.

The urge to connect stories is ingrained, a journalistic instinct. The most you can do is resist a bit when it becomes too farfetched.

Telephone Numbers and Addresses

It should be obvious that a listener cannot memorize a telephone number or address in one quick hearing and without notice. If you are going to give a special police telephone number or an address to which viewers can write for more information on a particular subject, tell your viewers in advance to be ready with pencil and paper. By "in advance" I mean earlier than the first half of the sentence that ends with the information.

When you give the information, it should be supplemented by a graphic that stays on the screen for more than a millisecond, and it should be repeated. Also, post it in the newsroom so it can be given to all the viewers who miss it and flood your switchboard with calls.

Preventing this flood on the switchboard is an incentive for doing it right. Another incentive is public service. The great majority of people who miss the information will shrug and forget about it. A person who is hesitant about reporting a crime tip will have an excuse not to do it. A woman who dreads finding out that she has breast cancer will have an excuse for not sending for that pamphlet on self-examination.

Be sure to verify phone numbers and addresses before announcing them on the air. Especially phone numbers. *Pick up the phone yourself and dial the number:* "Hi, is this the right number to call for the breast cancer pamphlet? Good. We're announcing it on TV news in about an hour so be ready for a lot of calls."

And when I say a lot of calls, I mean a lot. Normally we don't think about the hugeness of the audience, but then there is a reason to call and the calls come in astounding numbers, and we are reminded of all those people out there—and of course the viewers who call represent only a fraction of the total audience. If you put an incorrect phone number on the air, your error is compounded by every frustrating call to that wrong number. And for at least one person you have created a living nightmare: imagine the poor old man whose telephone rings with fifteen thousand requests for a meatloaf recipe or a free map of the city bus system.

PART 3

The News Career

17

Getting a Job

I have been a job giver and a job seeker, and I can testify that the process is considerably less objective than both sides like to think.

The job giver may take pride in his discerning evaluation of applicants, but especially when it comes to hiring untested beginners, the deciding factor tends to be intuitive.

The job seeker expects to be judged by his qualifications and professional potential. He is unaware of other factors that might make the difference, including factors beyond his control. Are they looking to hire a Hispanic or a woman or are they only going through the motions before giving the job to the bright kid from the station owner's country club? Does it help to have graduated from the nearby state college or to have newspaper experience or to be as different as possible from the person being replaced? The job seeker must be qualified, but as Napoleon said of his generals, the most important thing is to be lucky.

It is a common mistake to assume that luck and the hirer's intuitive response to you must be left entirely to fate. It is also a common mistake among young people to be oblivious to a basic reality about jobs: even if you are a fine prospect, you will not be hired unless there is an opening on the staff. The news business, like other businesses, has departmental budgets setting the number of employees in each position. Someone must quit or be promoted or fired before a job becomes open. If there is no opening, you cannot get a job.

News departments are besieged by job seekers. This puts a heavy strain on the executive in charge of hiring. He has many other pressing duties, so dealing with job seekers is a low and bothersome priority—until a staff opening occurs.

Then the low priority becomes a top priority. He is under pressure to act quickly—the newsroom needs a replacement without much delay. He does not have time to undertake a systematic talent hunt. And he does not like the thought of pulling open the drawer he's stuffed so chaotically with resumés and letters and writing samples.

This is the moment. If your name comes to mind, favorably, you have a strong chance of getting the job. He might have interviewed dozens of people in previous months, but only a few stand out in his memory (as an aid to his memory staple a photo to your resumé); of those few, most or all have drifted away or gotten jobs elsewhere. The parade of candidates has dwindled to a very few. Starting with the new opening on the staff, the hirer becomes the seeker.

Needless to say, this is the luckiest time to come strolling in for your job interview. A more systematic approach to luck would be to have taken a low-level job in the newsroom, such as desk assistant, and to know from the office grapevine that a job is up for grabs. Don't wait for the hirer to think of you—march in and nominate yourself for the job. You are already an insider, and most news departments encourage the morale-raising practice of promoting from within. If you have made a good impression, you have an enormous advantage over unknown outsiders, even if they seem better qualified.

You can also cultivate familiarity from outside the office. If your initial job interview goes well enough to create reasonable hope, follow up by taking any excuse to call or visit the newsroom— to remind the hirer of your existence and availability. Don't be a pest, but be persistent.

Of course, the best timing in the world won't get you the job if you appear unqualified or if the hirer doesn't get that intuitive feeling that you can handle the job. The required qualifications differ everywhere, but here are some thoughts that might help you make the right impression.

1. Present an energetic personality.

I think the most important personal quality in television work is energy. Just plain energy—physical, mental, emotional. There is so much to do to make a TV news show every day. Human energy, especially youthful energy, is the fuel that keeps the machine in motion. A TV-hirer will be attracted to vitality; he is likely to prefer a doer to a deliberate or reflective type.

Television work favors extroverts. It is a team effort, often highly stressful, and it helps to be vigorous, enthusiastic, and good-humored. If people like the idea of working with you, you are more likely to get the job.

2. Don't be too wonderful.

Do not tell the interviewer that you have "lots of great ideas" for the show. He has heard this all too often: the ideas usually turn out to be the same obvious ideas everyone else has had, or they are impractical or bad ideas that prove you don't really understand the show.

There are plenty of ideas but never enough capable people to execute them. So sell yourself as a good soldier who can carry out assignments. Have ideas later, once you know the terrain.

If an interviewer invites you to criticize the show, be diplomatic. Be *very* diplomatic. He may be asking for criticism, but he really doesn't want to hear it, especially from a novice. Couch your minor negatives in major positives.

About ambition: long-range ambition is attractive, but it is not attractive to appear to want *this* job as a springboard to the next one. I was once about to hire a young woman to be a researcher until she asked, "How long will I have to be a researcher until I get promoted?" That told me that she had no zest for the job; I lost the incentive to hire her and instead hired someone who *wanted* to be a researcher.

3. Don't lose credibility by overinflating your resumé.

Something about resumés brings out the shameless huckster in people. They seem to think they are not personally accountable for the fibbing and embellishing or even the stilted resumé language that theoretically alchemizes every humble experience into a formidable achievement. But it doesn't work. It's transparent: "summer employment participating in research, newsgathering, and production process" means "desk assistant," and everybody knows it.

The resumé should not be regarded as an instrument of personal propaganda. Write an honest resumé, straight, no baloney. But design it to your advantage, stressing experience that is pertinent to the job you're seeking. It may be wise to design different resumés for different jobs: if you've acted in college plays, that's good background for an on-air reporter, but if you're after a writing job, you should emphasize your contribution to the college newspaper. If you're a beginner with nothing special to note in your resumé, admit it.

Most intelligent employers are skeptical about resumés. They know that dummies have graduated from Harvard, that second-raters have won prestigious awards, that having had an impressive job or title does not mean you performed impressively. In television some of the most dazzling resumés belong to people who are continually being fired; they are skilled at getting jobs but not at doing them, and each firing adds a handsome new line to a resumé that is, in fact, a list of failures.

4. Communicate a sense of realism.

Many young people are attracted by the apparent glamor of TV news; they yearn to *be* reporters or newswriters without realizing that they have no special taste for actually *doing* what reporters and writers do. They are chasing a fantasy. Fantasy is a bubble sure to burst, and an employer does not look forward to dealing with their inevitable and painful disappointment, not to mention the disappointing quality of their work.

They betray themselves in job interviews. They should be full of curiosity about the inner workings of the news operation, the atmosphere where they ostensibly wish to spend their professional lives. Instead they ask viewer questions or starstruck questions, outsider questions instead of potential-insider questions. A simple example: instead of asking, "What's Bill Anchorman really like?" they should want to know, "How is Bill to work with?"

Very often they commit the disastrous tactical sin of not knowing what job they want (actually, the sin is *admitting* that they don't know). Desk assistant? Newswriter leading to producer? Reporter leading to anchorman? Asked what they want to be they are speechless because they have not focused on the realities of the working world, where all jobs are specific and hirers measure you for specific functions. To float in and say, in effect, "I just want to be in TV news" is nebulous and annoying to a hirer. Don't be surprised if he suddenly loses interest in interviewing you, let alone hiring you, because you are so out of touch with his needs. Just wanting to be in TV news is an honest and simple aspiration that has probably been the seed of many great careers, but if you have not progressed beyond the wide-eyed stage, it might be a clue that you are not ready for a grown-up job.

A hirer does not expect a young person to be an expert, but he needs to know that you will catch on rapidly to the realities of the newsroom, that you will not be a bewildered moon-child, forever out of step. I think the best way to demonstrate that you are on earth instead of in outer space is to interview the interviewer. Ask him what he does, what he likes about it, what he did before and what he hopes to do next, what *he* thinks of the show, what *he* thinks it needs.

There are many plusses to this approach. One is that he, not you, is doing the answering. Another is that he is telling you what he considers important, so instead of floundering, you know what to talk about. Your follow-up questions show that you are alert and genuinely interested. Your questions need not be brilliant as long as they are sensible. Instead of sitting there scared and blank, like most job seekers, you are making a confidence-inspiring show of initiative. You have begun learning the job before his very eyes. If his intuitive response to you will indeed be the deciding factor, you have done everything possible to make that response favorable.

Here are some other notes on getting jobs.

Writing Tests

Many news departments require applicants for newswriting jobs to take a writing test. The applicant is handed a sheaf of wire copy, led to a vacant desk, and instructed to write a certain number of stories or the overall script of an imaginary newscast.

The writing test was invented to take the guesswork out of hiring writers, to objectify a subjective talent. When I first encountered the writing test, I thought it was the silliest thing I'd ever heard of. Since then I've *half* changed my mind. Writing tests are useful in screening out people who can't write. They are too limited and artificial to prove that you are good, but it only takes a few sentences to prove that you are bad.

Therefore, my advice for taking writing tests is: instead of trying to prove you're good, try to avoid proving that you're bad. In other words, don't make the mistakes that naturally result from trying too hard.

Unfortunately, your human nature will cause you a problem: you will have a powerful impulse to force your copy to be conspicuously spiffy. Your fantasy is that someone will read it and exclaim, "Wow, this guy's really talented!"

But that never happens. There are too many things working against you. One is the plain and even humble nature of newswriting, a self-effacing form that only rarely allows for virtuoso displays. Also, you are nervous and self-conscious. The newsroom is unfamiliar and full of distractions. You don't know the style or page format or how long your stories should be or how important it is to finish quickly. And the stories they've given you are terrible—boring or overcomplicated or incomplete. Plus one that's supposedly humorous. You think: I'll have to compensate for these weak stories with some fancy writing. And that's where you go wrong.

Come back to the strategy: no mistakes. Take no chances. Use no frilly adjectives. Remember to attribute. Don't try to improve a story by flavoring it with your wit or wisdom or offhand personal opinion. Don't interpret or try to draw large meanings; stick to concrete facts. And keep everything short; every extra word extends the possibility of error.

If you have questions, look for someone to ask. If you have doubts about something you've written, forget to turn it in. Read your copy critically, but remember that a first draft often has a smoothness and naturalness that tampering will destroy. Rewrite if you have a clear-cut reason, but don't let nervousness lead you into fiddling with copy, each new idea creating new writing problems and new ideas, sending you into an unstoppable spin like J. Alfred Prufrock's: "In a minute there is time / for decisions and revisions which a minute will reverse."

Don't rush; rushing will cause mistakes. You may hear an imaginary clock ticking as you work, but in most writing test situations no one bothers to time you; your speed won't be noticed unless it's recklessly fast or inordinately slow.

And don't be seen drafting stories in longhand, even if you type them when you're done. If you haven't learned to type, you're not ready for a writing job in a professional newsroom.

Contacts

When it comes to job-getting and job-changing, nothing beats good contacts. If you establish friends and a good reputation in your first job, you will become part of an informal job network or professional grapevine. Friends who have moved to other stations will alert you about new openings and opportunities. Their recommendations will help; hirers are reassured by personal endorsements coming from people they know and trust. Being part of a job network makes you an insider, which is a whole lot better than being an outsider.

Generally you need that first job before you can penetrate a job network. But even without a job you can cultivate contacts. If Mr. A likes you but can't offer a job, perhaps he can at least get you an interview with Mr. B. Mr. B might allow you to use his name in letters to Mr. C and Mr. D. Mr. D might send your resumé over to Mr. E, who may pick up the phone and mention you to Mr. F. So now you know *six* hirers, A through F, and if you can keep all or some of these relationships alive, you'll probably wind up with a job. The point: when turned away, don't go off empty-handed. Make contacts and keep asking for more.

Never on Fridays

This is a small point but small points often make a big difference. Never call about a job on a Friday. Never schedule a job interview for a Friday. On Fridays people are weary. Their interest in the future is shrinking to an interest in their weekend recreation. They want to leave the office as early as possible. They don't want to prolong the day by gabbing with you.

Call on Monday when they're fresh and rested.

The Lure of the Big Time

The big cities—called "major markets" in TV lingo—are the capitals of TV news, and it is understandable that many young people want to rush to the nerve centers instead of dawdling in the hinterlands.

My feeling is that while jobs in New York, Washington, Los Angeles, Chicago, and Atlanta might be impressive, it is the local stations and small newspapers that offer the most fulfilling experience in the early part of a journalistic career. You may outgrow it, but if you haven't been there you've missed something. The richest memories of most veteran newsmen go back to their early days in small places, where they saw the news profession at the grass roots level and fell in love with it for life.

This is more than nostalgia. The small places are less pressurized, less compartmentalized; you get to try almost everything yourself. Your mistakes are forgiven, your excesses are corrected. You have a strong sense of involvement and progress. You have a lot of fun, and you accumulate stories you will tell for years.

The air gets colder as you climb the network peaks. The sense of play is quickly squelched. The atmosphere is hardball: authoritarian, political, tense. The number of viewers is seven or eight digits long, and there is no tolerance for blundering. You will work with talented people on important stories, but you will have to make more personal sacrifices than you bargained for and you will live with no small amount of anxiety and stress. You do not want to arrive in this arena until you are well prepared. Let it wait.

18

Random Thoughts and Exhortations

Viewers

The eternal questions in TV-land are: Who is out there watching us? How do we communicate with that vast unseen audience? How can we "get them into the tent" (i.e., get them to watch our program)? *Who are they?*

No one has a satisfying answer. High executives commission expensive audience research and demographic studies which even they don't trust, preferring intuitive or "gut" notions which are usually formulated in handy stereotypes (the famous "lady from Dubuque," the time-honored "Kansas City milkman," the newer "woman in the laundromat," the gloriously lowbrow "Joe Sixpack") or peculiar biases (such as the bias against people who live in apartments instead of houses and presumably have less typically American tastes than house-dwellers).

Other answers come from other quarters. In Jerzy Kozinski's *Being There,* viewers are portrayed as docile, passive, manipulable tube-gazers. In the late Paddy Chayefsky's *Network,* viewers are alert and angry, "mad as hell" at the way TV offends their intelligence. Another answer, for TV insiders, is that viewers are whoever and whatever your boss says they are. Here's a newsroom dialogue:

Person A: This economics story is boring and arcane and no one will understand it and no one will listen.

Person B: Are you kidding? This is a pocketbook subject, a bread and butter subject, and everybody knows that's the *only* kind of story people always listen to.

The boss decides. But he doesn't really have the answers, he is only leading the guessing. Of course no one admits it is guessing (unless it fails horrendously), and no one calls attention to its inconsistencies. The boss is free to be contradictory. Frequently, he juggles precepts to support impulsive or expedient judgments. In one script he demands extended clarification because "you can't make any assumptions about what viewers will understand." In another he deletes clarifications because "you don't have to waste valuable time going over what everybody already knows." One day he loves a ballet story because it adds "class" to the broadcast; the next day he kills an opera piece because Joe Sixpack despises high culture.

If enough of his guesses are successful, they are analyzed and the analysis becomes doctrine. It is hailed as brilliant, widely adopted, outrageously imitated. Then it wanes and finally dies. But of course we are no longer talking journalism; this is marketing.

To my mind, the only certainties about the audience are its vastness and diversity. Every night about half the population of the United States watches television. More than forty million people watch the network evening newscasts. Millions more watch local newscasts, morning newscasts, middle-of-the-night newscasts, and magazine programs, including *60 Minutes,* whose great ratings success is persuasively cited as proof that the mass audience is not solely escapist and responds positively to well-produced TV journalism.

Who is out there? *Everyone:* brain surgeons and dock workers and insurance salesmen, blacks and whites, old folks and teenagers, German-Americans and Samoan-Americans and Native Americans, Jews and Rastafarians and Buddhists, geniuses and morons, dentists, gangsters, barbers, hod carriers, athletes, derelicts, ministers, fishermen, mental patients, students, grandmothers, ad infinitum. How much sense does it make to conceptualize this spectrum of humanity in the person of a "lady from Dubuque" or a "Kansas City milkman"—stereotypes that deny the diversity of the audience in a vain effort to make its diversity comprehensible? Walter Lippmann wrote that a purpose of stereotypes is "substituting order for the great blooming, buzzing confusion of reality." TV journalists should resist the stereotypes and accept this idea of blooming, buzzing diversity.

So now we turn to the newswriter and ask him how he intends to communicate with this unfathomably diverse audience of laborers, astronomers, clerk-typists, etc. Does he write for none of them, choosing instead a nonexistent "average" viewer? Does he write down to them or up to them, or a little of both? Once he has accepted the audience's diversity, how does he cope with it?

I think the answer is easy to state and difficult to do: he concentrates on writing as *clearly* as he can. He observes the fundamental rules of good writing. He does not think about writing up or down to people or whether they *ought* to understand him or have to be teased into listening to him.

If he writes clearly, he can be confident that all but a few boneheads will understand him. Nobody's intelligence will be offended, and no one will be left behind. As long as it's clear, his writing can be plain or it can be stylish. Everyone can understand plain, and a brightly expressed bit of writing can be illuminating even to dull-witted people.

Of course, clear writing is not simple. And I think it requires something more than mastery of writing technique: it requires a commitment to get across to the audience. This commitment is presumed to be ever-present, but in fact it is ever-vanishing, slipping away unnoticed. Newswriters and other insiders are highly susceptible to *forgetting* the audience—perhaps because they are daunted by its unfathomability, or because they are caught up in the whirl of the newsroom and the internal imperatives that seem to take precedence over larger purpose.

Newswriters tend to think their work is done when the script is finished or when it is read on the air. But it is not written for the anchorman to read—it is for an audience to hear. It must travel across that great vale of fog and static and enter the viewer's mind; otherwise it's just an exercise. Ultimately, clarity requires the writer to be able to put himself in the place of viewers, to see what they will see and hear as they will hear. Then he will understand the difference between talking *at* them and talking *to* them.

Earlier I suggested that when you become bogged down writing a story it is helpful to imagine how you would tell it to your aunt. Along the same lines I noted that Turner Catledge suggested "a curious but somewhat dumb younger brother." And Arthur Godfrey said of radio broadcasting, "There is no audience, just one guy or gal in a room." Putting a real individual in your mind is an aid in loosening the knots you've made for yourself and re-engaging your naturalness at communicating. But be wary of creating your own stereotype and using it as a crutch. The audience is not your aunt or your dumb brother or a guy or girl in a room. It's all of them. And a lot more.

See It Feelingly

Getting facts is fairly easy; the higher art of journalism is getting the *story*. This requires imagination and empathy. In *King Lear* Gloucester tells how he sees the world despite his blindness: "I see it feelingly."

Do the same. Use your senses. Use your life experience. There is almost always a fuller truth to events that newsmen miss because they do not attempt to see with their imaginations. If you doubt that, think of the most profound event in *your* life and imagine how much of it would be lost in the normal journalistic telling.

So if you are standing on the lawn of a family that has had a relative taken hostage overseas, it is not enough to think, "I wonder when they'll make a statement." Beyond that, wonder what they are going through in there, what they are *doing,* what the State Department is telling them, what they feel about the reporters waiting outside, what they will do if the situation is unresolved for a long time and how it will strain their family or health or jobs, how they feel when the telephone rings—or when it doesn't ring.

If you are covering a public official's resignation in disgrace, consider whether he thinks his life is ruined. Think about where he'll go after he makes the announcement—to his wife, his mother, a church, a race track, a saloon? The news event may be over, but the personal story is far from complete, and posing these questions in your mind will sharpen your awareness. Think about the effect of the summer humidity in a jury room. Try to imagine the pain of a bullet wound. Consider what it's like to wake up the morning after winning a lottery or losing an election.

There is an old notion in journalism that an ace newsman gets the Who, What, When, Where, and How and shuns everything else as "soft." I think this is stupidity—as well as an implicit confession of inadequacy as a story-teller. Beneath a story's surface facts are even better facts, and deeper than all the facts are meanings that are no less important because they are subjective.

Using your imagination will reveal different possibilities of a story. It will also suggest good questions, good ideas, good tactics. Don't be blind to things you can't literally see. Emulate Gloucester; see them feelingly.

Freebie Fever

In every news office there is at least one person who is constantly on the telephone hustling freebies. This person will accept *anything* that is free—free tickets to plays or movie screenings or sports events, free meals, free books, invitations to cocktail parties, complimentary gifts whether large or small. Not only will he accept them, he will come close to *extorting* them: refusal to offer the freebie, he implies, will not be forgotten when it comes to news coverage.

Freebie Fever is a disease. Low-salaried employees might say they couldn't afford to pay for these things, and what's the harm of taking a little freebie that no one else wants? But the truth is that salary has nothing to do with it—the appeal is the wicked pleasure of getting something for nothing. I could (but won't) name a news celebrity with a six-digit salary who is known for leaping at freebies that the most impoverished desk assistant would reject.

Most freebies are easily resistable. But not all of them. "Joe, you're a hell of an anchorman, and I'd be thrilled if you and a friend [lecherous wink] would fly down to my place in the Virgin Islands [or Mexico, or Morocco] and stay as long as you like."

Whether the freebie is a token or a whopper, accepting it is the beginning of corruption. I must admit that I do not know of a news business freebie that was accepted in *explicit* exchange for coverage or favorable treatment on the air. But that's not the way it's done.

A big man in the clothing business makes a call to a local reporter:

"Mike, I was thinking that you'd be the perfect reporter to cover the gala opening of my new store. We'll have celebrities, famous ballplayers, beautiful models, gimmicks, you name it. Lots of fun. And I want you to try on one of our sheepskin coats. Very elegant, Mike. So, do you think they'll send you?"

Well, maybe Mike will suggest it to the assignment desk (not mentioning the coat), and if nothing better is happening maybe they'll send him. And maybe he'll come back with a free coat. What the hell, it's not as if there were some big public issue here. He's not *slanting* anything, he's not *compromising* his integrity. It's a coat, not a bribe.

But of course it's a bribe. And of course it's a compromise. And once you start compromising, what will make you stop?

A friend of mine was hired as a press secretary for a politician running for an important office. Press coverage was tepid. The candidate was furious and blamed my friend for "not getting these reporters on our side." He said, "You know how you get reporters on your side? You take 'em into a back room and give 'em a bottle of booze and stick a few bucks into their pocket. *That's* how you make friends in the press!'"

I would say that anyone in the news business who accepts freebies, large or small, is encouraging that perception of journalists and dishonoring everyone in the profession. The least you can do, when you see it happening, is to fail to conceal your contempt.

T-and-A

Earlier I said that T-and-A (Tits and Ass) stories were the traditional quick fix for TV news organizations seeking a way to perk up ratings. Sex stories have always been a part of the news, and sometimes they are legitimate, but what is repugnant is the cloak of Serious Journalism under which a news department tries to justify its Peeping Tom-ism. Often there is also a thickly applied layer of Puritan disapproval which fortifies the program's defense against charges that it is advertising or exploiting immoral behavior.

When the motive is hypocritical, as it so frequently is, the news organization is as guilty of prostitution as the scurrying streetwalkers its cameras pursue so avidly. Prostituting the news, like prostituting your body, leaves an invisible stain that is not easily washed away.

While you may not have the power to prevent your station from going the T-and-A route, it is in your self-interest to keep a distance from it. Sexy stories reap instant hoopla in the newsroom, and it may be tempting to join in for a share of the big reaction. But today's big reaction is tomorrow's tainted memory. People will remember your association with the sex story and it will do you no good.

Especially if you are female. An attractive young woman newswriter I worked with became an instant star shortly after her trial promotion to reporter when she closed a story on the New York Playboy Club dressed in a scanty bunny costume. Her personal T-and-A were eye-poppingly revealed. The station's logo was pinned to her bunny tail, and naturally the camera zoomed in on it. The on-camera close lasted about fifteen seconds. It was sensational in its impact and undoubtedly helped her win a permanent position on the reporting staff. Years later, the mention of her name among staff or viewers still evoked leering memories of her self-display in that bunny costume. She was a charming and intelligent woman who was never quite taken seriously after fifteen seconds in which she went too far.

Ho-Hum, Another Controversy

Every day there are new controversies, and newsmen gobble them up. Broadcasts are filled with accusations, charges, disclosures, threats, criticisms, protests. Resignations are called for, investigations are demanded, lawsuits are filed, prompt action is urged. The journalist churns out these stories, and in weary moments he wonders about their real importance. They flare up and then subside; they are quickly replaced by newer stories, newer uproars. Do they make any difference? Do they have any impact at all?

Yes, they do have impact. Newsmen are so wrapped up in the daily details of TV news that they tend to lose sight of its awesome power—the power to briefly focus the attention of thousands or millions of people. When this power is turned *on you*, it hits like a bolt of lightning. When it is turned on an organization such as a government agency or a business, it sends shock waves throughout the structure. There are urgent meetings, confrontations, recriminations, firings; media advisers and lawyers are rushed in; the boss goes on the warpath; and the repercussions and reverberations might continue long after the story fades out of the news.

That's impact. But the newsman has little notion of its intensity. He has probably never been on the receiving end of TV's power. He does not appreciate the tremors his work has set off.

And even if very few people are personally affected by the story, they are usually the ones who are in a position to determine the consequences. The police chief confronted by a protest about law enforcement feels a pressure to do something about the problem; the leadership of a chemical company accused of polluting a river feels a pressure to find another place to dump its wastes. These officials, prodded by news reports, might not do the right thing, but a *reaction* is guaranteed. No one involved in a controversy reported on television will yawn about it.

"Who Cares?"

The most devastating words inside a newsroom are "Who cares?" They are generally spoken in peevish tones when a reporter or writer receives an assignment that does not spark his interest or seems trivial or catches him in a cranky moment.

"Aw, *who cares* about that? Why *bother* with that? Do we *have to* do that?"

The complaint rarely kills off the story. More often, it forces the complainer into a face-saving position in which he makes every effort to find flaws with the story or makes himself a pest with his continuing whining about it. This is not one of the proud scenes in journalism.

The worst thing about "Who cares?" is that it is so arbitrary, it can be said of *any* story, for any reason. I know a man who was running a network assignment desk in the late 1960s until he said it about a certain civil rights march. "Just another protest. Who cares?" he grumped, declining to assign the story. The march became one of Martin Luther King's greatest triumphs, covered by most of the world press *except* this man's network.

He was not a bigot or an incompetent. He was just a grouch. When this incident illustrated the possible consequences of his grouchiness, his career was effectively ruined.

"How Dare You Ask a Journalist of My Stature to . . ."

Young people are always eager to perform functions that are *above* them, but some of them make the mistake of balking at doing things they consider *beneath* them. It's a mistake, for at least two reasons.

One is that a grudging attitude toward minor tasks (such as answering that incessantly ringing telephone) is extremely unattractive to seniors. To them, getting the task done is the only thing; they do not care to hear a lot of petty bickering about why you shouldn't have to do it. If this is your attitude, it will be noticed and held against you, believe me.

The other reason is personal. Once you get into the habit of finding things you resist doing, it will be easy to find more and more things you don't want to do. Finally you will arrive at a mentality that is often attributed to civil servants, in which your energies are primarily devoted to *evading* work. This is worse than laziness—it is a kind of reflex negativism that turns every task into a stifling burden. You become sour, petulant, and bored. And not just about your job.

Across the Street

I would bet that for just about every news office in the universe there is a place "across the street," usually a bar, where people go after work (or even during work) to unwind and decompress after the high-intensity scramble before and during airtime.

There is much to be learned in this environment. Indeed, it rounds out classroom and on-the-job training so well that it might be considered part of the triad of a young journalist's education.

In the bar you will find out about the folklore of journalism—the stories that are told, the legends of admirable, hilarious, or blundering behavior from your own office and others. These stories give you a sense of prevailing values: what your colleagues respect, what amuses them, what they frown upon. Perhaps the most important thing you learn in these conversations is what *not* to do.

You will pick up how-to tips that you will mentally file away and retrieve when needed, perhaps years later. You will learn about relationships in the office: rivalries, friendships, feuds, foibles, jealousies, insecurities—this is knowledge that might keep you from wandering into crossfire. You will learn the pleasure of swapping gossip with great gossipers, although it is wise for a youngster to keep his own contributions to gossip to a discreet minimum.

The bar is often a better learning place than the office because there is more time and candor and less inhibition regarding status. A low-level beginner with only a month on the job finds himself conversing in groups or individually with anchorpeople and executives.

Often he finds to his surprise that they enjoy his presence, his newness. They like to tell him things about the work they share. As I've said elsewhere in this book, people like to talk about what they do. If you are a good listener, you will be astonished by the things that even very important people will tell you and how much they appreciate your earnest attention.

Of course, there are also some cautions about hanging out in the bar. Avoid becoming associated with the negative contingent, the embittered complainers. It is worth hearing what they have to say, but don't take a chance of becoming infected with their cynicism.

Don't let your personal life revolve around the bar. This happens because journalists, like actors, athletes, police, or hospital teams, tend to finish work in a state of highly revved emotions, wanting to rehash the day's events in lively postmortems that outsiders can't take part in. It is natural that they cluster "across the street," spending their free time with the same people they've worked with all day.

But this camaraderie can be destructive. Their world starts to narrow. They are likely to drink too much or find other trouble. So be careful. As with wine, moderation is the key.

"Oh, Did Someone Kick a Touchdown?"

It is no longer acceptable for women to know nothing about sports or for journalists of either sex to be ignorant of the arts. Not only ignorant, but *proudly* ignorant.

Sports and high culture are bona fide news subjects, taken seriously by many viewers. Even if your station has a sports reporter and a reviewer or "arts editor," these subjects will eventually come your way. At that point, an attitude of smirking ignorance is more than unattractive, it is a professional liability. A producer or editor assigning a sports or culture story will not be pleased by a response such as "Basketball, isn't that the game where beanpoles run around in their underwear throwing passes at hoops?" or "Ballet, yeah, a bunch of fruitcakes flitting around in swan costumes."

You need not be a fan or devotee, but you should at least read the newspapers, know the names of the stars, and have a general idea of what's going on. Try to make yourself an exception to what H. L. Mencken described as "the old fond theory that it is somehow discreditable for a reporter to show any sign of education and culture, that he is most competent and laudable when his intellectual baggage most closely approaches that of a bootlegger."

Be Nice to Desk Assistants

Desk assistants usually work hard for pathetically little pay and seldom hear a word of appreciation. It is good to be nice to them. It's also smart, because at least one person you knew as a desk assistant will sooner or later rocket past you in the hierarchy, and she will always remember how you treated her.

Another possibility is that a certain desk assistant catches your eye, and one thing leads to another, and the day comes when you find yourself standing together at the altar. That's a good reason to be nice to the desk assistant: you might marry her. I did.

19

The TV News Career

At the age of thirty-seven I gave up my career in TV news, just eight weeks after my status and salary had jumped to a new level. After years of steering away from producer jobs, I had accepted one and become senior New York producer of the ABC News program *Nightline*. As I noted in the preface to this book, I missed writing and I quit. But there was more to it than that.

Early in your career, maybe even within the first weeks, you notice that there are surprisingly few older people in the newsroom—and by "older" I mean people *beyond their mid-thirties*.* At first the youthful atmosphere seems liberating and exciting. Ahead of you is an open field, with few entrenched seniors to block your way upward, so you hurl yourself into it, investing more and more of yourself in it, and several years might go by until you grasp the warning you could have seen at the start.

As I said earlier, I think the paramount requirement in TV news is energy. Daily journalism has a relentless and gluttonous appetite; it devours work, and the people who do it are driven at a consuming pace. Most daily journalism does not challenge your brain anywhere near as much as it challenges your sheer uncritical energy—your willingness *to rush out and do it* and then *to rush back and tell it* (blasting through all the obstacles in between). Ability is important, but energy is indispensable. Every day you must have the energy. Every day challenges your capacity to renew it and commit it to your work.

The virtues associated with experience—judgment, perspective, restraint, even sophistication—are not to be underrated, but it is the raw horsepower associated with youth that keeps the news

---

*The average age of *broadcast* journalists is 30.9 as compared to 37.2 for *print* journalists, according to *The American Journalist* by Cleveland Wilhoit, Richard Gray, and David Weaver (Bloomington, Ind., 1985).

machine in motion. Young people arrive brimming over with this energy. Their tanks are full, their motors are revving. Their minds are fresh and ready to absorb new things in great leaps of learning. Given this freshness and drive, the fundamental skills of journalism are rapidly mastered. Formal preparation is a desirable asset, but certainly a journalist can go into action without advanced training. Basic training will do—he is more like a Marine than a doctor.

With his energies so perfectly harnessed, the young TV journalist is capable of prodigious effort and vaulting progress. He is always *willing;* his adrenaline flows abundantly and indiscriminately. The wailing siren of a news event galvanizes him; even the routine flurry of the newsroom galvanizes him. Old hands stand back to let him through on his crest of energy, and he passes them in a breathless rush, spurred on by the exciting newness that confronts him each day and the exciting opportunities that stretch before him.

With some talent and luck, he becomes an overnight star of his news department. He is on the air with big stories (and already sending audition cassettes to the networks), or he is a twenty-five-year-old producer leading crews in the field, gallivanting around, tackling all challenges, mastering techniques, taking on the world.

TV news is a paradise for young hotshots. There is so much to do, and they are welcome to do it. They surge to the front, and acclaim pours in, and the most ambitious heights seem attainable. And attainable *soon,* just a few years—none of this working your way up for three decades!

In my tenth month in TV news I was offered a promotion: I could produce the Sunday evening newscast (of the leading station in the biggest local TV market in the country). Had I earned this in ten *months?* It seemed like something that should have taken ten *years!* I had come from a newspaper where it took five years before you dared to ask to be taken off the night shift. And yet here I was with Producership dangled before me. Small producerships would quickly lead to big producerships. I was on the way! Or was I?

The executive who offered the promotion was a certified hotshot himself, only two or three years older than I but clearly marked for big things. My reaction was not the euphoria he expected. I was astonished, bumbling—and ambivalent. When I told him I had doubts about my readiness for the producer's job, he actually laughed. Of course you're ready, he said. I told him I was still learning newswriting and film and hadn't even *started* to want to be a producer. "You're not turning this down, are you?" he asked in amazement. And I said, "Uh, yes, I guess I am."

In that instant, this executive who had just declared his interest in furthering my career decided that my career was an insult to his creed of meteoric success. *"I don't want anyone without ambition working for me,"* he said, his voice trembling with anger.

I was stunned by the intensity of his emotion. He made it clear that he wanted to fire me. But I had union protection. He tried to ship me off to a far outpost of the corporate boondocks, but I had a union veto over this exile and I used it. I stayed, knowing he would punish me in every petty way possible—and he did—but I took the punishment without alarm, because I knew he was angling for a news director post in another city and I was sure he would get it and leave. And he did.

Two or three years later, still in his early thirties, he attained his dream of becoming executive producer of the network evening news. After one year he was removed from this awesome position, having proved himself *unready* for it. And then *he* was sent to the boondocks.

So it goes for so many high-flying hotshots. Gravity brings them down.

The flaw with a career in daily journalism turns out to be the same quality that made it so attractive at the start: it is promiscuous. It shares many of the drawbacks of sexual promiscuity, notably the elusiveness of depth. Every day the newsman is thrown into new encounters, and his work is rich in variety, but finally variety is a hollow substitute for meaning. The original excitement that came from newness wanes as things inevitably become less new; the excitement of boundless opportunities fades as he sees that they are only opportunities to keep doing the same thing (though perhaps at a more prestigious level).

Each day he faces the same stories: the same crimes, fires, disasters, strikes, the same rituals by public officials, the same uproars and crises. The reality of daily journalism is that the day ends and is immediately forgotten and the next day you return and start from scratch. And that's the essence of promiscuity: every episode begins with fresh promise but ends in sameness, and there is so little carryover, so little sense of something building or deepening. Perpetual running is the one constant; the running that seemed so exhilarating at the beginning takes on a different feeling when the newsman senses that instead of running *toward* something he is running in circles and his career is just so many laps around the track.

When a TV newsman begins to seek depth as well as action,

he looks first to his work. But he knows its limitations—there's not much time to dig into a story and not much encouragement to do so when the final product will be only an extended headline, maybe twenty seconds long, maybe a minute and a half, at most a multi-part series of hyped-up reports designed more for ratings than for journalism. So he reverts to his instinctive pattern and seeks the answer in variety. He changes jobs, changes stations, changes cities, maybe he moves up to the networks or tries a position in management. Newsmen are always moving on, or at least talking about moving on. It is a journeyman's profession. Fleeing promiscuity, they keep jumping into its arms.

Not all newsmen are afflicted with unsatisfiable longing for depth. Some are gifted with a lifelong enthusiasm that saves them from this gnawing disappointment. They are the worst and the best: the hacks who don't recognize superficiality or tire of it, and the born journalists who believe there is something special and exceptional that makes every story worth the effort. But many are in between.

The most common strategy for fighting the promiscuity of daily journalism is to get out of general assignments and stake out a specialty—politics, education, environment, consumerism, etc. Such specialties offer, at least for a while, the satisfaction of getting into something with continuity and substance. (Newspapers offer this sort of specializing more than local TV news. For most local stations, "in-depth reporting" exists only in publicity department prose.) An alternative is the short-term and intensive specializing that TV reporters and producers undertake in special report units, documentaries, or news magazine programs like *60 Minutes*. But these jobs are few and highly coveted; not many can get them.

By the time I was in a position to get them, I was running out of steam. I was not cynical or lazy, not negative, not even unenthusiastic, but my enthusiasm was no longer automatic. I had stopped caring about stories *just because they were stories*. Unless I was convinced that a story was indisputably worth the effort, I could not muster the instant energy or the uncritical willingness *to rush out and do it*. My flame was burning low. I was on the way to becoming deadweight. Every organization has its deadweight, but I didn't want it to be me.

In TV news the career is accelerated, and the professional midlife crisis arrives relatively early, perhaps around the ten-year point (just when your childhood friends and former classmates are *beginning* to make their marks in law or business or other careers).

Newsmen come through this stage in different ways, but a significant number find themselves prematurely weary and disillusioned with a career that started seeming empty when the original momentum wore off.

Some stay anyway, in dead-end jobs. Others drift away. They are fired or they quit or they are transferred off the fast track into some corporate corner. They go into related fields, or unrelated fields. They just go.

And that is why you see so few older people when you take your first long look around your first TV newsroom. The warning was there, but you were too excited to grasp it: the action, the glamor, the dizzying variety—these things are the dessert, not the main course. When they become less gratifying, you may no longer be willing to pay the price in vital energy. And then *you* will be going too.

So maybe you should forget about journalism and sell toothpicks. Or soap. Or life insurance.

The truth is that if you are *serious* about journalism or one of those lucky people who have it in their blood and feel called to it, you will not be a bit discouraged by what I've just said. It wouldn't have discouraged me either. But I think I would have appreciated the warning about a fact of life that lay ahead and would have to be reckoned with.

A final word should be said about my own case, because it is far from typical. As I mentioned earlier, I am the son of a TV newsman; my father was a member of the Murrow generation and indeed a member of the Murrow team that made such inspiring history at CBS in the 1950s. I remember him coming home from the office each night still caught up with the day's excitement. The scotch bottle came out, drinks were poured, and the day's events were recounted in gripping narrative. It was a time of extraordinary creative fertility for TV news, a time of heroes and villains, a time of momentous achievement; it is no surprise if those electrifying stories raised my expectations to an unsustainable pitch and made me vulnerable to disappointment.

Undoubtedly, TV news is less electrifying now than when it was new. TV newsmen then were thrilled by their work; I think the nation was thrilled to watch it. The thrill had to fade, for everyone. TV news is now an institution (instead of an adventure); it is gigantic, a nationwide system run by thousands of able professionals (instead of an elite cluster in New York); it is technologically awesome, brilliantly coordinated, and the nightly news product is many times more sophisticated.

Yet I would suggest that some of its energizing sense of mission has worn off. The TV news people I have worked with are not, I think, as keenly stirred as their predecessors by a dramatic sense of commitment to great social purpose. Their purpose is more professional than social; their work is more likely to be good, less likely to be great.

Lacking the old tingling feeling of participation in Murrow-esque endeavor, newsmen are more apt to think of themselves as individuals rather than members of a team united by higher purpose. As individuals, they lose the group energy and become prey to the kind of fatigue that in my case became terminal.

But I would not overstate this loss of motivation. TV newsmen continue to think of their profession as *special*. All other jobs seem so deadly boring and narrow and so dismally remote from the great exhilarating parade of life. Unlike most people, newsmen believe that what they do is *important,* and also that it is *fun.*

And it is! Having left it, I already feel pulled back to it. Even the negatives have positive aspects. Here are the reasons why I think it is a wonderful career.

The people you work with are lively and bright, and what a difference that makes to your outlook and spirit. Newsroom camaraderie and hijinks are a delight. Personal relationships formed in the sharing of intense experiences are special and enduring, and TV production provides enough intensity for a wealth of such relationships. The teamwork brings people together in a frequently invigorating creative chemistry. Journalism tends to be done in an atmosphere of free expression; dissidents and eccentrics are tolerated and sometimes valued. There is a minimum of pressure to conform or stifle yourself—a pressure that is palpable in corporate corridors where people must dress the same, think the same, and comport themselves with decorum and circumspection.

The excitement may be shallow, but it's still excitement. Here's where the Fundamental Duality pays off: there's no business like Show Business and there's no business like the News Business when things are hopping. Even if you sink to the depths of ennui, there will be times of magical rejuvenation when the blood pounds and the senses are sharp and you spring into action like a young tiger.

You are a part of your times, allowed by your journalistic passport to enter the circle of famous people and historic events. There is a hazard—the seductive temptation to think of yourself as part of the news instead of a witness to it—but as long as you keep your bearings, the view from up close can be an unforgettable and priceless privilege. (And you acquire terrific anecdotes to tell at parties.)

You get around. Whether you are globe-trotting for a network or working for a local station, you continually find yourself in a range of places where no other profession would send you. One day the opulent chambers of the mighty, the next day a terrifying hellhole in a wretched ghetto. And *you encounter a vast range of people.* Some are miraculous in their human value, others are more despicable than you could have imagined. You meet likable villains and "most admired" people who turn your stomach. It is an unparalleled education.

And you get paid for it! *The money is good,* especially considering that most journalists are liberal arts generalists with no particular money-making potential. For some on-camera talent, the financial reward is fabulous, and many off-camera people find themselves earning more than they ever dreamed possible.

You are given a public voice. Even if you do not appear on camera, your words and ideas go out to a vast audience. Most young people get no serious attention from anyone, but the work of a young TV journalist gets attention from hundreds of thousands or even millions of people. Sometimes your work is routine, but there are occasions when it lifts a broadcast. You can feel the difference, and it feels very good.

What's more, *you are not smothered by your bosses* because daily journalism is so hectic that they do not have time to stand over your shoulder (unless you give signs of wandering astray). The endless urgency precludes the let's-have-a-meeting-about-that mentality so common in corporate life; instead of sitting around for hours trading views or playing politics while the vitality of your project seeps away, you just go and do it. This is refreshing, and to some extent it compensates for the lack of depth; *you do not become bogged down.*

Above all, *you are doing something worthwhile,* and for the most part you can be proud of what you do. The satisfaction that comes from the sense of serving your community or nation is a bonus that surpasses the more concrete rewards. I have warned against journalists setting out to be do-gooders, but often they *do* do good; even when their days are unexceptional, they keep huge numbers of people in touch with events outside their lives. No other country is so well informed; we take it for granted, but it is an

American asset of incalculable value. The broadcast journalist who suffers doubts about his role needs only to think of the Murrows and other fine professionals who have preceded him; their record is a reminder that he is following in a tradition of men and women who have distinguished not only themselves but their nation.

A good friend of mine tells a story about a guest lecturer who addressed his class at a graduate school of business. The lecturer was a senior executive of a major corporation whose principal product was a well-known brand of dog food. He was gung-ho enthusiastic, extolling the virtues of his field, discussing profits and marketing and packaging and expansion plans and executive benefits.

His objective, of course, was to attract and recruit some of the brightest students in the audience. But my friend spoiled the effort, rising to ask the question that had tugged at his mind from the start:

"Sir, when you retire and reflect on your career, will you have any regrets about devoting your life's work to selling *dog food?*"

Few journalists will ever hear such a trivializing question. But if they do, they need not fear the answer.